WE MUST REMEMBER:

THE VIETNAM WAR SERVICE OF MEN FROM NELSON COUNTY, KENTUCKY

Dr. Harry Spalding and
Don Parrish

ISBN: 978-1-935497-57-8

Designed by: Scott Stortz

Published by:
Butler Books
P.O. Box 7311
Louisville, KY 40257
(502) 897–9393
Fax (502) 897–9797

www.butlerbooks.com

DEDICATION

We extend our deepest thanks to all members of the armed forces who served in the Vietnam War. This book is dedicated to those men with links to Nelson County, Kentucky, who served in Vietnam and—most especially—to those who died in such service.[1]

Army Staff Sergeant Harold Milton Brown, died June 11, 1969

National Guard First Sergeant Luther Malcolm Chappel, died June 19, 1969

National Guard Specialist David Burr Collins, died June 19, 1969

Air Force Captain James J. Crawford, died February 3, 1972

Army Specialist Raymond Sylvester Ford, died February 20, 1966

Marines Private First Class Albert William Hawkins, died May 17, 1968

Army Staff Sergeant Nicholas Gerald Johnson, died August 13, 1970

Army Sergeant Paul Allen Johnson, died August 4, 1970

National Guard Specialist Joseph Ronald McIlvoy, died June 19, 1969

National Guard Staff Sergeant James Thomas Moore, died June 24, 1969

Army Staff Sergeant James Raphael Norris, died November 3, 1968

Army Private William David Price, died March 18, 1968

National Guard Sergeant Ronald Earl Simpson, died June 19, 1969

Army Specialist Charles David St. Clair, died January 16, 1971

Marine Corporal William Russell Taylor, died August 28, 1966

Army Specialist Barry Neal Thompson, died June 25, 1969

National Guard Specialist Jim Allen Wray, died July 2, 1969

CONTENTS

Acknowledgments

We would like to thank all of the people who made this book possible. First, we wish to thank all who served, those who accepted it as their duty to America and to the free world. Many of the younger people of today do not realize the threat that Communism posed at the time of the Vietnam War politically, ideologically, and militarily. Those who served did so to help stop the spread of such an evil threatening the whole free world and we owe them our thanks.

Secondly, we would like to thank all of those who told us their stories. There is no substitute for personal recollections of experiences. Thirdly, we would like to thank the Kentucky Standard. Without its "People in the Service" column and other news stories, we would not have had much of the information contained in this book.

We would like to acknowledge the fine books, We Were Soldiers Once . . . and Young and The Sons of Bardstown, which supplied information about two of the critical battles involving Nelson Countians.

To a great extent, we would like to acknowledge our wives for their help and forbearance. Lastly, thanks to Karen Ricketts for her perseverance as a transcriptionist.

AUTHOR'S NOTE

When writing this book on Nelson County's experience in the Vietnam war, we decided to write it in chronological order of the war— the history of the war—and, in so far as possible, place Nelson County's servicemen in these times and places. In doing so, we hope the reader can better understand the war and the people involved. It was a vicious and emotionally stressful war in which Americans, and Nelson Countians in particular, did themselves proud most of the time, and deserve our thanks.

Unfortunately, we have not been able to record the experiences of every Nelson Countian who served in Vietnam. We were unable to contact many of them. Others not preferred to talk about the war. For those who did give us their stories, we are most grateful. For those whose stories we missed, we are sorry. Most of the servicemen mentioned in this book are Nelson County natives. Those who aren't Nelson Countians have very close connections to the county.

As we wrote this book, we were amazed by the number of medals and commendations awarded to Nelson Countians. There were so many they almost seemed commonplace. Their number echoed Admiral Chester Nimitz's comment about Iwo Jima's veterans, "Uncommon valor was a common virtue."

CHAPTER 1

VIETNAM AND NELSON COUNTY

This book is about a small town and county in Kentucky, and a war that became very unpopular as it went along. Democracies tire quickly of war. The Vietnam War seemed to drag on indefinitely without an end in sight, with ever-increasing casualties and deaths. Nelson County, about which this book is written, had more deaths in the Vietnam War per population than any other county in America.

However, despite this, the war was mostly supported locally, as it was in many small towns and counties in the heartland of America. Many people still believed that, as the bastion of the free world, the United States was fighting Communism. In late 1964, opinion polls showed that 85 percent of the American public agreed with the administration's stance on Vietnam. In early 1965, "nearly 80 percent believed that an American withdrawal would open Southeast Asia to Communist domination, and an equal proportion favored a US combat troop commitment to block that possibility.[2]

Some Americans were disillusioned by leadership in Washington, and generalship in Vietnam, but believed that the cause was right. Nelson County servicemen, when they came home, were respected and were not afraid to wear their uniforms, as happened in many of the large cities and on some college campuses. They were respected for what they were, common young men, many of them neighbors. Most didn't want to go, but did; didn't want to fight, but did; and didn't want to die, but some did. They were young people, who often lived in a hellhole of desperation, not for personal gain, but for their country, freedom from world communism, for their families and the ideals they stood for, and for the men who were fighting next to them. The last, in the end, proved one of the greatest incentives.

Most who went were draftees, but Nelson County had a higher number of volunteers than the national average. The county also had a large number who were in a local National Guard artillery battery that was called up. Those who went were spread around in all branches of the services involved, and in most of the fighting units. They were in practically every major action that was fought all up and down the length of Vietnam.

As stated before, the county had an unusual number of deaths for its size. Many were killed in a single night, when the Bardstown National Guard battery was overrun—a night of terror, death, and courage. Over half of the county's deaths were killed in a one-month period. The others were killed all over Vietnam, almost from the first to the very end. Each was duly mourned. A number who died had unborn children they would never see.

One of Bardstown's sons was the first big hero of the war, and had his picture on the front of *Time* magazine. He was a tough, self-effacing lieutenant colonel. Though outnumbered four to one, his battalion came out victorious in a place that had been enemy country. He was a real leader, who thought of his men and duty before himself. A book (*We Were Soldiers Once . . . And Young*) and a movie (*We Were Soldiers*) were made of his exploits.

The county also had a pilot, a lieutenant colonel, who was shot down, captured, tortured, but never gave in to the enemy's demands for a false confession. He spent almost four years in enemy prisons, the last two in the infamous Hanoi Hilton. He was in the last batch of prisoners to be released after the treaty in 1973. He had scars, physical and mental, that would last a lifetime. The county had a pilot and squadron commander, who flew B-52s in tactical and strategic air missions. Nelson County had Green Berets who were there before America's first major land forces became involved in early 1965, the marines who landed at Da Nang. The county also had members of those first marine units. One was an artillery forward observer who was decorated for saving more than 100 American lives. Another re-enlisted three times, was wounded several times, and ended being an advisor for South Vietnamese troops. He also had two brothers who served in the marines, one of whom was killed in action. The county had a naval lieutenant commander who was in charge of docking in Cam Ranh Bay harbor, one of the biggest port facilities.

Nelson County had a major who went in with the first deployment of the First Division in 1965, and a captain in the Air Force who was killed in 1972, the last year of American involvement in Vietnam. The list goes on. The county had an unusually large number of servicemen who were decorated for bravery, such as five helicopter pilots who received the Distinguished Flying Cross.

Many more who served got no fame or notoriety—young American men, who went, did their jobs and came home with no fanfare. They just wanted to get on with their lives. Many had hellish memories that they wanted to forget. Others were not marked as much, but they were all marked to some extent. This book was written to tell the stories of many of them, and in a larger sense, to tell the story of the American experience in Vietnam.

Nelson County's experience was so remarkable that journalist Dan Rather did a special on it on his evening news broadcast, and Charles Kuralt visited Bardstown twice for his Sunday morning show. Bardstown and Nelson

County were also highlighted around the world for their participation in Vietnam in more than 100 news media outlets, including the *London Times*. A German team spent a week in Nelson County to write a feature story for their television station.

CHAPTER 2

VIETNAM AND AMERICA

_____

The Best

They were the best, the best I've ever known,
With their sweat-soaked shirts and hair
Curled in wet ringlets, and their curses
Flailing the unfriendly clime with welts
Of anger. They chided the fates that filled
The air with heat, and insects, and noises
Of calling death; but they fought and dug,
And crawled, and trooped. No brass buttons
Or mirrored shoes passed their inspections.
Their dirty fatigues were their earned badges,
And brave fellowship their shining medals,
Their unsought glory. They stanched the blood
Of loneliness with their laughter,
And brotherhood of flaming trial.
Where have they gone, these brave men
Released from the ruins of yesterday,
And the firefights of tomorrow?
In what campaign are they waging now
Their lonely battle to survive a day?
In what unlistening street, in what dark bar
Do they share their fears, their needs,
Their laughter? With what faceless men,

Uncaring and distant, are they forgetting
Their victories and their victims? I sit
Reflecting the shared stygian shadows
And wonder in the long, quiet hours
If ever the brave and good will meet
Again, and seen in the eyes
Of a man courage, and in his heart care.

—Dr. Harry Spalding

The Vietnam War was the longest and most unpopular in which America has ever been involved. It was a war in which the United States supplied most of its combat personnel with the draft. It was the last war for which the United States would do so. Later in the war, as in Iraq, National Guard and reserve units were called up to fill the army's and marines' needs to build up a fighting force that reached 500,000 at its maximum in Vietnam. Nelson County and Bardstown sent their shares. The number of those who were killed from Nelson County was greater than any other county in America per capita. In addition, many others served and had harrowing tours of duty; many came back with scars, both physical and mental. Most came back to live productive lives, but hid their memories, some so bad that the men couldn't even talk about their experiences.

Who were the men who served? They came from all strata of society. Many were volunteers. It seems from interviews conducted for this book that Nelson County had more than its share of volunteers. As the war went on and became more unpopular, a number of Americans of draft age went to Canada or out of the country to avoid the draft. As far as the authors know, no one from Nelson County took that course. As long as a student was in college and making passing grades, he was deferred from the draft. A number of locals took that route, but they would probably have gone to college anyway. Many of those who did go to college were drafted after they graduated. Having dependents often kept men from being drafted, but not always. One soldier from Nelson County, who was drafted and later killed, had two children.

Most of the men who served, whether they were drafted or volunteered, were between 18 and 21; most were just out of high school. A few were high school dropouts. Those in the county's National Guard unit who went to Vietnam were older, in their early or mid 20s.

Many who went became "grunts," as the combat soldiers or marines were called. They were the ones who bore the brunt of the fighting, the ones who went out on patrol to find and fight the Vietcong or North Vietnamese, or who flew by helicopter into a hot zone where a battle raged. It was a different type of war than the United States had ever fought before. There was no definite front. The enemy could be anywhere or everywhere. Frequently, sweeps were done to clear the enemy out of a section of the country. As soon as the Americans left, the enemy would move back in. The Vietcong looked just like the rest of the natives, and could slip in or out of so-called safe areas to do their damage.

The Vietcong were indoctrinated South Vietnamese insurgents who knew the land, and frequently cowed the peaceful village natives, and assassinated mayors or other local officials loyal to the government. The North Vietnamese army came down the Ho Chi Minh Trail through neutral Laos and Cambodia. They could attack across the border, and pull back if the situation got tough or they were at a disadvantage, fighting hit-and-run battles. Rarely would they stay and fight it out when confronted by sizeable air and ground power. In addition, they had the jungle in which to hide. They dug an extensive tunnel system that would make the catacombs of Rome look insignificant. In those tunnels, they hid out and lived with bunks, kitchens, hospitals, and places to store their arms and food.

Against such an enemy and the accompanying disadvantages, American soldiers had to wage war. Most often, they waged it well, average people from Bardstown and similar towns all over the nation. Most admitted that they were scared, but did their jobs anyway. Most said their tours were often boring, but when action happened, it happened fast, and was accompanied by sheer terror. However, these soldiers and marines from Bardstown and the rest of the nation didn't run. They stayed and fought with a regularity that seems improbable.

During their tours of duty, the respect and caring of these men for others in their outfit grew. Frequently they stayed and fought because they did not want to let their fellow soldiers down or lose their respect. Often they would take care of the "short-timers" in their outfits. American servicemen had to serve only one year in Vietnam. When a man had only a few weeks to go on his tour, he was given less dangerous jobs, particularly if he was married and had children. They were taken off the point (the lead soldier on patrol) and if possible, were not sent out on dangerous patrols. Unfortunately, this did not always happen, and short-timers were sometimes killed. However, there was an unspoken brotherhood among the men that often lasted long after their fighting days were over.

Later in the war, when it became obvious that America was pulling out, men were less likely to take chances. They were wary of orders they thought were ill advised and would put them in a dangerous position. Some men refused to follow orders. Some officers were careless in their efforts to make a name for themselves at their men's expense. Sometimes, soldiers would "frag" these officers (throw a fragmentation grenade at them), or kill them in battle to get rid of them.

In all of the authors' interviews with local veterans, not one indicated that he had been part of any such actions. They were not angels, but they had ideas of what was right and wrong.

The movie *Platoon* depicted some soldiers as sadistic. Surely, there were such men, but by far, the rank and file were not. They had a distasteful and dangerous job to do, and did it. As far as atrocities were concerned, they happened. In such a war, it is hard to tell friend from foe, and innocent people are sometimes killed. However, unconscionable massacres such as My Lai were very rare, even on a smaller scale.

In none of the interviews conducted for this book, however, did the authors hear of a person known to be completely innocent being killed. In the horrors of war, villages were burned to rout out the Vietcong. Innocent people were caught up in those fights, and suspected Vietcong were captured or shot. Many a quick decision had to be made as to who was the enemy and who wasn't. To a certain extent, this was inevitable. During the war, protests were carried on in some cities and university campuses. Sometimes veterans of Vietnam would join in. Few, if any, local veterans did, despite the brutality, horrors, and seeming senselessness of the war. Most felt it was their duty and did it, and they wondered why those who escaped the war by going to college would be the loudest in protesting it. Many felt it was their guilt.

Much was heard of alcohol and drug abuse by US servicemen, particularly during the latter stages of the war. In such a frustrating, never-ending and pressure-filled war, the use of both is understandable, if not to be condoned. It was common for beer to be used frequently, almost like rum rations were in the British army. Soldiers drank to temporarily escape their situation. Nelson County servicemen probably drank their share. As far as the use of drugs, such as marijuana or cocaine, was concerned, some did use drugs and a few came home addicted to them, but addiction was not the rule. Most did not use drugs when they came home.

When soldiers came home to other cities or counties, they were sometimes called baby killers and spat upon, or worse. Such action would have been repulsive to the people of Nelson County. These soldiers were young Americans who were pulled from their normal lives by the draft, or who volunteered because they thought it was their duty, and went through a hellish experience because their country called them. Nelson Countians thought they were to be honored, not spat upon.

These men were not born killers. Some had never shot a gun before. However, it was "kill or be killed." War is a very distasteful, inhuman thing. Killing is not something to brag about. Frequently it was done to protect one's unit as well as one's own scalp. Most soldiers shuddered when they thought about it, and tried to block it out of their consciousness.

Nelson County soldiers were not saints. They did things out of fear and anger. They hung one on with alcohol every now and then. Some used pot. However, they usually did their jobs, fought their battles, and took care of each other. They were scared at times, almost panicky. They felt their hands sweat and their hearts race. They knew the chaos of battle. At times they felt like bugging out, but didn't. They did things that, in retrospect, they would have changed, but most often did the best they could, and the best that could have been expected of them. They were the best of American manhood.

CHAPTER 3

EARLY HISTORY OF THE VIETNAM CONFLICT

The recorded history of Vietnam began in 208 BCE when a group of Mongols migrated south.[3] Off and on for more than 1,000 years, the Chinese dominated the area. In 1426, the Chinese were finally defeated, and the Vietnamese became independent.[4] Their independence lasted until the 18th century when French missionaries and adventurers arrived. French influence and power grew, and the French captured Saigon in 1859.[5] France took over Vietnam as a protectorate in 1883 after a 26-year war of conquest.[6] It became part of an Indochinese union in 1887 comprising Tonkin (north)[7], Annam (central), and Cochin China (south), Cambodia and Laos.

Despite this, a feeling of nationalism persisted. The Vietnamese hoped for independence, and tried to meet with President Woodrow Wilson to present an eight-point program at the post-World War I peace conference in Paris. They were turned away. One of the group's spokesmen was Nguyen Ai Quoc, who would later change his name to Ho Chi Minh.[8] French Indochina after World War I continued to be ruled as a French puppet government.

Nguyen Ai Quoc founded the Youth League of Vietnam in 1925, the precursor of the Communist party.[9] At the same time, the Vietnamese Nationalist Party was founded in opposition to the Youth League. An uprising in 1930 was ruthlessly put down, and the Vietnamese Nationalist Party almost became defunct.[10] Several political groups persisted underground, resisting the French.

After the fall of France in World War II in 1940, Japan took over French Indochina by treaty and force, leaving some French in an administrative capacity. In 1941, the Viet Minh, a Communist front, was founded.[11] It collaborated with several other nationalist groups. Under the direction of Vo Nguyen Giap, a schoolteacher, it became the most effective guerrilla group against the Japanese.

Nguyen Ai Quoc (Ho Chi Minh) went to Nationalist China seeking its support. The Chinese, who had their own designs on Indochina, took him prisoner. When he was released in 1943 with Chinese help, the Viet Minh and other resistance units sabotaged the Japanese, and assisted some downed Allied flyers.[12] In late 1944, under Giap, the Viet Minh attacked puppet French outposts in northern Vietnam, their first armed attacks against the French.[13] In early 1945, American OSS (Office of Strategic Services) agents parachuted in to assist these guerilla groups[14], bringing some American aid. After August 1945 and the end of World War II, because of OSS help, Ho Chi Minh thought the US to be friendly, and even sent letters to President Truman asking for support. In September 1945, with OSS help present, he proclaimed the Independent Republic of Vietnam, even quoting from the American Declaration of Independence.

However, British units moved into the power vacuum, according to terms of the Potsdam Conference, to accept the Japanese surrender at Saigon. They released 1,400 French legionnaires, who went on a rampage against the Viet Minh.[15] Other nationalist Vietnamese groups, French colonialists, and Chinese troops arriving in northern Vietnam also opposed the Viet Minh.[16] General Jacques LeClerc arrived on September 24, claiming, "We have come to reclaim our heritage." Ten days later, Colonel Peter Dewey, the head of the OSS mission to Vietnam, was killed at the airport, mistaken as French. He was the first of almost 60,000 Americans killed in the Vietnam strife.

The US agreed to supply France with trucks and other equipment in September 1945. This was seen as endorsement of French colonialism despite the fact that many Americans were against colonialism in any form.[17]

In resistance, the Viet Minh signed an agreement in November 1945 with the other nationalist factions. Ho Chi Minh was recognized as the leader of the group that called itself the Democratic Government of Vietnam. In March 1946, France recognized that republic as a free state within the Indochina Federation and French Union. French forces landed in the north.[18] This agreement fell apart in June 1946 when France proclaimed a separate government for Cochin China (southern Vietnam).[19]

In December 1946, the Democratic Republic of Vietnam launched its first attack against the French government, following deteriorating relations and oppressive French actions.[20] This was considered the beginning of the Indochina war. In the meanwhile, Ho Chi Minh switched sides with the Chinese, 200,000 of whom had come south after World War II. He also switched with the French and other nationalist factions to gain control of the nationalist movement. He succeeded. As French troops gained control of the country, the Viet Minh army moved to the mountainous region north of Hanoi.[21]

In the meantime, the United States was focused primarily on the Communist threat in Europe and China. Its interest in Vietnam was secondary. Although pro-French and anti-Communistic, American leaders felt Vietnam was a less urgent threat.

The post-WWII world was polarized. As Russia set up puppet communistic governments in the eastern European nations that it had overrun, and fostered aggressive communistic parties in France, Italy, and

Greece, the western free world reacted with countermeasures. Russian belligerence, in denying the West land connections with West Berlin, worsened the situation. The fall of China to the communists and the invasion of South Korea by communistic troops from North Korea further polarized East and West into two armed camps, where little diplomacy was possible.

France appointed Bao Dai as chief of state of Vietnam within the French Union, and in 1950, Ho Chi Minh declared that the only true legal government was the Democratic Republic of Vietnam.[22]

In 1949, the communist Chinese army under Mao Tse-tung had overrun all of China, defeating Chiang Kai-shek, and forcing him to flee to set up his government on the island of Taiwan. This opened up the northern border of Vietnam and the accessibility of Chinese aid directly to the Viet Minh. They slowly consolidated their position, and by October, they occupied northern Tonkin from the sea to the Red River. In 1951, they tried a much more ambitious offensive in the Red River Valley, and were defeated with 6,000 dead and 8,000 wounded.[23]

President Truman announced an acceleration of US arms to help the French with a military mission and military advisors. By late 1951, aid had reached $500 million.[24] With the introduction of the Eisenhower administration in January 1953, the war changed from a colonial war to one of communism against the free world. Aid in 1954 reached $2 billion.

In 1953, a reinforced Giap drove into Laos.[25] Overstretched, he pulled back. The French decided to build a fort at Dien Bien Phu along the route to Laos to prevent another such attack and to serve as a mooring point. They retook the area with five battalions and built their fort.[26]

Giap decided to confront them there. He moved an army of multiple infantry, artillery, and anti-aircraft battalions into the mountains around Dien Bien Phu. He surrounded it and cut off its supply lines. The attempts at air reinforcements failed. The second American killed in the Vietnam War, Captain James McGovern, died while trying to fly support into the beleaguered fortress.

Giap attacked with an army of 50,000 men, buttressed by 24 American howitzers captured from the Chinese Nationalists after their fall, and Russian and Chinese artillery pulled by hand over rugged, mountainous terrain.[27] His tactics included building ever-encircling and compressing trenches and tunnels until he closed with human wave attacks against French soldiers under Colonel Christian de Castries. He finally subdued them. His casualties were 23,000 compared to French casualties of 8,500.[28] However, he had won a major battle against the French.

After Dien Bien Phu, the four powers—Britain, the United States, France, and Russia—agreed to set up a conference on Korea and Indochina in Geneva in April. Before the investment of Dien Bien Phu, President Eisenhower stated his "row of dominoes" theory, the systematic falling of non-communist countries, of which Indochina was the first domino in Southeast Asia. He considered massive aerial bombardment of enemy forces.[29] Allies talked him out of that, and on April 26, 1954, the eastern conference started in Geneva. It included nine delegations, including China. After the fall of Dien Bien Phu in May, the French publicly decried a partition, but privately considered a compromise that would salvage part of Indochina. The Viet Minh, flushed with victory, were against compromise, but after two months of debate, they were persuaded by Russia and China to agree to a partition of Vietnam at the 17th parallel and a general election in two years. Cambodia and Laos were to be free independent nations.[30] Representatives from India,

Canada, and Poland were to supervise the agreement.

While this was going on, Bao Dai, who had been appointed chief of state for Vietnam by the French, appointed Ngo Dinh Diem as premier[31], a role he would maintain for nine years. A Catholic, Diem was initially considered a patriotic, conservative, efficient, and supportive politician.[32] He would rule South Vietnam until 1963.

Unfortunately, Diem was not outgoing, did not reach out to other factions of the country, and became isolated from the common peasants. He failed to win the minds and hearts of the common people, pandering more to the landlords and the upper class. Within three months, part of the army was in revolt. They surrounded his palace with tanks. He stalled long enough to allow supportive troops to come to his rescue.[33] Some members of his cabinet resigned, and he began replacing them with family members. He was forced, however, to form a coalition government with six members[34] of other sects to form a national consensus. In October 1954, a threatened withdrawal of American backing helped solidify the consensus. When reforms were agreed upon, the United States began to send increasing aid.[35]

After prodding, Diem introduced some agrarian reforms, but they were insufficient and too poorly run to help the peasants much, and they allowed the landlords to take back what the peasants had been given by the Viet Minh. In five years, 15 percent of the people owned 75 percent of the land.[36]

In the first year, Diem won out over rebellious factions in the south. His enemies withdrew to the Mekong Delta and later joined the Vietcong.[37] Diem also refused to have elections as dictated by the Geneva Conference, stating that he did not sign the agreement.[38] In a rigged election in the south,

Diem received 98.2 percent of the votes over Bao Dai to become the chief of state. He became the country's first president and supreme commander of its armed forces.[39]

The popularity of the Diem regime remained fair for several years due to "local leadership, US assistance, and the natural wealth of one million acres of abandoned rice farm land."[40] Thereafter, Diem continued to lose popularity as the effort to keep himself and his family in power became more contrived.

With time, forces loyal to the Viet Minh began to reassert their power by building up cohesive units in the Mekong Delta and other places, assassinating loyal local politicians, and increasing the flow of insurgents from the north. By December 1958, a directive from the North ordered active insurgency.[41] From 1959 until 1961, the number of assassinations of local officials increased from 1,200 to 4,000 a year.[42]

Diem reacted by appointing more military to administrative posts, failing to take care of the social and economic needs of the local people. In 1959, land reforms were not carried out, and agrovilles (strategic hamlets) were formed.[43] For security against insurgents, displaced peasants were moved into protected villages. In 1959, Diem not only rigged a government election, but also sent some of the opposition to jail.[44]

In December 1960, Hanoi announced the formation of the National Liberation Front[45] of over a dozen political parties and religious sects, a communist coalition that was dubbed the Vietcong by the Saigon government. In many cases, the peasants were more allied with the Vietcong, which was closer to them than the Saigon government. In addition, the Vietcong's merciless actions earned them a reputation of "omnipotence and omnipresence."[46]

Diem sought the favor of the influential landowners, and spent little on schools, medical care, and other services for the peasants. In 1960, in an effort to force land reforms, paratroopers surrounded the presidential palace. Diem again stalled until loyal troops arrived.[47]

When John F. Kennedy won the 1960 presidential election, he inherited a deteriorating situation. The Vietcong were increasing their attacks. In July 1961 alone, there were 41 attacks.[48] At first, Kennedy was cautious, but adhered to the domino theory. In April 1961, he instituted a program of social, political, economic, and military assistance, and decided to stay with Diem. He was reluctant to introduce sizable American military combat units, but did increase the number of advisors and helicopter units. In September 1961, the Fifth Special Forces Group was activated at Fort Bragg, North Carolina. President Kennedy gave them distinctive headgear and the name "Green Berets."[49]

Despite the buildup of American advisors and strengthening of the Army of the Republic of Vietnam (ARVN), the Vietcong were still often winning local battles. America's stance at the time was as the bastion of the free world, as described in a letter from President Kennedy to the sister of one of the advisors who was killed.

DEAR MRS. PENDERGRASS:

I WOULD LIKE TO EXPRESS TO YOU MY DEEPEST AND SINCERE SYMPATHY IN THE LOSS OF YOUR BROTHER. I CAN, OF COURSE UNDERSTAND YOUR BEREAVEMENT AND THE FEELINGS WHICH PROMPTED YOU TO WRITE.

THE QUESTION WHICH YOU POSED IN YOUR LETTER CAN, I BELIEVE, BEST BE ANSWERED BY REALIZING WHY YOUR BROTHER AND OTHER AMERICAN MEN WENT TO VIETNAM IN THE FIRST PLACE. WHEN THIS IS UNDERSTOOD, I AM SURE THAT THE OTHER RELATED QUESTIONS WILL BE ANSWERED.

AMERICANS ARE IN VIETNAM BECAUSE WE HAVE DETERMINED THAT THIS COUNTRY SHALL NOT FALL UNDER COMMUNIST DOMINATION. EVER SINCE VIETNAM WAS DIVIDED, THE VIETNAMESE HAVE FOUGHT VALIANTLY TO MAINTAIN THEIR INDEPENDENCE IN THE FACE OF THE CONTINUING THREAT FROM THE NORTH. SHORTLY AFTER THE DIVISION EIGHT YEARS AGO, IT BECAME APPARENT THAT THEY COULD NOT BE SUCCESSFUL IN THEIR DEFENSE WITHOUT EXTENSIVE ASSISTANCE FROM OTHER NATIONS OF THE FREE WORLD.

IN THE LATE SUMMER OF 1955, WITH APPROVAL OF PRESIDENT EISENHOWER, AN ADVISORY GROUP WAS ESTABLISHED IN VIETNAM TO PROVIDE THEM WITH THE ADEQUATE WEAPONS, AND EQUIPMENT AND TRAINING IN BASIC MILITARY SKILLS, WHICH ARE ESSENTIAL TO SURVIVAL ON THE BATTLEFIELD. EVEN WITH THIS HELP, THE SITUATION GREW STEADILY WORSE UNDER THE PRESSURE OF THE VIETCONG. BY 1961, IT BECAME APPARENT THAT THE TROUBLE IN LAOS AND THE TROUBLES IN VIETNAM COULD EASILY EXPAND. IT IS ALSO APPARENT THAT THE COMMUNIST ATTEMPT TO TAKE OVER VIETNAM COULD EASILY EXPAND. IT IS ALSO APPARENT THAT THEIR ATTEMPT

TO TAKE OVER VIETNAM IS ONLY A PART OF A LARGER PLAN FOR BRINGING THE ENTIRE AREA OF SOUTHEAST ASIA UNDER THEIR DOMINATION. EVEN THOUGH IT IS ONLY A SMALL PART OF THE AREA GEOGRAPHICALLY, VIETNAM IS NOW THE MOST CRITICAL.

If Vietnam should fall, it would indicate to the people of Southeast Asia that Communist domination of their part of the world is almost inevitable. Your brother was in South Vietnam because the threat to the Vietnamese people is, in the long run, a threat to the free world community, and ultimately a threat to us also. For when freedom is destroyed in one country, it is threatened throughout the world.

Sincerely,
John F. Kennedy[50]

A program of "nation building"[51] was started with the belief that Vietnam's society, government, and economy could be "Americanized." The strategic hamlet idea was reenergized to deprive the Vietcong of the peasants' support, with the result that 33 percent of the peasants ended up in hamlets.[52] The strategic hamlets crumbled in 1962 due to removing people from their traditional land, bureaucratic abuses, corruption, some Vietcong infiltration, and other causes.

Despite American efforts, Diem's reaction to economic and social reform stiffened, and the South Vietnamese military responded poorly. They relied more and more on US aircraft and helicopters than becoming aggressive fighters. Diem seemed more interested in using the army to keep himself and his family in power than in fighting the enemy.[53]

Another detriment to the Diem regime was his installation of his brother Nhu as internal security chief of the nation. He formed cells of five men to do covert intelligence work in the army and government bureaucracy to spy on dissidents.[54] Nhu's actions and the flaunting of power by Nhu and his wife, who was known as "Madam Nhu," added to the disenchantment with the government.

Anti-Diem feeling increased in South Vietnam. Two South Vietnamese Air Force planes bombed the presidential palace in February 1962, but failed to injure Diem.[55] The Military Assistance Command Vietnam (MACV) was established under General Harkin in 1962[56], and the number of military advisors was increased from 3,000 to 11,300[57] as the situation continued to fester. In December 1962, a report from the State Department director of intelligence stated that a communist coup could occur at any time.

Meanwhile, the war was not going well against the Vietcong. In early 1963, 2,500 South Vietnamese troops, well armed with armored personnel carriers and using American helicopters for the first time, were roundly defeated by 300 Vietcong at Ap Bac in the delta. The VC succeeded in killing many of the ARVN troops, and escaped intact.[58]

In May 1963, government troops fired upon 20,000 Buddhists, celebrating the traditional birthday of Buddha, for flying the Buddhist flag. Nine were killed, including seven children. Buddhist protests added to the growing resentment. One of their leaders blamed Diem and his American backers.[57] Rallies and large strikes occurred, and a Buddhist monk immolated himself on June 11 at a busy Saigon intersection. Pictures of the incident were seen around the world.[60] Other monks immolated themselves as the government repeatedly blamed the Vietcong for the shooting incident in May.

For the first time, President Kennedy and some of his aides considered the possibility of a coup to get rid of Diem and Nhu.[61] Conversations about a coup had already occurred among South Vietnamese generals, and in private, they talked to a CIA agent.[62] Their plotting was complicated when truckloads of Nhu's men dressed in army uniforms attacked the Buddhist conclaves in Saigon, Hue, and other places, and rounded up more than 1,000 monks and other citizens. Urban youth rallied quickly to protest the actions.[63]

Ambassador Henry Cabot Lodge got the truth from his staff; he also learned that the generals had sought American support for a coup. Lodge initially suggested waiting. When Washington received the messages, local American policy decisions went back to Lodge.[64] Crucial debates were carried on at the highest circles of the US government, including with the president, for four days. The plotters would not move without American approval. Kennedy gave Lodge complete discretion to cut off aid to Diem, a signal the plotters needed.[65] However, the army plotters were slow to act. Delays occurred, with many secondary misgivings by the generals and in Washington, too.

Finally, when the generals learned that Nhu had gotten word of the proposed coup, and was planning a counter coup, they acted on the night of November 1, 1963. Diem and Nhu got word and fled the presidential palace to hide in a church. Later that night, they called the generals and received assurances that they would be given asylum in another country.[66] They were picked up in a troop carrier, and assassinated on the way back to the palace.[67]

Lodge had been assured that their lives would be spared. Kennedy was shocked. In the countryside, the peasants demolished many of the strategic hamlets. Lodge later cabled the president that he could neither manage nor stop the coup.[68]

On November 4, 1963, a new government started, with the real power residing in the revolutionary committee headed by General Duong Van Minh.[69] In less than two months, General Nguyen Khanh overthrew Minh, but kept Minh as titular head of state.[70]

"They rapidly disrupted the administrative system by replacing Diem's officials with their own cronies, many more corrupt than their predecessors."[71]

"The junta was ineffective and drifting," said Defense Secretary Robert McNamara.[72]

In 1964, a greater number of sectarian riots occurred, as the Buddhists became more militant, and felt slighted by the Khanh regime.[73] A coup against Khanh was attempted, but faltered when backed down by the air force. The administration was juggled a number of times to satisfy the disgruntled factions, but Khanh remained in control, if at times in the background.[74] He spent more time guarding against internal rivals and neglected his administrative duties.

In the United States, less than three weeks after Diem's demise, President Kennedy was assassinated on November 22 in Dallas. Within two days, his successor, Lyndon Johnson, confirmed that US support would continue in South Vietnam. By the end of the year, there were more than 15,000 American military advisors. In January 1964, General William

Westmoreland arrived as General Paul D. Harkins's deputy. He would eventually replace him in June, as Harkins's overly optimistic reports came under suspicion.[75]

The new government was no more effective against the Vietcong than Diem's had been. In early 1964, the Vietcong staged numerous bombings and hit-and-run attacks. In the delta, 3,000 ARVN troops encircled 600 Vietcong, but the South Vietnamese army lacked aggressiveness and the VC fought their way out.[76]

The Ho Chi Minh Trail in Laos was improved so that parts of it could handle truck traffic. The trail had previously been used mostly by indigenous communistic southerners returning south to fight with the Vietcong, but by April 1964, regular North Vietnamese Army (NVA) soldiers were going south. By the end of 1964, complete tactical units (up to 10,000 men) went down the trail.[77] Several pitched battles occurred. McNamara reported to President Johnson that 40 percent of the countryside was under Vietcong control and, in some provinces, such as Long An in the delta, as much as 90 percent was under VC control.[78]

The situation was getting worse even though the United States was spending millions of dollars for pacification purposes, such as teaching Vietnamese peasants to breed pigs, dig wells, and build houses. There were American doctors, schoolteachers, accountants, mechanics, and even disc jockeys in Vietnam.[79] US aid financed all of these, plus weapons and other products needed by Saigon to expand its armed forces to 600,000 men. The number of American military advisors or Green Berets was also steadily increasing.

CHAPTER 4

GREEN BERETS

"In September 1961, the US Army's Fifth Special Forces Group, First Special Forces, was activated at Fort Bragg, North Carolina, and eventually became in charge of all Special Forces in Vietnam, according to author Shelby L. Stanton.[80] Several years later, the headquarters was moved to Nha Trang in Vietnam.

Many of the advisors were working out in the field, helping build a multiple approach of counter insurgency. One group, the Civilian Irregular Defense Group (CIDG), was established to help prevent Vietcong control of the minorities. The CIDG worked with the Montagnards, Nungs, Khmers, and other religious groups. Originally, the CIA ran CIDG, but eventually turned it over to MACV (Military Assistance Command Vietnam). One of its purposes was to monitor infiltration of Vietcong and North Vietnamese Army troops across the border from Laos and Cambodia. These listening posts would become a thorn in the side of enemy infiltrators, and they tried to overrun them on numerous occasions. Sometimes the enemy succeeded, but sometimes the camps' defenses against overwhelming numbers were amazing successes.

The Green Berets also had numerous other jobs, spying and patrolling in Laos and Cambodia, and the more specific job of trying to win the minds and hearts of the common people with medical clinics, farming advice, etc. It was a most difficult job. They would go in by day to do their work, and by night, the Vietcong would undo what they had accomplished. The people were swayed more by the Vietcong, whom they feared, than by any effort the Special Forces might make.

The Green Berets, or Special Forces, were a swashbuckling group, usually marine or army non-commissioned officers (NCOs), who worked alone or in small groups. Some of them were considered legendary. Many acted independently from the regular army, and it was only later that they came under control of MACV. Over time, the Green Berets trained more than 54,000 CIDG troops, and established more than 80 fortified CIDG camps.[81]

Dr. Bob Hendren was one of the first, if not the first, Nelson Countian to serve in Vietnam.[82] He went to Vietnam in early 1965 and was there for nearly a year. The buildup of American troops started during that time. There were around 15,000 troops when he first went into the country, and probably close to 100,000 when he went home.

He was with the Army Fifth Special Forces Group, the Green Berets. He was the junior medic on a 12-man Special Forces A-Team. He was on the Cambodian border west of Saigon (now Ho Chi Minh City) at Long Khot, and then further south at Chou Duc on the Cambodian border. Their mission was border reconnaissance, training their Vietnamese counterparts and the local popular force.

Another agenda was to try to create goodwill in the area. That was the time of Chieu Hoa (open arms). This was a failed amnesty plan by the South Vietnamese for the Vietcong. The plan appeared to succeed for a while, but in the end, resulted in the VC infiltrating villages and military camps.

Hendren was one of two medics on the team, and spent most days with the engineers traveling up and down the river doing community projects and medical work. As a Special Forces medic, he had to train for a year, much longer than the ordinary medic or corpsman. The final eight weeks was the most intensive, when they learned to do gunshot wound debridement, give open drop anesthesia, do venous cut downs when necessary for rapid infusion of fluids, and even do emergency amputations, as well as give medicines. He treated patients with oral tetracycline, sulfonamides, and injectable penicillin in powder form in single-dose vials. He had otic (related to the ear) and ophthalmic preparations. The most popular medication at that time was the APC headache tablet and they had a large supply of those. They had chloroquine and a chloroquine-primaquine combo tablet that they took once a week to suppress malaria. Hendren gave gamma globulin injections to the men in the unit every three months as an attempt to prevent hepatitis. He had intravenous solutions of dextran, dextrose, and water, and normal saline to treat shock.

When they traveled up and down the river to small villages, they were greeted kindly. They would usually be served tea with the village elders before they started. They had an outpatient clinic that was open for the villagers as well as anyone else who wanted to come. They tried to take care of emergencies at any time. They had various suture material and orthopedic supplies. The majority of the patients were children. They had an interpreter with them. A government nurse was in the area, but no physician.

Barry Sadler, who wrote the "Ballad of Green Berets," was a medic, and was in Hendren's medical class and finished with them. He was also in Company D of the Fifth Special Forces Group with Bob and went to Vietnam at the same time. Charles Williams, who received the first Medal of Honor awarded in Vietnam, was also in D Company.

Hendren treated all kinds of diseases in the villages, and was frequently in danger of being captured by the Vietcong. Two members of his team were wounded while he was there. Their senior medic, James Jackson, was captured and not released until 1967, when Hendren was in his first year of medical school. There was a news story on TV about his release. Jane Fonda's husband and peace activist, Tom Hayden, went to Cambodia to get Jackson and another soldier named Fister. The VC had held them in leg irons in a four-by-six-foot bamboo cage, in the U Minh forest area in southern Vietnam for 18 months.

About the same time, Hendren learned of the death of Hubert Van Poll, a close friend and team member. He received the nation's second highest award, the Distinguished Service Cross, when he was killed in action. He was the most decorated soldier at the time, having previously received the Silver Star and Bronze Star.

Five of the team members stayed in touch, and try to get together every year at the Special Forces convention.

John Blevins, who lives on the outskirts of Bardstown, was typical of the Green Berets. He was a clerk typist when he first went into the army. He volunteered for jump school as a paratrooper, and afterwards was in the 101st (Screaming Eagle) Airborne Division at Fort Campbell. He went to Morse code school and became a radio operator, and then went to the Special Forces training group at Fort Bragg. He was then assigned to Germany to do undercover work, collecting and passing on intelligence. If the Russians attacked, they were to stay where they were, and operate behind Russian lines.

He got out of the army after that, but didn't much like civilian life.

He re-enlisted and went to helicopter flight school for three months. From there, he went to Vietnam with Special Forces, where he was assigned to Camp 415 at Tuyen Nhon, close to the Cambodian border (where it sticks out like a fishhook into South Vietnam). There were twelve Special Forces men there and around 200 CIDGs. Camp 415 was actually in the northern Mekong Delta in the Plain of Reeds. It was backed by a branch of the Mekong River and faced out onto the Plain of Reeds.

Blevins was one of two radio operators who sent intelligence back to B team at Moc Toy twice a day. All of the Special Forces went out on patrols—usually two Special Forces men and about 100 CIDGs. One of the radio operators stayed in camp. The CIDG was about 35 percent Cambodians; the rest were Vietnamese with a few Vietcong who had infiltrated. According to Blevins, the men could tell who the Vietcong were in battle. If the CIDG rifles were pointed toward the enemy, the CIDGs were friendlies. If they were pointed toward US troops, they were Vietcong. The patrols and raids were to collect information and set up ambushes along the heavily vegetated river branches and canals. Sometimes they used small motor boats (Boston Whalers®). Sometimes they went by small sampans or canoes at night. That was the scariest for the men, because they never knew what would come out of the vegetation while they were rowing silently. Most of the patrols were dry runs, but occasionally firefights developed when Vietcong were ambushed. The Vietcong hated the CIDG troops, and sometimes would commit atrocities against them, as if to teach the others a lesson.

The camp was four-sided with heavily armed blockhouses at the corners, connected by barbed wire and booby traps with ditches in front of them. The delta would frequently flood during the monsoon season. Blevins has a photo of himself standing waist deep in water in the compound. One CIDG camp was under water for months.

The Special Forces didn't often wear their green berets, except for special occasions. Blevins said they usually wore a camouflaged "boonie" hat. They were on their own for food. They were each given $70 a week for rations, and obtained their food wherever they could. Most often, they got it from a close-by camp with a mess hall. They would pool their money and one would go get the food. They frequently traded captured weapons or flags for food. They were irregulars and seemed to like their independence. Occasionally in their mission for food, they would go to Saigon for a couple of days, have a few beers, and relax.

In addition to their ambushes and patrols, some of which included slogging for miles through swamps and ditches, they had outposts up to 10 miles from their base camp. These were primitive posts with thatched roofs, and were in a circular shape for protection. Their function was to collect information, and one or two Special Forces men and some CIDG forces would man the outposts.

One of the Special Forces or Green Berets' main jobs was to stop infiltration across the Cambodian and Laotian borders by the Vietcong and NVA soldiers. Compared to the rest of the American activities in Vietnam, they were more successful. Their jobs were lonely, and occasionally the CIDG would revolt against them. In Blevins's camp, there were three such revolts, one of which was very scary, but they were resolved without anyone being killed. Overall, they did their job very well.

CHAPTER 5

PATH TO FULL WAR

—————————

On August 2, 1964, the destroyer USS *Maddox* was sailing off the North Vietnamese coast doing electronic surveillance. The *Maddox* was in international waters. Three North Vietnamese PT boats attacked the destroyer. At the same time, the South Vietnamese Navy was carrying on a few raids along the North Vietnamese coast using CIA-hired mercenaries from around the world, and the US Navy was carrying on DeSoto patrols by destroyers, designed for plotting coastal radar and intercepting communications. The destroyers had gotten within eight miles of the coast, although they were 28 miles out to sea when North Vietnamese patrol boats attacked them. Nine torpedoes were fired at the *Maddox*. The *Maddox* used evasive action to escape and returned fire, sinking two of the three PT boats. The carrier USS *Ticonderoga* deployed American planes and helped to chase away the other PT boat.

President Johnson did not take aggressive action at that time, but warned Russia and North Vietnam that any other warlike action would be met with force. Two days later, the *Maddox*, accompanied by the destroyer *Turner Joy*, returned to its surveillance job. At night, they heard North Vietnamese transmissions that sounded as if they were going to take action. Two blips showed up on the radarscope. It was a dark, windy, and cloudy night, and the blips came and went. The sonar operator on the *Maddox* thought he heard torpedo sounds and evasive action was taken. Because of poor visibility, the *Turner Joy* fired a number of rounds toward where the blips seemed to be coming from. The men thought they saw an explosion out in the darkness. Finally, the blips were gone. Because of the rough areas, the sonar soundings were questionable, but the Americans felt that the PT boats had tried to sink their ships.

The next day, President Johnson authorized retaliatory strikes. Carrier planes bombed and strafed two patrol boat anchorages. They also bombed the oil storage area at Vinh, and knocked out approximately 10 percent of North Vietnam's petroleum supply.

The president also asked for and got from Congress a resolution by 88 to 2 allowing him to respond to any aggressive action by the North Vietnamese. The resolution read: "Congress approves and supports the determination of the President as Commander in Chief to take all necessary measures to repel any armed attack against the forces of the United States. And to prevent further aggression, the United States is prepared, as the President determines, to take all necessary steps including the use of armed forces to assist any member of the Southeast Asia Collective/Defense treaty, requesting assistance in defense of its freedom."[83]

The Tonkin Gulf Resolution was, in effect, a war powers act. With it, the president was allowed to make war.[84]

In June of 1964, General Westmoreland took over MACV from General Harkins. Westmoreland wanted a greater American presence in Vietnam, but by January 1965, it had increased only slightly. The Special Forces Command was moved to Qui Nhon on the Vietnamese coast. The Fifth Special Forces Group (airborne), with four aviation battalions, moved in. They were primarily located in Saigon, Bien Hoa, Qui Nhon, and Pleiku in the highlands, and Da Nang, with Special Forces outposts along the

Cambodian and Laos borders.

On February 7, 1965, the Vietcong attacked the barracks of Camp Holloway at Pleiku with mortar rounds and satchel charges.[85] Eight Americans were killed and 128 injured, and a number of aircraft damaged or destroyed. Three days later, the Vietcong exploded the hotel billets in Qui Nhon, killing 23 Americans and injuring 22 others.[86] For some time, the military command had been urging a strong presence of American combat units in Vietnam to protect American bases. These two attacks strengthened that argument. Such units also would facilitate the defeat of the Vietcong who were besting the South Vietnamese Army. Westmoreland and the high service officers prevailed in their urgent demands, and the United States decided to send in combat troops. Reprisal air raids in the north, called Avodart I and Avodart II, were carried out.

At this time, a decision was made at the highest levels to start a bombing campaign of the North to force the Hanoi government to desist in their aid to the South. This campaign was called Rolling Thunder. In order to build a consensus of opinion for Rolling Thunder, Daniel Ellsberg of the Defense Department researched and gave stories of Vietcong atrocities, such as the mining of buses, mutilation of American advisors, and assassination of local officials and their families. Ellsberg would later become a harsh critic of the war. However, at the time he felt like many Americans, and said, "I thought our retreat from Vietnam would cause us much trouble in our worldwide conflict with Communism" and "embolden the Soviets, and Chinese, and insurgents worldwide, and discourage our allies."[87]

Many of the initial flights would be out of Da Nang. Its airfield would need protection.

CHAPTER 6

THE AMERICANS LAND

In 1965, the first American ground forces of any size were sent to Vietnam. America was at war. On March 8, 1965, two marine battalions from the Third Marine Division landed at Da Nang. One battalion landed on the beach, and advanced in battle-like formations, but were met only by girls who gave them flowers. The other battalion flew in to Da Nang airfield. The planes received some fire from the adjacent countryside, but had no casualties. In mid-April, two other battalions joined them to beef up the Da Nang garrison, and establish a base at Phu Bai, 40 miles north of Da Nang toward the old capital of Hue.[88]

On April 20, two more battalions landed 60 miles south of Da Nang at Chu Lai. Engineer Mate Third Class Carl Pash was aboard the USS *Canberra*, which brought the Fourth Marines ashore. The marine command totaled 8,600 men, and included one battalion of the Fourth Marine Regiment. Ten Huey helicopters were also located at Phu Bai. Enclaves were set up in all of these places. The operation was known as the Third Marine Amphibious Force.

Sergeant George Taylor of Balltown, Kentucky (south of Bardstown), was in this early detachment, as was Lieutenant Robert Downard. Sergeant Taylor was later joined by two brothers in the marines, one of whom would be killed.

Their main job initially was to protect the airfields. The local South Vietnamese Army officials denied them any offensive action, even patrolling outside of their bases.[89] In three weeks, their role expanded to limited action.

On July 1, the Vietcong attacked on the air force side of the Da Nang airfield. The marines drove off the VC after they had destroyed a number of aircraft parked on the field. After that, unrestrained authority was given for marine offensive operations. Two battalions of the Seventh Regiment, First Division landed at Chu Lai on August 14.

Lieutenant Kenneth Sympson, from the Cox's Creek area near Bardstown, Kentucky, landed with the First Battalion. His unit first landed at Qui Nhon off the assault ship *Iwo Jima*, but shortly re-embarked and moved to Chu Lai. As an artillery forward observer, Sympson had one of the most exposed jobs in the army, and was frequently out in front of the infantry with little protection.

Commanders decided it was time to clean the Vietcong out of the adjacent countryside. Intelligence indicated that the First Vietcong Regiment was on a peninsula 14 miles south of Chu Lai. An operation called Starlite was planned. It would involve troops primarily from the Third and Fourth Regiments, and was a multi-pronged attack. One group would land by amtracs on the beachhead; they would be reinforced by M48 tanks and Ontos vehicles armed with six recoilless rifles. Marines advancing up the beach were met by rifle and automatic weapon fire from entrenched Vietcong. Despite fire from six-inch guns from the supporting USS *Galveston*, the Vietcong bunkers held out, and had to be charged by marines with bayonets. The trenches were taken after fierce hand-to-hand fighting, and the beach was secured.

Inland, the Second Battalion of the Fourth Marines landed aboard helicopters. They ran into a VC-controlled ridgeline, and soon had it cleared by bayonet attack. Another company landed almost on top of a VC battalion headquarters. After a hot landing against rocket-propelled grenades (RPGs) and machine-gun fire, the company pulled back into an operational perimeter. One attack up the hill against concentrated gunfire failed. Tanks and Ontos vehicles came up and bombarded the hill. The marines attacked again using rifle and grenade fire, and gradually cleared the Vietcong from the summit.[90]

Advancing through two hamlets they thought were friendly, the marines ran into more tough resistance. A mortar barrage rained down on them, and machine-gun fire came from two directions. A relief column of tanks and Ontos vehicles was met by a hail of RPG and recoilless rifle fire. The vehicles were immobilized. More marines were called up to take the two fortified villages. The enemy tried to overrun the Americans through the night, and many marines and VC died. The next morning, a unit from the Seventh Marines helicoptered in, and joined the other units pushing towards the coast. They pushed the VC back into pockets of defense, where they were annihilated as the marines pushed on to the coast in a pincer movement. Operation Starlite was a success. The First VC regiment had been badly mauled when caught by surprise.

Lieutenant Sympson wrote:

> OPERATION STARLITE HAD JUST BEGUN FOR ME AND FOR THE HANDFUL OF YOUNG MARINES WHO COMPRISED MY ARTILLERY OBSERVATION TEAM. THIS WAS NOT THE FIRST TIME WE HAD LANDED IN THIS COUNTRY, BUT IT WAS THE FIRST TIME WE WOULD FACE THE ENEMY.

THE FIGHTING HAD BEEN GOING ON ALL DAY WITH ABOUT THREE BATTALIONS OF MARINE INFANTRY ASSAULTING THE FIRST VIETCONG REGIMENT. WE HAD CAUGHT HIM, AND THE ENEMY WAS FIGHTING FOR HIS LIFE, FRANTICALLY. IT WOULD DO LITTLE GOOD.

AS WE CLOSED ON THE ENEMY NEAR VAN TUONG, WE MARCHED OVER GROUND WHERE A FURIOUS FIREFIGHT HAD OCCURRED EARLIER THAT MORNING, PERHAPS AN HOUR BEFORE. THE EARTH, SHRUBS, AND TREES WERE FRESHLY SCORCHED FROM THE MORTAR AND ARTILLERY FIRE, AND NAPALM DROPS.

STONE WALLS AND MONUMENTS WERE PITTED AND SCARRED FROM RIFLE AND MACHINE-GUN FIRE, BROKEN FROM THE CONCUSSION OF BOMBS AND HAND GRENADES; BURNT-OUT PEASANT HOMES, PERHAPS THE TARGET OF NAPALM OR FLAMETHROWERS. THESE ARE THE KIND OF THINGS THAT COME EASILY TO MIND; WHAT THE MIND TRIES TO PROTECT ITSELF FROM—THAT IS THE MOST DEVASTATED—THE PEOPLE WHO BATTLED EACH OTHER HERE. YOU DON'T PICK UP AFTER YOURSELF IN THE MIDDLE OF A FIREFIGHT, AND THE MARINES WHO PRECEDED US HERE LEFT BEHIND THINGS WE DID NOT WANT TO SEE, THINGS WE DID NOT WANT TO SMELL, THINGS THAT OUR MINDS FOUND HARD TO UNDERSTAND. THE MARINE DEAD AND WOUNDED HAD BEEN EVACUATED. THE VIETCONG WOUNDED WERE HIDING, AND CAME TO BE OUR TARGETS, AS WELL. THE VIETCONG DEAD WERE ROTTING IN THE HEAT AND HUMIDITY, AND THE STENCH OF THE PLACE MADE YOU WANT TO PUKE.

THE DEAD WERE EVERYWHERE. THEY WERE IN THE RICE PADDIES AND IN THE TRENCH LINES THAT DIDN'T PROTECT THEM ENOUGH. LIKE THE TREES, LIMBS, AND OTHER THINGS, THEY WERE

RIPPED APART AND SCORCHED. THEY WERE THROWN ABOUT. SOME
WERE WHOLE, BUT HAD GAPING MORTAL WOUNDS. SOME WERE
NEARLY VAPORIZED, WITH LITTLE BUT ENOUGH EVIDENCE THAT
THEY HAD EXISTED AT ALL. THEY LOOKED LIKE THINGS THAT COULD
NOT MAKE IT ACROSS THE HIGHWAY, BUT BIGGER AND WITH DARK
CLOTHES SCRAMBLED WITH THEIR FLESH. THEY COULD NOT BE
REASSEMBLED, AND THEY COULD NOT WORK ANYMORE.

SUCH IS THE TERROR OF WAR, WITH TORN AND BATTERED
BODIES, THE AFTERMATH OF BATTLE, AND THE TORN VEGETATION
ABOUT THEM. THE VEGETATION WOULD GROW BACK, BUT THE
BODIES WOULD NOT.[91]

Operation Starlite was an undoubted success. It gutted a Vietcong
regiment, and cleared the area south of Chu Lai. It rivaled the later, more
heralded, battle of the Ia Drang. Six-hundred and fourteen of the enemy
soldiers were killed compared to 45 marines killed in action and 203
wounded.

Operation Piranha, another amphibious and helicopter assault,
followed Starlite on September 7. It resulted in the destruction of a large
Vietcong cave. Following this assault, the Vietcong avoided the marines until
December.

From then on until 1971, the marines would stay heavily engaged. The
most available army unit for the buildup was the 173rd Airborne Brigade.[92]
It was composed of the First and Second Battalions of the 503rd Airborne
Infantry Regiment. They were called the "herd." They were brought in on
April 14, 1965, and stationed at Bien Hoa. At first, one battalion guarded
the port of Vung Tau, the landing port for troops. The other battalion

guarded the airfield at Bien Hoa. In early June, they were pulled together, and an Australian battalion added. Then they trained as airmobile infantry. In late June, the brigade had a training action involving 144 helicopters, the 173rd Brigade, and two ARVN battalions. They went into the jungles of War Zone D, which had previously been Vietcong territory. They had little combat, but they got the feel of jungle warfare. The brigade had an attack in War Zone D in July and at Pleiku on August 10 after an attack on the Special Forces camp at Duc Co. This would be their mission throughout their stay in Vietnam, to go wherever they were urgently needed to put out fires.

While in Pleiku, they held the Thanh Binh Pass on Highway 19, through which the ARVN troops were retreating, and stayed around Kon Tum province for a while before returning to Bien Hoa. In October, they were back in the jungles of War Zone D north of Saigon, where they ran into sniper fire and occasional ambushes, but no serious battles.

The Second Brigade of the First Division came into Vietnam on July 16, 1965, as part of the buildup. The Big Red One Division left Fort Riley, Kansas, and was directed to secure the coastal town of Qui Nhon. The division's supplies were sent there. However, two days before the division's scheduled arrival, its ships were shunted to Saigon for the city's protection. The division had to wait for its equipment. The Fifth Artillery Battalion was attached to the First Infantry Division. The battalion's executive officer was Malcolm Geoghegan of Bardstown.[93]

Geoghegan had been in the navy in World War II, and had served on a ship off Okinawa during the deadly kamikaze attacks. After the war, he returned to college, joined ROTC, and got a commission in the army. He steadily rose in rank, and went to Fort Sill for artillery training. He then went to the Army War College. By the time he went to Vietnam, he was a major and the number-two man in his battalion.

His battalion was followed by the First Cavalry Airmobile Division, which went to the Central Highlands to prevent the enemy from driving to the coast along Highway 19 and cutting the country in two.

On October 19, the Special Forces Camp of Plei Mei was garrisoned by 12 Special Forces men and by 415 Civilian Irregular Defense Group (CIDG) soldiers. The 32nd, 33rd, and 66th NVA regiments had moved into the area. After midnight, they overran an outpost, and mortar-barraged the camp. Then they assaulted it, running with AK-47s blazing. Despite intensive defensive fire, they were able to blow up the perimeter barriers. Then they came pouring through the gaps. They were illuminated with flares, and scores were machine-gunned down. Enemy rockets illuminated the night. Around 3:45 a.m., jets came in and napalmed the area around the camp. Intense fighting persisted, but Special Forces held on. At dawn, a flight of medevacs came in, escorted by helicopter gunships. One medevac was shot down and all hands were lost.

A Special Forces unit with two ARVN companies came in the next day to Pleiku to try to reinforce the camp. A force of 1,200 mechanized ARVN soldiers also tried to reach the camp. They ran into opposition and a lack of aggressiveness kept them from reaching the camp until October 25. The Special Forces unit, called Project Delta, helicoptered in about four miles from the camp on October 21. They had to cut their way through dense jungle, a very slow and exhausting procedure. The next morning, they fought their way through machine-gun fire into the perimeter to help relieve the battered camp defenders who were still hanging on. That afternoon, a clearing force of three companies was sent out of the perimeter, but met stiff resistance, and had to withdraw. When the armored relief column finally reached the camp, the enemy withdrew.[94]

The next day Colonel Elvy B. Roberts, commanding officer of the First Brigade, First Cavalry, helicoptered in for a briefing. After that, he moved his entire brigade to Camp Holloway at Pleiku, determined to punish the attackers of Plei Mei. The First Cavalry was drawn into one of the early major battles of the war.[95]

CHAPTER 7

1965: LA DRANG AND HARVEST MOON

The first major land battle between American forces and the communists occurred in 1965. By that time, the United States had deployed parts of several divisions to Vietnam. One of the first divisions was the First Cavalry Airmobile. In time, the division would be known as the first team, but in 1965, they were as unproven as the other units. However, they had several great assets. They were well trained, had helicopters to give them rapid battlefield mobility, and one of their battalions was led by an outstanding soldier and officer, Lieutenant Colonel Harold G. Moore, Jr.

Lieutenant Colonel Moore was born in Bardstown, Kentucky, in the early 1920s.[96] Moore was an excellent athlete, and played end on the high school football team. At the time, they used what was called the "sleeper play." A player would run to the sidelines as if he were being substituted for, but he would stay inbounds at the edge of the playing field, unnoticed. With the next play, he would take off downfield unguarded. If the team had a good passer, they could usually achieve a good gain or a touchdown. It was perfectly legitimate, and Moore played it perfectly.

However, his ambition wasn't in sports. He had made up his mind early that he wanted to go to the United States Military Academy at West Point and become an army officer. He was disappointed when the senator from Kentucky, who had promised an appointment, failed to come through.

He went to Washington, and worked in the national capital, trying to find some connection and an appointment to the Military Academy. After about a year, a congressman from another state got him an appointment to Annapolis, the Naval Academy. He didn't want that, and after some finagling, exchanged it with another congressman for an appointment to West Point. His persistence paid off.

He entered the academy just after World War II started, so he didn't see any action in that war. He graduated in 1945, just as the war was ending. He earned a master's degree in international affairs, and received a yearlong fellowship for advanced studies at Harvard. While at West Point, he attended church on an almost daily basis.

He became a paratrooper with the 11th Airborne Division in Japan, and then returned to serve with the 82nd Airborne. He volunteered for the Airborne's test section, and jump-tested experimental parachutes and associated equipment for the army, air force, and the CIA. He had 135 jumps, and experienced several near-death incidents. This experience helped train him for coolness and courage under fire.

Even though Moore missed World War II, he had plenty of war service after that. He commanded two companies in Korea, seeing some of the bitterest fighting at such places as Pork Chop Hill and Old Baldy, among others, where the attrition rate was high on both sides. After that, he returned to West Point to teach tactics, and then had a year of study at the Army Command and General Staff College. He served for two and a half years in the Air Mobility Division of the Army's Research and Development Office. Following other assignments, he was sent to NATO duty for three years in Oslo, Norway, where he was responsible for planning the ground defense of Northern Germany, Denmark, and Norway.[97]

After a year in the Navy War College, he served for 18 months as an Air Assault Infantry Battalion commander in the 11th Air Assault Division at Fort Benning, and in the same position in the First Cavalry Division in Vietnam. While at Fort Benning, he was given a commendation for saving a soldier's life with CPR when he passed out on a long march.[98]

While in Vietnam, Moore led his battalion into the war's first major battle with North Vietnamese troops. The North Vietnamese had decided that the Central Highlands of South Vietnam were critical. They had previously had no large units of their army in South Vietnam. However, they sent elements of several divisions, three full regiments, down the arduous Ho Chi Minh Trail in Laos and Cambodia into that area along the Chu Pong Massif, 3,700 feet high. Until that time, the Vietcong had done most of the fighting. The NVA had just arrived and was setting up their staging areas for the development of the Central Highlands invasion. Their advance units had been blunted six weeks before by a surprise attack of companies of the First Cavalry Division. They had lost their medical supplies and stocks of other supplies, including rice, from a planned staging area. That attack made them more aware of the enemy and gave them a chance to prepare.

Moore had orders to fly with his battalion deeper into the rugged highlands—into the area around the Ia Drang Valley—to find the enemy and destroy them. He did an exploratory flight over the area to find a suitable landing site. He found three, but only one was big enough to land eight helicopters at one time with approximately 80 men. He had to bring them in fast. Otherwise, the lead elements would be extremely vulnerable to attack. He called the larger area "X-ray," because of an X on the map.[99] He also located a suitable clearing to the rear for the artillery support called Falcon. Two batteries of 105 howitzers were airlifted to this site by large Chinook helicopters.

When this was done, his companies were taken in one at a time: Bravo Company first, Alpha Company second, and Charlie Company last. His battalion was under strength, down to fewer than 500 men, due to rotation of troops, malaria, and other causes. At full strength, it would have been about 700. However, he had his orders and he was going to follow them. His helicopter-supporting group was down to 16 (half strength). They would have to take in 80 men in eight helicopters, and quickly return to pick up another load. This was cutting the safety margin thin. Any glitch along the way could strand those already landed without support.

X-ray landing zone was blasted around its fringes with artillery, helicopter rockets, and machine-gun fire. Moore went in with the first group of eight Huey helicopters, and the first 80 men of Bravo Company. He was the first man on the ground.[100] His second-in-command would remain aloft in an observation helicopter to give rapid intelligence to the ground troops. Fortunately, Bravo Company landed without mishap.

This was all going on below the Chu Pong Massif, and the North Vietnamese could look down on them. They rapidly sprang into action.

The American troops were told to advance uphill as rapidly as possible to find the enemy, and more importantly, to be in position to protect the landing zone—the lifeline of the battalion.

At first, it seemed easy, too easy. While the platoons of Bravo Company were advancing, Moore reconnoitered the area to visualize the terrain for a protective perimeter. It wasn't long until he heard rifle fire.

One of the lead platoons under Lieutenant Henry Herrick saw enemy soldiers as they were moving out, and they took off after them.[101]

After a short distance, they were sprayed by a hail of gunfire, and went to ground, taking casualties. Before they realized what was happening, there were enemy soldiers all around them. As best as they could, they set up an oval defensive perimeter under Herrick's direction in a depressed swatch of land. They fought off the enemy, but they were surrounded. They were separated from Bravo Company and the rest of the battalion. Over the next two days, they would repel enemy attacks, gradually losing more men, but a handful of them survived on sheer courage and ingenuity.

Meanwhile, the rest of the battalion landed, and the enemy—tough NVA soldiers—tried to surround and overrun them. Moore was busy trying to set up a good defensive perimeter. A dry creek bed looked like a potentially dangerous spot, where enemy soldiers could infiltrate into the perimeter and the landing zone. M60 machine guns were placed there. The rest of Moore's men got down behind any cover they could find. This initial period was very fluid, with American soldiers moving to various parts of the defensive line, and the enemy moving to find a soft spot where they could penetrate and overrun.

The next two days were touch and go, but the first two hours were particularly perilous. As more troops helicoptered in with ammunition, the wounded were taken out. Moore was particularly concerned about protecting the landing zone (LZ). It was his lifeline. Helicopters would come in, unload men and supplies, and reload within a matter of a few minutes. Sometimes they didn't even touch down. They were good targets for enemy fire, but fortunately, even though some were damaged, none of them was lost.

After Bravo Company was ferried in, Alpha Company, under Captain Tony Nadal, was brought in next, and hustled up to the left flank of Bravo Company. The perimeter was beginning to take shape. The lead elements of Charlie Company followed, but until they could be positioned on Alpha Company's left, the perimeter couldn't be established.[102]

In the meantime, Moore set up a command post from which he and Sergeant Major Basil Plumley could operate. Captain Matt Dillon, Moore's second-in-command, was in a helicopter overhead, radioing in obvious enemy movements and relaying how the battle was developing. Moore set up his radioman next to a large termite hill. From there, Moore could call in artillery fire and air support, and he would spend a good bit of the next two days there. He wanted to get out and check on his men, but there was grazing fire all over the area. Sergeant Plumley told him that if he, as their commander was lost, the whole battalion would be lost. For a while, they were the only reserve.

As the battle developed, the NVA commanders tried to figure out the area the Americans held, so they could outflank it with their troops boiling down from the Chu Pong Massif. At first, the Americans thought they were fighting the Vietcong, but Nadal recognized that they were North Vietnamese Army troops. He shouted over the radio, "They're PAVN, they're PAVN," meaning that they were well-trained, disciplined troops, and good shots. Both frontal assault and flanking attacks were tried.

American troops arrived just in time to plug gaps in the line. The 112 men of Company C, under Captain Bob Edwards, was one such unit. They stopped a charge of 150 enemy troops, surprising and decimating them.[103]

Captain Ray Lefebvre, with some of his men from Delta Company, arrived just in time to prevent another attack from penetrating the perimeter and the landing zone. Lefebvre was wounded, but his heroic action earned a high decoration. Specialists Russell Adams and Bill Beck set up their M60 machine-gun about 100 feet ahead of the perimeter. They and another M60 crew warded off a company-sized attack on the dry creek bed. Adams became a casualty and Beck continued to hold his position and repel the enemy. More than 30 years later, Beck met the commander of that company, who said, "So you're the man who wiped out my command."[104]

Meanwhile, the mayhem persisted all over the battlefield. Men had their own little individual battles. One soldier had only a M79 grenade launcher, and using an anthill for protection, was able to kill two enemy soldiers. Others used M-16s, M60s, and grenades, having little cover other than tree stumps and high grass.

Moore's casualties, including officers and men, increased. He had told his command not to leave any casualties, killed or wounded, out in the battle line, and his men didn't, often at risk to themselves. However, if the Americans were taking casualties, the enemy was taking much worse.

In addition to small-arms fire from the ground troops, artillery fire was crashing down on them, encircling the perimeter with a curtain of fire. There were twelve howitzers in LZ Falcon, an artillery base set up five miles away to support their operation. They were amazingly accurate at five miles. They were not only able to protect the main perimeter, but also Herrick's isolated platoon. In addition to the field artillery, Moore's air assets played a big part in his defense. There were Skyraiders, World War II single-engine planes, which could carry an enormous amount of armament, and stay over the target longer because of their slow speed. There were jets carrying 250-pound bombs and napalm. There were the Air Rocket Artillery (ARA) helicopters, which could attack a target like a "gaggle of geese," darting forward and sideways and sometimes even backwards. Each helicopter carried multiple rockets, and six helicopters per unit could bring a lot of firepower to bear.

That afternoon, the helicopters all went back to refuel several times. They not only bombarded the attacking enemy, but also their reserves on the Chu Pong Massif. Moore said that these extra assets were the difference between his forces and those of the enemy. Both sides had well-trained elite soldiers. Moore failed to say that his leadership played a big role.

After the lines had been somewhat stabilized, the command decided to send out men on a mission to try to reach the isolated platoon. By that time, only seven men of the original platoon were uninjured; 13 were wounded and nine were dead. Herrick was killed after setting up the perimeter, and Sergeant Ernie Savage was in command. They had beaten off several attacks, and were grimly holding on. They still had radio communication. Captain Tony Nadal of Alpha Company and Lieutenant Dennis Deal of Bravo Company led the relief mission. They hadn't gotten very far before they ran into blistering small-arms fire, and started taking casualties, one of which was Sergeant Jack Gell, whose dying words were, "Tell my wife I love her." The enemy machine gunner and his squad had killed Gell and wounded several others from behind a termite mound. They had the whole front pinned down when Lieutenant Joe Marm stood up and charged the mound. He threw a grenade behind it, then shot or bayoneted the rest of the enemy soldiers. Later, a dead officer and 11 dead soldiers were found behind that mound. Marm was wounded, but earned the Congressional Medal of Honor for his heroism.[105]

Little forward movement had been accomplished and casualties were mounting. Nadal radioed for permission to fall back. There was danger of another platoon being cut off if they didn't. The first attempt to reach the isolated platoon failed. White phosphorus artillery shells covered their retreat with their wounded. Deal and a sergeant would later wildly dash 100 yards to retrieve an M-16 sitting on a stump.

In the meantime, Moore was anxious to get more reinforcements. The LZ had become so hot and dangerous because of enemy fire that it had to be temporarily shut down. Ammunition was running low. Two helicopter pilots who were to enjoy increasing fame during the war, Captain Bruce Crandall and "Too Tall" Captain Ed Freeman, loaded their helicopters with ammo and decided they would try to make it in. They radioed Moore and told him they were on their way. When they got to the LZ X-ray, they found Moore himself there to help guide them in away from the worst enemy fire. Moore asked that the remaining elements of companies C and D be flown in as soon as possible. With better consolidation of their position and the LZ, those elements flew in, with Moore guiding in the lead helicopters. Another company, Bravo Company of the Seventh Cavalry, Second Battalion, under Captain Myron Diduryk, was also sent in. They would serve as the battalion reserve.[106]

Night was coming, so Moore strengthened and shortened his lines. He put one of Diduryk's platoons with Company C, and brought in his second-in-command, Captain Matt Dillon, who had been in a helicopter overhead helping to visualize the battlefield.[107] Moore decided that Dillon was needed more on the ground, assisting with operations.

Enemy activity had fallen off and Moore had time to assess his losses. Alpha Company had lost three officers and 31 enlisted men. Bravo Company had lost one officer and 46 enlisted men, in addition to the lost platoon. C Company had lost only four men.[108] His command was wounded, but still a virile, determined group of soldiers. The enemy had been wounded much worse, but it, too, was still determined, and far outnumbered the Americans. Moore and Plumley made walking rounds of the perimeter. Morale was still high.

As night settled in, the men were told to stay on alert. They couldn't dig deep foxholes because of the noise involved and roots in the ground.[109] All through the night, there were probes of the perimeter, which were easily driven off. The LZ was set up for night landings with flashlights and radio contact. New supplies of ammunition and water came in. Water, transported in large plastic containers, was almost as important as ammunition. As supplies were brought in, the wounded were loaded up and taken out. A small first aid station was jerry-rigged up with ponchos to keep in the light.

On one of the helicopter runs, the one that Matt Dillon came in on, a young correspondent by the name of Joe Galloway came in.[110] He and Moore would become fast friends, and the two would later write a book about the campaign (*We Were Soldiers Once . . . and Young: Ia Drang: The Battle that Changed the War in Vietnam*). As Dillon and Galloway flew in, they noticed hundreds of blinking lights coming down from the Chu Pong Massif, presumably NVA soldiers coming down to get in position for an early morning attack. Moore called in artillery on them, and they heard at least one large explosion. The men got little, if any, sleep, despite the rigorous day they had put in.[111]

As dawn broke, Moore planned how to relieve the isolated platoon. He noticed that everything was quiet, too quiet. He ordered recon squads to move out from Charlie Company to see what the enemy was doing. It was about 6:30 a.m. The recon squads hadn't gone 150 yards into the high grass before shots were heard. The squads ran back and alerted their buddies. The NVA soldiers were right behind them.

The enemy had planned an attack at 6:30, and the recon squads ignited it.[112] Originally, they had planned to attack at 2 a.m., but hadn't gotten into the right position. They attacked in battalion strength, supported by a Vietcong main force unit. The enemy got into American lines before protecting artillery could be brought to bear. Much of the fighting was hand-to-hand. The two platoons of Company C were hit the worst. It was 60 men against the massed forces of the attack. Two American machine guns cut down the enemy, but not fast enough.

Within 15 or 20 minutes, both lieutenants commanding the platoons, Lieutenant Neil Kroger and Lieutenant John Geoghegan, were killed, and their men were being chewed up, but *somehow they were holding.* The company commander, Captain Bob Edwards, was wounded in the shoulder and hunkered down in the command foxhole with his radioman. His executive officer, Lieutenant John Arrington, was called over to take command of the company, but he, too, was wounded. Another wounded officer was with them in the command foxhole with one enlisted man.[113]

Edwards called for help for his company, but Moore felt it was too early to commit his reserve. Finally, he sent a squad from Alpha Company to assist the thinning C Company. Of the 16 men in the squad, two were killed and two were wounded by grazing fire before they even reached the Company C lines. Artillery was called in, but much of the enemy forces had gotten too close to American lines to fire safely. However, they did fire at the reinforcing NVA and Vietcong units. The "Broken Arrow" call went out, which meant that they were about to be overrun, and every plane in the area flew in to give what relief they could. Unfortunately, because enemy units were into the American lines, the planes' help was limited. The moment of truth had come.

The noise of the fighting was deafening, with every weapon in the arsenal of both sides firing. Moore had seen a lot of tough fighting in Korea, but he had never heard anything so deafening. Most of the officers and many of the NCOs were down. It was up to them, the thin line of C Company, to hold. It was so tenuous that the men of Alpha Company and Bravo Company on the other side of the perimeter were preparing to turn around and meet any serious breakthrough.

Moore called the regiment, and asked for another company. Fortunately, the Alpha Company of the Second Battalion, Seventh Cavalry, was prepared and ready to go. Within a short time, they were on their way in helicopters. With the battle developing as it did, it was obvious to Moore that the main thrust of the battle was all going to be in C Company's area.[114] Just getting to the area from anywhere in the perimeter was dangerous because of the grazing fire. Two machine-gun groups were responsible for most of the enemy casualties, scything down the charging enemy. At the end of the morning's battle, two American machine gunners were found dead at their gun, with enemy dead stacked up in front of them. On the other M60, only one of the gunners was uninjured and still firing when the battle ended. With more troops coming into action on the friendly side, the situation stabilized after a few hours.

Private First Class Larry Stephenson of Delta Company, who was situated on C Company's flank, held an area 50 feet wide to keep C Company's position stable.[115] He calmly dropped to one knee, and killed 15 of the enemy before help came. Help soon arrived in the form of the battalion recon platoon, which helped stabilize the perimeter where the two hard-hit C Company platoons had been.

Moore looked up as two F100 jets flew right toward his position. He was alarmed to see two canisters of napalm drop from one jet toward his lines. The second jet was about to follow with its load of napalm. Frantically, he got his flight radio officer to call off the second plane just in time. Fire from the first plane hit at the edge of his position, and badly burned two men.[116] Some of the fiery jelly landed on the ammunition pile. Plumley, while under fire, calmly swept it off before it blew up the reserve ammunition, and possibly maimed numerous men. A medic ran out to help the burned men, and was shot in the head.

Finally, with the additional help, the battle was winding down. Captain Diduryk's Bravo Company of the Second Battalion and a platoon from Alpha Company were ordered up to take care of the area where three platoons had been badly shot up. Of the 106 men who started the day in Charlie Company, 46 officers and men were dead, and 20 more were wounded.[117] Hundreds of slain North Vietnamese soldiers littered the battlefield. The wounded, including Captain Edwards, were brought back to the battalion aid station, patched up, and given plasma as necessary.

The enemy withdrew and the battlefield was policed. The dead were brought in, as well as the firearms and equipment, both American and NVA. What was left of Company C was brought back to form the battalion reserve. Helicopters came in to pick up the wounded and the dead.

To the east, more help was coming. The Second Battalion of the Fifth Cavalry, under Lieutenant Colonel Bob Tully, was marching in. They encountered no opposition until they ran into a NVA strong point half a mile from LZ X-ray. Tully's men outflanked it and the resistance was broken. They marched in through the edge of the battlefield and were amazed at the carnage. One soldier carried an American flag and put it up on a broken tree, where it stayed until the battle was over.[118]

With the addition of Tully's battalion, he and Moore decided it was time to send out a force to rescue the lost and trapped platoon. Tully would lead the mission, and two of his companies, plus Captain John Herren's

Bravo Company, of which the lost platoon was a member, would participate. They started after a preliminary barrage of the area around the platoon's site. They initially met no resistance. Later they received some sniper fire. When they finally reached the small perimeter of the platoon, they hardly recognized the men, because they were covered with dust from all of the artillery fire. A blocking force was placed around the site. The men were given water and their wounds dressed.

Of the 29 men in the platoon, nine were dead, including Lieutenant Herrick, 13 were wounded, and seven were extremely tired, but unwounded. More sniper fire came in. The men who could move on their own were assisted. Stretchers were made of ponchos, and the wounded and dead were carried back to LZ X-ray along with their weapons. It was a slow, tedious, sad parade in the steaming heat.

Tully called in when they were 15 minutes out, and medevacs were summoned. Snipers hit a couple of men from the rescuing force. The ordeal of the isolated platoon was over. For more than 24 hours, they had been attacked off and on, knowing that at any time their little pocket could be crushed. One medic had saved the lives of many of the wounded. The platoon had finally been saved.[119]

The second night was coming on. It was again too quiet. Moore laid out his defenses for the night. Tully's battalion was stationed north and northwest of LZ X-ray. Moore's men, with two companies from the Second Battalion, Seventh Cavalry, would stay in their old positions facing the mountain. Diduryk's company, reinforced with a platoon from Alpha Company, Second Battalion, were placed where C Company had been so brutally cut up in the morning battle; they were linked in tight with the companies on their flanks. The men shortened their lines, and placed rigged grenades and trip flares in position forward to their lines. They figured artillery sitings and ranges. At dusk, the men were given ample supplies of ammunition. Harassment and interdiction artillery fire started, and continued off and on through the night.

At about midnight, a strange call came through. General Westmoreland sent a message that he wanted Moore to leave X-ray early in the morning and fly to Saigon to brief him on the battle. Moore felt that his place was with his men, and right then they were the most important thing to him. No further messages came through.[120]

Intermittent firing came through the night without any organized attack, but all of the men at LZ X-ray felt that one was coming. Booby trap grenades went off in the dark, trip flares started going off after 4 a.m., and at 4:22, the main attack started.[121] A reinforced NVA battalion and a VC battalion attacked in human waves. Artillery was called in, and shells with flares illuminated the battlefield. The enemy attacked from the same direction as they had on the previous morning. They were met primarily by Diduryk's company.[122]

A C-123 plane, "Smoky the Bear," flew over and dropped parachute flares to take over the task from the artillery. The plane would stay over the battlefield until 5:50 a.m. when it ran out of flares. One flare fell into the ammunition supply, and Plumley ran in and threw it safely away from the grenade boxes.

The enemy charged recklessly with screams, shouts, and whistles into the smoky killing field. Diduryk's rifles and machine guns mowed them down. When the flares were the brightest, the enemy sought cover in the tall grass and trees, but then they got up and charged again. A few managed to get within 10 to

15 feet from the American foxholes, but were killed with rifle fire and grenades. The enemy sent RPGs, and AK-47 and machine-gun fire into the American lines, but the soldiers had good cover in their foxholes. The Americans fought off the initial attack in about half an hour. At 4:31, the attack resumed. The intensity of the attack increased, and the enemy assaulted all three of Diduryk's platoons. American troops fired all of their mortars and, added to the artillery fire, made a cauldron of the field in front of their lines. That, plus the rifle and machine-gun fire, was too much, and the enemy broke and ran.

At 6:22, the NVA commander launched another attack with waves of soldiers coming straight down from the mountain. They ran into a hail of gunfire, and kept on coming despite their losses. They were mowed down. Artillery and mortar fire again came into play. Finally, the attack ended with hundreds of dead soldiers added to the dead from the previous morning battle.[123] The smell was sickening. In Diduryk's company, which bore the brunt of the attack, only six men were slightly wounded.

After the attack finally subsided, Moore directed that, since they had plenty of ammunition, the whole area around the perimeter should be sprayed with gunfire to get rid of snipers and any other enemy remaining around LZ X-ray. He gave the order for every gun to fire repeatedly for two minutes into the area immediately adjacent to the perimeter. The sound was deafening. A few shots were returned, but afterwards, all was silent. He then ordered his men to advance several hundred feet beyond the perimeter in a sweep. Bayonets were fixed and they advanced. A little opposition was met, but not much.

They then policed the battlefield. When one soldier mentioned to Moore the carnage the enemy had suffered, he answered that they, too, had mothers. He respected his foe as human beings, fighting for what they believed. He personally walked around the battlefield, looking for any dead American soldiers. He wasn't going to go back on his word that he'd leave no men behind, that he'd bring them all back. When he saw a body being dragged by its feet, he made four men pick it up. He said, "These are my men. They will be treated with dignity."[124]

When it was all over and the enemy had obviously withdrawn, the media came in to get their stories. It had been the biggest battle to date. Orders came down for the First Battalion to fly back to LZ Falcon and then to Camp Holloway. A company from the Second Battalion that had participated in the battle would accompany them. The others would march out. Moore made sure that every man of his battalion, dead or alive, was loaded onto a helicopter before he got on the last one. He was literally the last man of his outfit off the ground.[125]

When Moore landed at LZ Falcon before going back to Camp Holloway, he went over and shook the hands of the men of his command—they were dirty, bedraggled, and sitting on the ground. Only 240 of his command had not been killed or wounded. Mutual respect existed between the commander and his men. More than a few tears were shed by the exhausted troops. Moore also thanked the artillery battery that had fired 10,000 rounds in their defense. They all had gotten very little sleep for 72 hours, particularly Moore.[126]

When Moore got back to Camp Holloway, he went to the Officers' Club to get a drink. The bartender refused to serve Moore because he was dirty and his clothes were caked with dust. Moore put his M-16 on the counter and, in no uncertain terms, reordered the drink. When the bartender heard the whole story, he sheepishly complied.[127] After Moore was sure that his men were all taken care of, he went to his barracks for a well-deserved rest.

As night settled in at LZ X-ray, the men remained on alert. Things were too quiet. Where had the enemy gone? Bob McDade's Second Battalion, Seventh Cavalry remained (except for the company that flew out with the First Battalion), and Bob Tully's Second Battalion, Fifth Cavalry, was still there. They were posted about the perimeter vacated by Moore's men, and had orders to march out the next day.

After an uneventful night, they marched out in column; Tully's battalion was first and McDade's second, with one company of the Fifth Cavalry Battalion. Their orders were to stay together until they split up. Tully's battalion would go to LZ Columbus, one of the artillery sites from the previous day's fighting, where they would be picked up by helicopters and flown back to Camp Holloway. McDade's battalion was to continue on to a small opening called LZ Albany, and from there to LZ Crook eight miles away, where they would be picked up.[128]

The terrain they had to march through varied, but was mostly high elephant grass with patches of trees. The lead was an inverted V with the recon platoon, followed by the headquarters company, and the rest of the battalion. McDade was halfway back on the column. Flankers were out 30 yards. It was a miserable day. The men were fatigued from the last two days without much sleep, and most were carrying 40 pounds. Some, such as the radiomen and the mortar men, carried much more. Although most tried to stay alert, it was difficult. As they neared LZ Albany, they found two NVA soldiers whom they captured. McDade came forward. Many of the other officers came forward at McDade's request to see what was going on, and to interrogate the prisoners. The men took advantage of the stop and rested, sitting in the high grass. The men had inadvertently stopped at the base camp of the Eighth Battalion of the 66th NVA Regiment, and the under-strength Third Battalion of the 33rd NVA Regiment.[129] The flankers had come in to rest when all hell broke loose. Rifle fire broke out, and mortar shells came in. Staff back at brigade headquarters heard cries over the radio calling for fire support, and voices saying, "We are surrounded."[130]

The attack came along the right flank assisted by mortar fire. McDade and the command group were able to form some semblance of a perimeter with the recon platoon at the head of the column.[131] The first two platoons of Alpha Company were badly handled. Though overrun and unprepared, they fought as best they could, but the unit's cohesion was gone. They fought hand to hand alone or in small groups, but were overwhelmed. The field in their area soon became littered with bodies of Americans and NVA. Their company commander wanted to come back to them, but NVA soldiers blocked the way.

Captain John Fesmire of Charlie Company tried to make it back to his company, but was unable to do so. He radioed First Lieutenant Donald Cornett, his executive officer, and told him to move forward around Delta Company to LZ Albany, but the company met elements of the 66th Regiment head on. They were outnumbered and had an intense hand-to-hand fight. Losses mounted on both sides, but Charlie Company was badly chewed up. Of 112 men in the company, 45 were killed and 50 wounded. Only a dozen were uninjured.[132]

Delta Company was also badly battered. The commander, Captain Henry Thorpe, was in the command perimeter, and had helped organize it, but was unable to get to his own men. Some men tried to organize themselves in groups for resistance with partial success, but the enemy was among them. In small groups, they fought their battle in the tall grass and adjacent trees. They suffered 28 killed and many more severely wounded.[133]

When the firing started, Captain George Forrest of Alpha Company, Fifth Battalion[134] (the last company in the column), took off running down the left side of the column to be with his troops. He ran 600 yards and made it. He was able to set up a defensive perimeter with his company.

Mayhem was all around. Troops were able to establish perimeters at both ends of the column. A mixture of American and NVA soldiers between the perimeters fought it out. The NVA had the advantages of surprise, overwhelming numbers, position, and close leadership. Many of the Americans were down.

Brigade Commander Tim Brown flew overhead in a helicopter to observe. He called in fire support, and ordered a company from the First Battalion, Fifth Cavalry to march overland to give relief. He ordered Diduryk's Bravo Company, Second Battalion to get ready to fly into LZ Albany.[135] The help would be too little too late. Most of the casualties occurred in the first hour of fighting.[136]

Out in the column, after the first onslaught, men were fighting in small groups from any cover they could find. The NVA troops were walking all over where Americans lay dead or wounded, and firing down on them with AK-47s. Men in the perimeters could see them, but could do nothing about it.

After an hour, Skyraiders flew in and asked that smoke grenades mark the perimeters. The NVA was massing for an assault on the command perimeter. The planes started dropping napalm and 200-pound bombs, and fired their 20-mm machine guns into the enemy with good effect. It appeared that the battalion command perimeter would survive. Artillery fire also began to come in.[137]

Skyraiders then turned their attention to the GIs out in the column, with mixed results. Some American soldiers were helped by it, but others were injured, or killed, but the overall effect of the bombing and artillery support helped save LZ Albany.[138] Bravo Company of the Second Battalion, First Cavalry, under Diduryk flew in after dark, and helped stabilize the command perimeter and guarantee its safety.

Alpha Company, Fifth Battalion, Fifth Cavalry marched three miles overland from LZ Columbus.[139] They were met by some enemy troops, but drove them off, and finally linked up with Alpha Company of the Second Battalion, Fifth Cavalry at the rear of the column. After calling in medevacs to take out the wounded, the two companies joined and set out to reach the other companies of the march. They started in a V formation. When they reached a rise in the ground, they were met with enemy fire. It was late in the day. Dusk was coming, so they formed a perimeter for the night and planned to move out in the morning at daybreak.[140]

Night brought more terror to the wounded men of Charlie and Delta companies. There were more assassinations by enemy troops patrolling no-man's land between the perimeters. However, the dark also allowed individuals and small groups of soldiers, wounded or not, to escape the battlefield.[141]

In the morning, the enemy withdrew for the most part, leaving a few snipers and watchers behind. The troops in the reinforced perimeters cautiously ventured out onto the battlefield. They were horrified by the carnage. American bodies, especially those of Company C and D companies, littered the field. Their bodies were often entwined with the NVA soldiers with whom they had been fighting.[142] They had fought bravely, but were outnumbered. The men policed the battlefield and collected wounded who carried in and medevaced out. Then they had the sad job of collecting the dead and loading them up for their final journey home. Finally, the troops packed up and marched out to LZ Columbus. They had been through a terrifying experience that they would never forget.

The next day, elements of the 33rd NVA regiment attacked LZ Columbus, but they were driven off after a short fight. Most of the men were helicoptered to Camp Holloway. The rest were taken to hospitals.[143]

In essence, the battle of the Ia Drang was over. In many homes, parents, spouses, and friends received "The Secretary of the Army reports . . ." telegrams. The first big battle of the American Vietnam war was over. It was a harbinger of things to come for the next seven and a half years. Death tolls rose steadily, much more for the enemy than for America, but saddened families found no solace in that. American troops fought bravely. Many acted heroically, including Hal Moore. He would end up being one of the biggest heroes of the war. He didn't ask for fame, but he got it. He not only proved he was an intelligent and courageous man, but he was also a caring one, deeply respected by his men.

Despite the carnage outside of LZ Albany, the casualty rates for the whole five days of battle heavily favored the US soldiers. However, the NVA salvaged something out of it, a little prestige. They would fight on tenaciously.

The last battle of 1965 was Operation Harvest Moon, which started on December 8. For more than a month, the Vietcong had been aggressive in the midst of the monsoon season. They moved back into Phuoc Ha Valley, west of Da Nang. An entrapment attack was planned.

Two ARVN battalions were to move overland, and two marine battalions were to be helicoptered beyond the VC force to compress them in a pincer movement. However, operations don't always develop as planned. One of the ARVN columns was attacked furiously on its flank and almost disintegrated. The other ARVN battalion tried to help, but it, too, became enmeshed and encircled. A marine battalion was sent to link up with the beleaguered troops. The battalion fought a running battle for 24 hours before it linked up with the ARVN troops, and started putting pressure on the Vietcong.[144]

Meanwhile, two marine battalions helicoptered in behind them in two different landing zones. A third battalion flew in between the two already on the ground to make a more cohesive force. Soldiers in the lead company of the third battalion ran into a hail of fire after landing in a rice paddy, and had to fight for their lives. The company took heavy casualties. Using the dike berm of the paddy for cover, marine corpsmen slid from one wounded man to another. The rest of the battalion met heavy resistance, but fought through to link up with the imperiled company.[145]

After being consolidated, the battalion moved forward with the other two marine forces, compressing the VC positions. Progress was slow and costly to both sides. B-52 attacks were made on December 12 and 14 on suspected enemy positions. When the marines moved in, they found the enemy gone. They found extensive tunnel systems, with large caches of supplies and manufacturing equipment. The VC tried an ambush on December 18, but a marine counterattack routed them. Harvest Moon was over, and the enemy pushed out of Phuoc Ha Valley for the time being. It would be the last marine offensive during the monsoon season.

The last division to come to Vietnam in 1965 was the 25th Division, which had been stationed in Hawaii. It had been supplying helicopter door gunners since 1963. It was the army's Pacific reserve. The spearhead of the 25th into Vietnam was the division's Third Brigade, which landed at Pleiku on December 23 to help shore up the Central Highland area.[146]

CHAPTER 8

1966: WESTMORELAND TAKES THE OFFENSIVE

The year 1966 continued to be one of aggressive action by the American army as it built up. The enemy were to be tracked down wherever they were and destroyed as a fighting unit. It became a war of attrition and body counts. General Westmoreland figured that if enough of the enemy were killed, eventually they would quit, but they had no quitting in them.

Operation after operation continued, from Marauder, to Abilene, to Birmingham, to El Paso, to Hawthorne, to Crazy Horse, and so on for the duration. The operations involved all of the provinces from I Corps in the north to the Mekong Delta in the south.

I Corps, just across the demilitarized zone (DMZ) from North Vietnam, was primarily the responsibility of the marines. The Second and Third Corps areas were the bailiwick of the First Cavalry Division and the 25th Division, to be joined later by the Fourth Division. The Fourth Corps area of the delta and adjacent territory was the area of action for the First and Ninth Divisions. The 173rd Airborne Brigade and the 101st Airborne Division (as available) were sent wherever they were needed. The 173rd Airborne rushed to put out fires, wherever they occurred. In the following years, these divisions were to be in two of the biggest battles of the Vietnam War—Dak To and Ap Bia Mountain (Hamburger Hill), two years later. In mid-1966, the mobile fire brigade of the first brigade of the 101st Airborne joined the 173rd Airborne Brigade. The first brigade, too, was moved from hot spot to hot spot. The full 101st Airborne Division was moved to Vietnam in late 1967.

Brigades of multi-division battalions carried out many of the actions, so that a division's regiments and battalions might be spread out through several operations.[147] Thus the war was fought throughout the whole of South Vietnam, from the DMZ in the north to the Mekong Delta—a massive spreading delta, one of the biggest on earth.

The war was fought through mountainous areas, jungles, lowland plains with beautiful green rice paddies, peasant villages, and urban areas. The Vietcong and North Vietnamese Army were everywhere, mostly hidden in jungle sanctuaries. Frequently, they lived in and around small villages where they blended in with the local farmers, defying Americans to tell the difference. In the locals' hutches, the NVA dug holes to store weapons and ammunition, or sometimes to conceal themselves, covered with a thatch of straw.

In the jungles, which were frequently double and tripled canopied, the enemy set up their strongholds. In these strongholds, they had caches of weapons, ammunition, and food—whatever they needed to survive and conduct the war. Around these sites, the enemy often set up a series of heavily built bunkers, where they could entrench themselves, and become very difficult to dislodge. Often these fortifications connected to deep tunnels, to which the enemy could retreat under heavy artillery or air bombardment. The tunnels were impervious to the most destructive of weapons. Such were the strongholds in the Iron Triangle, west of Saigon, and the A Shau Valley, close to the Laotian border.[148] So also was the Dak To area in the Central Highlands, and numerous other areas, which were smaller and unnamed, but were just as deadly when attacked.

The enemy may have been the best diggers, or at least the most persistent diggers, on earth. They had tunnels, bunkers, and redoubts all over the country. They were also mobile diggers. In ambushes and at battle sites, they would fortify ridges, tree lines of fields and paddies, hedgerows, hilltops, or any other suitable places of defense in a matter of hours. It became instinctive to them, and they never seemed to tire. Rarely were they caught in the open or in an indefensible stance. Most often, they knew when the Americans were coming and were ready.

In 1966, the American strategy was to recapture as much of South Vietnam as possible, and to destroy the enemy whenever and wherever they were met. It was a bold plan, but success was completely elusive. No amount of firepower was going to do it. The best-armed army, navy, and air force in the world would fail to do it. However, in 1966, they tried.

Enemy leadership seemed to believe that the best defense was a good offense. The enemy would attack the patrols of squads, platoons, or companies. They would try to overrun American units, to bloody the nose of anyone intruding in their territory, and discourage them from any intervention. From their hiding places, they would cut down as many Americans as they could with an initial burst of fire, and charge with their AK-47s and SKSs blazing. Occasionally they would succeed in wiping out a unit, but most often American forces would fall back into defensive perimeters and survive despite their losses. Frequently, it came down to hand-to-hand fighting. Americans often depended upon artillery and air backup, or reinforcement to repel the enemy.

Fortunately, the relatively raw American soldiers and marines proved the equal of their attackers. Despite their losses, they gave as good as they got, and the enemy suffered many losses. Small unit actions happened everywhere along the length of the narrow country; their timing was unpredictable. The years 1964, 1965, and 1966 were a learning time on an increasing curve.

The tactics of the individual units had to be changed, honed, and hardened. It took a while for the American troops to become savvy, to learn how best to confront the enemy, and beat him in individual battles. It was a war of seek and find. Americans had to look for the enemy, who could pretty much dictate when and where they wanted to fight. The army estimated that the NVA or the Vietcong initiated 88 percent of contacts. Sixty-three percent of these contacts were against bunkers or fortified trenches. Forty-six percent began as ambushes.[149]

Patrolling troops would frequently come face to face with the enemy in camouflaged tree lines, rice paddy dikes, and fortified streams. The first five or 10 minutes would belong to the enemy. What happened after that would be decided by the American soldiers' response. If they could quickly find cover, return fire, and hold their ground until reinforcing elements came to their support, the tide of the battle could quickly turn, and enemy bunkers could be charged and knocked out. If the enemy fire was overwhelming, quick reaction in forming a defensive perimeter could save lives. Officers and sergeants had to respond quickly and call in artillery and air support to help even the odds given to the enemy, who could normally pick the time and place of battle. American troops had to learn to press the attack to strip the enemy of time to develop further ambushes or implement surrounding or flanking maneuvers.

Enemy snipers took advantage of the American propensity to go to the aid of the wounded.[150] Frequently, they would wound one man, and kill those who came to his aid.[151] As hard as it was, American soldiers learned to let the wounded lie until the battle was over, and spray all tree lines where snipers might hide. The rotation system was another big drawback to the American fighting mission. Men normally rotated out after one year of service in Vietnam. Men who had gotten the experience of fighting that type of war, and had become savvy and knowledgeable soldiers were shipped out at the end of a year, and raw, inexperienced men were brought in. Some, but not many, "re-upped" for a second year. The NVA and Vietcong were in the war for the duration.

In 1966, both sides were parrying, trying to find out the best way to beat the enemy. Westmoreland had 116,000 soldiers and 44,000 marines at the beginning of the year.[152] The number would grow to more than 350,000 by the end of the year. He was preparing his army, and was going after the enemy wherever he could find them. He was sending them out from enclaves at Saigon, Da Nang, Qui Nhon, and Pleiku. He was also building up a big logistical base for carrying on the war.

The US Army had decided on a strategy of search and destroy, and attrition—pulling the elusive Vietcong into battle and destroying them. Patrols of various sizes were sent into suspected enemy territory. There were no definite fronts; everywhere was no-man's land. These patrols usually had firebases within range that could destroy the attackers. Patrols often went out as bait. The policy met with some success, but often nothing happened. Only an estimated one percent of these patrols ever made contact with enemy soldiers. The wily Vietcong and NVA usually picked the time and place of the battle, when the odds might be in their favor. Even then, they would fight as long as the odds looked favorable, and slip away if they weren't.

In early 1966, the army decided to try a hammer-and-anvil type of sweep in Binh Dinh province. This area had long been in Vietcong hands, and they had been uncontested. The operation was originally called Operation Masher, but President Johnson objected, and the name was changed to White Wing. The anvil would be two South Vietnamese divisions, and the hammer would be a brigade of the First Cavalry, which would try to drive the Vietcong into the South Vietnamese forces. The marines in Operation Double Eagle would try to seal the northern border of the province.

Binh Dinh had been the most heavily populated area of Viet Minh in the south when Vietnam was divided. An estimated 90,000 Viet Minh lived there at the time of the French withdrawal. Only half chose to relocate to the north. The rest stayed and built up a formidable Vietcong force, forcing many of the local farmers to join and submit to lengthy indoctrination in the communist creed. They had been in virtual control of Binh Dinh[153], controlling all of it except a few urban areas.

The First Cavalry unit was under the command of Hal Moore, who had rapidly been promoted to colonel after the Ia Drang campaign.[154] He commanded the Third Brigade, which consisted of the First and Second Battalions, Seventh Cavalry, and the First and Second Battalions, 12th Cavalry Regiment, of which Specialist Raymond Ford of Bardstown, Kentucky, was a member. His fate would be determined in Operation White Wing.

The operation started at Bon Song, which was the first phase center for Third Brigade activities. From there, different units helicoptered out to landing zones calculated to entrap the Vietcong forces. The Second Battalion of the Seventh Cavalry, while moving north from Landing Zone Two, ran into stiff resistance and got bogged down. First, Company A was immobilized by sheets of machine-gun fire and sustained moderate losses. Company C came to its rescue, but ran into appreciable resistance. Moore was upset by the holdup and told his commanders to keep moving. Immobile men are useless men.

On the second day of the operation, Moore helicoptered in and personally took command. He first sent the Second Battalion of the 12th Cavalry to relieve the two floundering companies. (This was Raymond Ford's first action.)

Moore evacuated the wounded and realigned his troops. He then led a flanking attack of the enemy's position by the 12th Cavalry's Second Battalion troops, exposing himself to fire on several occasions.[155] He felt his presence helped return morale to his troops. Outflanking, attacking, and overrunning the Vietcong's position, he got Operation White Wing going again.

The Third Brigade ran into North Vietnamese Army units of platoon size on several occasions. Artillery and determination dislodged them with double envelopment procedures. Fleeing enemy soldiers were mowed down. One of Moore's old companies from the First Brigade, Seventh Cavalry got involved in a fierce firefight at night. A medevac helicopter flown by Major Bruce Crandall, a hero in the 1965 Ia Drang battle, again performed heroics. Flying in by intermittent use of a flashlight and headset, he twice landed in a small, close site in the jungle to medevac out wounded soldiers from a surrounded company.

The Third Brigade followed enemy soldiers as they attempted escape from the central portion of Binh Dinh through the jungle and rice paddies. Though it was the end of the rainy season, there was often misting rain with low-lying clouds, but the US forces completed phase one of the operation.

In the second phase, the Second Brigade of the First Cavalry joined the Third Brigade. Four battalions landed on the high elevations of the An Loc Valley and marched down to the valley floor. Although the enemy had fled, the three-day sweep of the valley revealed extensive tunnel systems with fortifications.

The third phase moved out in an area called the Eagle's Claw because of its many narrow valleys. Moore changed his tactics, using infantrymen as "beaters" to push the enemy into artillery fields of fire. Again, most of the enemy fled, but a platoon of Vietcong, reinforced by a company, stayed and fought. The enemy was finally overwhelmed. A large cache of Vietcong supplies was found, along with a mess hall, hospital, and a hand grenade factory. Their grenades were made out of old cans.

After the third phase, Moore's tired Third Brigade pulled out. The First Brigade joined the Second Brigade, which retained the Second Battalion of the 12th Cavalry. They had extensive battles in the rugged mountains, in an area called the Small Iron Triangle. They eventually encircled the Vietcong regimental headquarters, and a B-52 raid finished it off.

During this last stage, Specialist Raymond Ford was fatally injured by a mine (*Kentucky Standard*, February 14, 1966). Ford was a 21-year-old who had been urged by his mother to join the service, travel around, and become something in life. He came from a family of four brothers and seven sisters. Two of his brothers also served in the army. Ford joined the army in July 1963, one month after graduating from high school. The army seemed to suit him with its structured life. He remained close to his mother and family. His last visit home was in December; he left on December 14 to return to his outfit just before they deployed to Vietnam.

He was an infantryman, dependent on helicopters and his feet to get around. He had been in Vietnam for only two months before his death. His mother received a letter from him on February 19 saying he was fine; it was written the day before he died. The end can come quickly, even in a successful action.

Ford was the first Nelson Countian killed in the Vietnam War. In addition to the shock and sorrow for his family, his death came as a shock to the whole community. It was a wake-up call that the US was in a war, and results could reach anywhere in the nation. Before Ford's death, Vietnam was a war that was far away, for which most Americans had little feel, pro or con. Most Nelson Countians were patriotic and anti-communistic, but the cost of the war had not come home to them.

Ford's death made headlines in the local paper. The city government called for a special event on July 31 to honor him, his family, and all Vietnam servicemen and their families.[156] Colonel Hal Moore was home and participated in the event. Raymond Ford would be well remembered.

After Operation White Wing, a reporter asked Moore what would happen to Binh Dinh province after the American army left; if Moore thought the enemy would move back in. He said that he was just a soldier doing his duty, and that long-term results in the area depended on the actions of the South Vietnamese government. The Vietcong filtered back in, and another battle had to be fought there within six months.

After the Ia Drang battle and Operation White Wing, America had a national hero in Vietnam. Moore's troops had been responsible for 2,700 of the estimated 4,600 enemy killed thus far by the First Cavalry Division (*Kentucky Standard*, June 30, 1966). Moore's picture was on the cover of

Time magazine, and he was one of the first in the war promoted from battalion commander to brigade commander. All through the campaign, he was concerned about his men. He came home to Bardstown as often as possible to visit his mother. His father had died, and a younger brother was paralyzed by polio in the late 1940s.[157]

CHAPTER 9

OTHER 1966 BATTLES

In early 1966, the rest of the First Marine Division shipped to Vietnam. In conjunction with Operation White Wing, the marines started Operation Double Eagle. It was in Quang Ngai, the province next to Binh Dinh. The area around Chu Lai to the west had been an enemy stronghold, and the Second and Third NVA Divisions were stationed there, in addition to Vietcong units. In a three-battalion amphibious strike force, the marines moved into Quang Ngai province just below Chu Lai with the Second ARVN Division.[158] Their aim was to trap the NVA and Vietcong forces between themselves and the First Cavalry in Binh Dinh province.

Lieutenant Kenneth Sympson was in Operation Double Eagle. He recalled long marches, frequently at night through jungles and high grass, where each man had to hold on to the man in front of him, or risk being lost in enemy country with dire consequences. He also recalled the frequent rains, and how the marines stayed wet most of the time, with either rain or sweat inside their ponchos. There were small ambushes and firefights, but Sympson said, "I don't think they were ever trying to stop us as much as irritate us and cause a few additional casualties."[159] Despite all of the marching at night along jungle trails, Sympson had to stay aware of his approximate position in case he had to call in support artillery.[160]

On January 28, landing craft unloaded two marine battalions in rough seas 20 miles south of the city of Quang Ngai. Amtracs unloaded men and supplies. Two days later, the Marine Special Landing Force Battalion helicoptered into the old French fort five miles west of the beaches. Bad weather limited the use of helicopters. At the end of February, when the weather cleared, the marines "then split into helicopter search teams, which bounded from hilltop to hilltop, striking deep into suspected Vietcong regions."[161] Contact was light, mostly sniper fire. The enemy had withdrawn and was trying to figure out a way to combat the American methods of making war. Operation Double Eagle was frustrating and was discontinued in March.

About the same time, the marines were involved in two more operations where they came to the aid of South Vietnamese forces. One was Operation New York, in which a VC battalion was giving the ARVN a tough time on the Phu Thu Peninsula, west of Phu Bai. Three marine companies helicoptered in. Moving by flare light at night, they swept over the sandy peninsula. The enemy was waiting in bunkers, and had set up fire lanes for crossfire through the scrub grass. With artillery and air support, the marines crawled forward, and knocked out bunker after bunker, in an area that ran the length of two football fields. The enemy withdrew slowly, and mop-up continued for six weeks.

Operation Texas occurred when a VC regiment attacked the ARVN base at An Hoa. The South Vietnamese troops were about to be overrun and An Hoa lost. More ARVN troops helicoptered in without effect. Finally, a battalion of the Seventh Marines joined in and the VC started withdrawing. A battalion of the Fourth Marines flew in behind them, and the enemy was caught in a vise and decimated.

First Lieutenant Kenneth Sympson with the Fourth Marines, of Cox's Creek, Kentucky, earned a Bronze Star. A company of marines was surrounded and trapped. Sympson was responsible for saving their lives. He remained in his hazardous post as a forward observer 325 feet from a heavily fortified village. From there, he directed 2,500 rounds of artillery over a four-hour period. One hundred and twenty Vietcong died in the battle. Sympson had enlisted in 1963, and completed boot training at Quantico and artillery training at Fort Sill (*Kentucky Standard*, August 18, 1966).

The *Kentucky Standard* (March 3, 1966) also reported that Sergeant George K. Taylor of Balltown, Kentucky, was wounded on February 21 during these battles 12 miles south of Da Nang, and received the Purple Heart. Taylor was one of three brothers to serve in the marines in Vietnam at the same time. This occasion was one of three times that he was wounded.

While he recovered, the *Kentucky Standard* (May 6, 1966) interviewed him. He said that most villagers lived in small close villages in crude huts. "Villagers were only concerned about the war when it came to their rice paddies," he said.

Other Nelson County men served in Vietnam during this time. In March 1966, Lance Corporal John P. Downs served with the First Battalion, Ninth Marines (Golden Dragons) in a weapons platoon. James M. Norton was a marine corpsman at Chu Lai and Private First Class Larry White was with the Fifth Marine Regiment at Chu Lai.[162]

In early 1966, Sam Miles was reported to be at Cu Chi, which was the base for the 27th "Wolfhound" Regiment of the 25th Division. He was probably part of that division. The area was a hotbed of Vietcong activity, as it was astride one of their main supply routes from Cambodia. The Wolfhounds took a lot of tough fighting, facing deadly fire from bamboo thickets near small villages. Eventually the division's area of control extended out far enough that the headquarters was not within mortar range.

There was an extensive tunnel system around Cu Chi. Parts of the system still exist and are shown to tourists. The openings are very small and are accessible only to people about 120 pounds or smaller. In its original state, the tunnel system had dormitory rooms, kitchens, manufacturing rooms for explosives and firearm repair, and storage rooms for food and other supplies. Its ventilation openings were camouflaged, and the smoke exhaust pipe from the kitchen was hundreds of feet from the kitchen cooking area. As an engineering feat, the tunnel system would challenge the catacombs of Rome and the underground cities of Cappadocia. The VC and NVA were tough, wily, hardworking, and ingenious foes.

In early 1966, the First Infantry Division was ordered to push out northwest of Saigon. Occasionally units of that division would run into fierce resistance and engage in short firefights. When odds were not in the enemy's favor, they would withdraw.

The cost of entry for American troops into these firefights was often deadly. Some were deadlier than others. On February 24, Operation Rolling Stone began. Soon a unit of the First Infantry's Division came under severe attack 40 miles north of Saigon. The battle of Tan Binh had begun. The First Infantry's Fifth Artillery (Alexander Hamilton's Cannoneers) came under fire. The attack lasted from 2 a.m. to 7 a.m. and casualties were heavy, according to the *Kentucky Standard* (March 24, 1966).

Major Malcolm Geoghegan was executive officer of the Fifth Artillery. Geoghegan's artillery unit was never attacked in its home base. However, when the unit went out in the field to support the infantry, they were attacked in a human wave onslaught. Even though many of the

Vietcong were killed, they did penetrate the common perimeter of the infantry and artillery. During this attack, American losses were moderate. The enemy was driven off with many casualties.

Geoghegan's unit also suffered casualties in an ambush, and a number of men were killed by sniper fire. Geoghegan was in Vietnam from October 1965 until September 1966 and came out unscathed. He served in three wars and never got a scratch.

The Fifth Artillery was later involved in Operation Silver City in the same area. Later, Company C, Second Battalion, 16th Infantry was caught in an ambush and badly shot up by the D500 VC Battalion. Company C came close to being wiped out. They had been hacking their way through the jungle, and stumbled on the VC battalion's base camp. They were attacked from all sides. The decimated Americans fought off three assaults during the night. Artillery fire formed a ring around the beleaguered company, and relief broke through to them the next morning. Artillery saved many lives. More than 1,000 rounds were fired. Rope ladders, known as Jacob's ladders, were let down from helicopters through the jungle canopy to take out the wounded.[163]

Papers found on a dead VC lieutenant revealed that the VC planned to start an offensive against the city of Loc Ninh and the Loc Ninh Special Forces camp.

Major General William E. DePuy of the First Division decided to preempt the move. The Ninth VC Division was determined to prevent this. Massive battles followed. The 273rd VC Regiment ambushed a column of tanks. They knocked out first and rear tanks with recoilless rifle fire, and assaulted the column. After a furious four-hour battle, the attack broke off.[164]

Three days later, part of a company was helicoptered in to a rubber plantation, and the other part was mauled while trying to set up a pincer movement. They were met by fire from a hill and mortared it. When they charged up the hill, they were driven off by automatic weapon fire and grenades. Another company was called in to assist, and was met with fire from another hill. A dug-in battalion met them. Almost a whole recon platoon was wiped out by flanking machine-gun fire, but action by a reserve platoon saved the day, and the enemy was pushed out of their bunkers and off the hill. The last company of the battalion of the 28th Infantry was thrown into the action and, following an artillery barrage and air support with fragmentation bombs, a frontal assault with hand-to-hand fighting scattered the VC, and the second hill was taken. The battalion then mopped up what was left of the enemy in the rubber plantation.

Nelson Countian Tommy Armstrong was with the First Division, First Aviation Battalion, which was responsible for air mobility and support of the division.

The next encounter, called the battle of Srok Dong, occurred on June 30. The Second Battalion of the 28th Infantry and four tanks of the Fourth Cavalry swept around Quon Loi. They had just assisted an armored vehicle launch a scissor-type bridge across a small river when, as part of a returning column, they were ambushed by machine gun and recoilless rifle fire. The four tanks were knocked out by repeated hits on their turret top cupolas, and the infantry sustained casualties.[165] A tank-led column of armored personnel carriers came down the road to the rescue. The tank blasted enemy positions, and other armored vehicles formed a shield around the damaged tanks. Sixty rounds of tank shells poured into enemy positions. A flame-throwing tank burst through the thick undergrowth and sprayed the Vietcong stronghold.

During the action, George O'Hara of the Fourth Cavalry, received a Bronze Star for coming to the defense of the crews of several knocked-out tanks. He drove his tank back and forth in the face of enemy fire to keep the Vietcong away from the crippled tanks, and helped their crews escape. O'Hara had come to Vietnam in November 1965 (*Kentucky Standard,* June 30, 1966). His wife lived on Payne Street in Bardstown.

Nelson Countians continued to take part in the scattered battles and operations serving in practically all major divisions.

As the battle of Srok Dong waged, air and artillery power, and helicopter support forced the enemy to leave the field. DePuy said in a brief to General Westmoreland, "This was a complete surprise."[166] United States forces nearly lost the battle. However, air superiority proved to be a deciding factor, and inflicted severe losses on the enemy.

Fighting continued in War Zone C with a large ambush in reverse. American forces purposely leaked information of an attack moving in a single column. It was ambushed where it was expected, and the ambushers were hit with massive artillery and air attacks. The VC fought on, and even continued attacks, but eventually withdrew when it appeared they were going to be surrounded.

The 196th Light Infantry Brigade started Operation Attleboro to explore ever deeper into VC territory. The brigade found and destroyed large caches of rice. An attached 27th Infantry battalion ran into part of the Ninth Vietcong Division. Another battalion of the 27th was brought in to try to help it, and "engaged in a grisly, sustained battle for survival."[167]

Bardstown native John Cambron was in the 27th "Wolfhound"

Regiment of the 25th Division. Cambron didn't want to talk about his experiences. He had lived through hell once and didn't want to do it again. He humbly said he was no John Wayne. He was like most American soldiers who did their dangerous jobs bravely without fanfare against a tough and resilient foe.

Six massed assaults were made against First Battalion, 27th Infantry. Four reinforced VC regiments attacked them. Several battalions of the First Division, the Third Brigade of the Fourth Division, and the 173rd Airborne Brigade were thrown into the battle. Finally the Ninth VC Division retreated west in the face of overwhelming power. The 196th Infantry Brigade and the two battalions of the 27th were badly handled. The leadership of the 196th was changed.

In the northern province, information came through that the 324th NVA division was moving across the DMZ. The Fourth Marines were sent to investigate, and repel the enemy if necessary. In an attempt to helicopter two battalions in, two helicopters collided and crashed, sending their rotor blades spinning into some men. Another crashed into a tree, and a fourth was shot down. Henceforth, the area would be called Helicopter Valley.[168]

The Third Battalion pushed north against opposition until they reached the Song Be River at the DMZ. As they were pulling out and getting ready to demolish the crashed helicopters, they were suddenly hit by a 1,000-man charge. Though the marines fired as rapidly as they could, the enemy was among them. The marines formed small self-protecting groups, and fought their way hand-to-hand back to the main battalion that had formed behind them. It was a close action—bayoneting, clubbing, and firing—and the men carried their wounded back with them.

The marines called in artillery and air support. Napalm burst within 500 feet of the marines' line. The battle lasted four hours before the enemy withdrew. Helicopter Valley was abandoned, as it was of no practical value in the mobile defense system, and action with the NVA 324th Division petered out.

Lieutenant Kenneth Sympson of Nelson County was with the artillery that helped drive the enemy out.

Within a month, the NVA was back, and the marines moved back toward the DMZ in an operation called Prairie. The three battalions of the Fourth Marines were joined by a fourth, the First of the Ninth Marines. (John P. Downs of Nelson County served with this battalion.) The First Battalion of the 26th Marines made an amphibious landing to protect their flank.[169] They made heavy contact with the enemy after coming ashore, and after a seven-day battle, drove the NVA out of their bunkers and tunnels, and back across the DMZ.

About this time, the second of Nelson County's Vietnam deaths occurred. Marine Corporal William Russell Taylor, serving with the 26th Regiment outside of Da Nang, was killed by multiple small arms wounds on August 28, 1966.[170] He had been in Vietnam for only three days. He was from a large Balltown family, and had two other brothers serving concurrently in Vietnam. His wife was expecting and Taylor would never see his child. He had enlisted in 1963. The *Kentucky Standard* (September 2, 1966) reported that Taylor's last letter to his mother said, "Don't worry about me. The Marine Corps will take care of me, and God willing, I'll be home."

The other three battalions advancing by helicopter and foot fought isolated battles with groups of the enemy, and destroyed their strong points.

One particularly pitched battle was for "Mutter Ridge." Immense trees and bamboo thickets guarded the ridge and kept out the light. As the marines worked their way up the hill, NVA soldiers charged downhill, throwing grenades and firing AK-47s. From behind tree stumps and whatever other cover they could find, the American troops fired back, their M60 machine guns propped uphill. They stopped the charge.[171] Progress was slow, made doubly difficult by the terrible heat and humidity.

After a two-week, costly battle, Mutter's Ridge was topped.

Mutter Ridge

GREEN AND ANGRY, DRESSED IN BUNKERS
WITH BLINKING FIRE BENEATH THE EDGE
OF THE SKY, SUPERHEATED AND BREATHLESS
ROSE THE MASS OF MUTTER RIDGE.
STRETCHED TAUTLY AS FAR AS WE COULD SEE
FROM END TO END AN UNFORGIVING LEDGE,
THAT DEFIED OUR DRENCHING SWEAT AND BLOOD
AS WE CLAMBERED UP MUTTER RIDGE.
THROUGH BAMBOO TANGLES AND GRAPPLING VINES
WE CLIMBED UNTIL, LIKE A GARDEN HEDGE,
OUR LINES WERE MOWED BY SHEERING FIRE
BUT STILL WE CLIMBED UP MUTTER RIDGE.
WE REACHED THE TOP AND DROVE THEM OFF
OF A PLACE THAT SEEMED LIKE HELL'S OWN EDGE.
AND WE WONDERED IF THE PRICE OF FRIENDS
WAS WORTH SECURING MUTTER RIDGE.

—DR. HARRY SPALDING

Numerous other small unit engagements were fought, and the NVA was thrown back across the DMZ with substantial losses as the year ended. Brigadier General Lowell English said, "I'm sure of one thing. Although we've definitely killed more than 2,000 in Hastings and Prairie combined, and probably a lot more, they haven't quit."[172]

American forces were beefed up at year's end with four regular army divisions, two airborne brigades, two light infantry brigades, two marine divisions, and numerous supporting units. The Ninth Infantry Division had come in and had already seen one battle in the delta. Three Nelson County soldiers, Ronald Greenwell, Eddie Gritton, and Donald Stivers, came in with that division. They were all in the 39th Regiment, but in different companies (*Kentucky Standard*, January 12, 1967).

In 1966, these forces challenged the enemy deep in his territory with varying success. Often the NVA and VC were forced to leave the field, but they proved to be tenacious, tough fighters. As George Taylor said, most of the peasant farmers cared little for the war unless their rice paddy or village was involved, but the enemy moved in and out among their improvised closures. The jungles and mountains were the enemy's main strongholds, but they could be anywhere.

CHAPTER 10

HELICOPTER WAR

Helicopters and air mobility played an ever-increasing part in the Vietnam War. In a country of rice paddies and jungles, but few roads, helicopters played the most important roles of mobility, surprise, supply, reserves, and rescue, ever seen in any war. They could drop troops behind the enemy. No place was out of reach for American forces. Helicopters were one of the most valuable offensive weapons of the war.[173]

However, they were vulnerable. They made good targets for enemy gunners, and when flying into an area of enemy fortifications (as often happened), the helicopters and their cargoes of men could be and often were chewed up by automatic weapons fire. During the war, helicopter pilots and their crews accounted for one out of every nine deaths. Often they were called into hot landing zones (zones under intense enemy fire) to bring out the wounded in all kinds of weather. Extreme bravery was frequently shown in medevac service and in replenishing supplies to beleaguered units.

Tactics were developed to reduce losses. When bringing troops into an area of unknown concentrations of enemy troops, gunships would precede the landing force, and shoot up adjacent ridges and tree lines, or artillery and air support would encircle the area with a ring of fire. Then the troop-laden helicopters, called "Hueys" or "Hogs," flew in. Assault soldiers sat in the cargo doors or stood on the skids, ready to jump with their M-16 safeties off and ready to fire. Men and supplies were off-loaded, and the helicopter would be up and away as quickly as possible, sometimes without touching the ground. Meanwhile, the door gunmen blasted away at any suspected enemy sites. Sometimes, despite all of the preparations, the assaulting force was met by automatic weapons fire, and the losses of helicopters and men were horrendous.

Helicopter gunships proved to be very valuable weapons. They were armed with rockets and machine guns on both sides and under the nose. They could give close-in support that artillery and other air support could not provide. Frequently, they fought in groups of four or more, and were like a swarm of bees.

Special air ambulance companies used helicopters called medevacs to evacuate the wounded. They often saved lives. By getting seriously wounded men to critical care units on a timely basis, shock and death were frequently prevented, and limbs preserved. Those helicopters were specially equipped with litters, intravenous set-ups, breathing support equipment, and often a well-trained emergency medical technician. The chain of medical service— from the corpsman to the medevac choppers to the acute care facility— streamlined medical and surgical care better than in any previous war. Medical evacuation was not just limited to medevacs. The wounded were often loaded on any helicopter flying out after bringing in men and supplies. Their landings in hot zones, day or night, guided by smoke grenades or flashlights, were legendary. Many crews received the highest awards of valor, often posthumously. Their ability to extract the wounded from the most marginal of terrains was a great morale booster for the fighting troops, who knew that if they were wounded, their lives and limbs could be saved.[174]

The range of helicopters depended on their loads, and had to be calculated both out and back. They consumed tremendous amounts of fuel, and special depots had to be set up. In addition, the frequently used and damaged helicopters required maintenance, and special units were set up for this function. The largest was at Tan Son Nhut Air Base at Saigon.

To command and control this tremendous amount of aviation stock, the First Aviation Brigade was set up in May 1966.[175] It developed into a large military command, organized into groups, battalions, and air cavalry squadrons. The command eventually comprised 24,000 men and 4,200 aircraft of all descriptions. The brigade oversaw 142 aviation companies.

Weather played a big role in helicopter use. Flying conditions were often severely hampered. The northwest monsoons from September to April north of Phu Bai, and the southwest monsoons from April to September south of it, brought heavy clouds and poor visibility. The use of aviation over jungle areas was particularly restricted.

Other hazards were numerous. Crews of hovering helicopters had breathing problems from exhaust fumes pushed down by rotating blades, and cordite from the gunner's machine-gun fire. Pilots often had spatial disorientation, caused by vibration and frequent total viewing changes. The noise of the main rotor and weapons caused hearing loss, and subsequently, poor responses to orders. Sometimes the men suffered permanent damage to their eardrums and hearing.[176]

The Bell Huey or Hog was the main army helicopter. It was used primarily for hauling assault troops and supplies, but also became the most used helicopter for medical evacuation. It could carry a squad of troopers and their equipment, and as many as six stretchers. It also made an excellent gunship with multiple guns and rockets attached, and could produce a lot of firepower. The Apache, a later helicopter produced by Bell, was intended for scouting and attacking the enemy with multiple weapons. It was faster and more agile than the Huey. The Chinook, a bigger two-rotor helicopter, could carry a much bigger load. It was slower and more bulky and harder to get into landing zones. The Chinook was frequently used for extracting troops, or for hovering and letting troops descend by Jacob's ladders through double and triple canopied forests. Lastly, there was the flying crane, which could lift heavy loads, such as an army howitzer.

The marines primarily used the H34, which they considered sturdier, and which had wheels instead of struts. This allowed it to be used on small attack helicopter carriers for sea-to-air-to-ground attacks. The marines had their own aviation commands and, to a great extent, operated their aviation support units separately from the army.

During 1965 and 1966, the war expanded, and the number of Americans tripled. An acute shortage of helicopter pilots developed. There were not enough to keep up with the demands of the helicopter war. Many were shifted from commands in Europe and Korea to fill these needs. Inducements were offered, but few pilots signed up for another year after their rotation was up. There was a shortage until late 1967 and 1968, when the helicopter school at Fort Rucker began to turn out warrant officer pilots. Many of them were 18 or 19 years old. They liked the thrill and were would-be race drivers. They turned out to be excellent pilots and earned many medals for valor.[177]

Helicopters were also excellent for scouting, screening, and finding the enemy, as the cavalry scouts in the Indian wars had done. Not only could helicopters find the enemy, but as the battle progressed, they could see enemy development and movements from overhead, and help direct the course of battle. They proved so good for scouting that squadrons were formed strictly for this use, such as the First Squadron of the Ninth Cavalry Regiment, and of the 101st Airborne Division.[178]

Sergeant Paul Allen Johnson, a Nelson County man, belonged to the 17th Scout Squadron when he was killed in action in 1970.

Several Nelson County natives were involved in the helicopter war.

One of the most interesting stories is that of Denny Howard. He joined the army in October 1952 at the end of the Korean War, and ended up serving 24 years before retiring as a chief warrant officer (CWO-4). He first spent six years in the infantry, and then went to Nike missile fire control school at Fort Bliss, Texas. After graduation, he received an appointment as a warrant officer and was assigned to Pittsburgh, Pennsylvania, for three years and then to Greenland for a year. When he came back to the states, he went to primary helicopter flight school at Fort Walters, Texas, and next to the advanced helicopter flight school at Fort Rucker, Alabama, and then was assigned to Fort Carson, Colorado. After a year at Fort Carson, he attended the officers' aircraft maintenance school at Fort Eustis, Virginia, and then went to Germany for a three-year tour. He served only 18 months of it, however, as he was sent to Vietnam in July 1966.

Howard was assigned to the First Air Cavalry Division at An Khe in the Central Highlands. However, the division flew mostly out of landing zones, one of which was LZ Hammond near the coast. Howard flew Hueys (UH-1) on every kind of mission assigned to the unit. Many of the flights were combat assault missions, flown in all sorts of situations. Fortunately, the helicopters he flew were never damaged, and he never crashed. He was also the aircraft maintenance officer and flew some medical evacuation missions.

He is a modest man and speaks of his flights as almost commonplace. They were obviously anything but, as he was awarded three Bronze Stars and has three Army Commendation medals.

Every mission was potentially dangerous. Howard was also awarded the Distinguished Flying Cross when LZ Hammond was attacked. The enemy didn't get beyond the perimeter, but they fired mortars, rockets, and small-arms fire that ignited the ammunition dump. Munitions were going off everywhere, with rockets shooting like roman candles. Several helicopters and fixed-wing aircraft were destroyed, and many others damaged. The adjacent fuel point caught fire, adding to the conflagration. Howard flew some of the least damaged helicopters to safety and removed personnel who were in danger. He did this at risk to his own life. During his two tours in Vietnam, he was awarded nine Air Medals, one for every 25 flights.

Howard's first tour lasted until July 1967, and on his return, he was assigned to Fort Knox, Kentucky. From there he went to Corpus Christi, Texas, to prepare for duty on the aircraft maintenance ship, the *Corpus Christi Bay*. His second tour was from December 1968 to December 1969 onboard the *Corpus Christi Bay*. The ship docked at Vung Tau, at the mouth of the Saigon River. The ship completely rebuilt aircraft components, such as electrical, hydraulic, instruments, engines, and transmissions, and did some repair work for other branches of service. While Howard was there, he also did some taxi service, flying the ship's doctor and dentist to villages where they were needed, and picking up people and supplies for the ship. He enjoyed flying.

Howard said he didn't know whether the Vietnamese could be trusted. One night, when he returned to the ship from Vung Tau in a Lambretta, the driver and two others tried to mug him. Fortunately, he had a pistol and they were unsuccessful. The same people beat up another soldier from the ship. Howard also told of a case where a sister company allowed Vietnamese women on the LZ to fill sandbags. One morning, a pilot discovered hand grenades with the pins pulled and only tape keeping them from exploding, in the exhaust of every helicopter in the unit. Fortunately, they were found before the engines were started and no damage was done. No more Vietnamese women were allowed in the area.

After returning home in December 1969, Howard was stationed at Fort Knox for a while, and then went to the warrant officers career course at Fort Rucker, Alabama. After graduation, he was assigned to the school, and taught aircraft maintenance and records keeping. As an instrument flight instructor, he also renewed instrument flying tickets as time allowed. He attended the Alabama Institute of Aviation Technology, and became a licensed aircraft and power plant mechanic. When he retired in August 1976, he had about 4,000 flying hours, most in helicopters, but he also flew military fixed-wing aircraft and as a civilian flight instructor taught flying in civilian aircraft.

Denny Howard later served as the mayor of Bloomfield, Kentucky, and was one of a number of town's leading citizens who served in Vietnam. Others include Corporal Mike Simpson, Private First Class David Bishop, Danny Stewart, and Dr. Bob Hendren.

Sergeant Kenny Thomas was also a helicopter crewman. He volunteered for the marines at the age of 17. He had to get his mother to sign the permit because of his age. Four of his friends were joining, and he wanted to go with them. It was a little unusual for five to volunteer together, when much of the nation was protesting the war. Two volunteered for only two years, which guaranteed them a trip to Vietnam; and three signed up for four years on the promise that they would go to aviation school.

Thomas and two of his buddies followed the two-year people by two days, and went to Parris Island for boot camp. They spent eight weeks in tough boot camp where they could hardly talk to each other. They went next to Camp Geiger for advanced infantry training, since all marines are considered riflemen first and their specialty second. From there, they went to Memphis for avionics and electronics training, where Thomas learned all about radios (VHF), radar, and navigation by using radio signals. Finally, he went to Jacksonville, North Carolina, for helicopter school. He had a chance to stay there as an instructor, but he chose to go to Vietnam.

In the fall of 1968, he volunteered to go to Vietnam in place of his brother, who was in a National Guard company that was about to be called up.

In 1942, five brothers—the Sullivans—were killed in action after the sinking of the USS *Juneau*. Consequently, US military services did not normally send brothers into a combat area at the same time.

Thomas went to Camp Pendleton in San Diego for advanced helicopter training. He was then sent to Da Nang at Marble Mountain Air Base, which was used for both helicopters and fixed-wing planes (*Kentucky Standard*, November 23, 1968). While he was there, the base was under frequent attack by mortars and rockets. Marines are trained to take their M-16s and form a perimeter against ground attack in those circumstances. Because of the large size of the air base, Thomas had to go to the perimeter only about every fourth attack. Otherwise, he could go to his bunker.

In December 1968, he was transferred to the USS *Okinawa*, an attack ship that carried about 30 helicopters, and 400 to 500 combat marines.

The *Okinawa* would sail up and down the coast, its personnel engaging in support operations for other marines involved in battles, large or small. Sometimes there would be several support operations going on at the same time.

On the ship, Thomas served mostly as a repairman, but for two months, members of his group would fly out on helicopters as machine gunners. Every three weeks, the ship would off-load, and sail back to its base at Subic Bay in the Philippines. Thomas and his squadron, the HMM (helicopter, medium maintenance) served during this time out of Phu Bai and Quang Tri, from which they continued to give support operations. Then they would reload back on the Okinawa.

In March and April 1969, Thomas started flying as a gunner. Their helicopters, the UH34Ds, carried men (usually six to eight), ammunition, food, weapons, or whatever was needed into the operation site, occasionally even beer. Sometimes they medevaced out the wounded. Normally they flew every morning and came back at night. Before Thomas went on a flight, he had to check out a M60 machine gun, a 36-caliber pistol and a knife. Sometimes they flew "mortar rounds" at night, trying to see the flashes of mortars to pinpoint the enemy, but the enemy kept on the move after firing a few rounds from their mortars. Because they kept going, sometimes Thomas would get only two hours of sleep.

Sometimes they had to bring supplies to a unit under heavy attack; colored smoke grenades guided in them. The marines called it "pop smoke." When they flew into a hot zone under attack, it was frequently chaos, but they usually completed the mission. His helicopter was frequently hit, once right above his head. Most often, they kept on flying. One helicopter came back with 100 holes in it.

Thomas said their helicopter could take more damage and still fly than the more famous Huey helicopter.

"When you flew into hot zones, things happened so quick that you couldn't stop to reason things out; you had to act almost on reflex," Thomas said in an interview.

That is what marines are taught: *don't think; do it.* His unit lost a number of choppers, usually shot down, but occasionally in mid-air collisions in the hectic confusion of battle. They always had a wingman. Thomas lost none of his immediate friends.

The helicopters usually flew into the hilltops where the marine outposts were located. Usually, a clearing was laid out in the middle of a hill where the helicopters could land. One time, when the marines were about to be overrun, his 'copter had to take out the last group of marines—12 of them—which overloaded the helicopter. Under fire, they had to get a running start downhill and just barely made it over the perimeter concertina wire.

The helicopters usually flew in groups of three or more. Sometimes, in heavy fire, they called in Huey gunships, or fixed-wing planes with plenty of firepower. Sometimes they flew over "free-fire zones," where they shot at anything moving. They had to get clearance first to make sure friendly forces weren't in the area.

Thomas said he sometimes felt as if they were decoys trying to flush out the enemy. The enemy liked to knock out helicopters. Many of the enemy considered helicopters their worst killer. In close action, they often shot at the machine gunners first to take protection away from the helicopters. The life expectancy of a machine gunner in action was short.

After his two months of flying, Thomas was glad to get back on ship or ground permanently. He stayed with his outfit until October 13, 1969. One time, he asked for a day leave to visit the National Guard battery from Bardstown when they were on Hill 88. He stayed the night with them and woke up to an explosion. He grabbed his M-16 and headed for the perimeter, until he learned it was outgoing fire rather than incoming.

After he came home, he was assigned to a training squadron at Jacksonville, North Carolina, and even served as a lifeguard. At the end of his enlistment, he was able to get out two months early so he could sign up for college. He felt his two months of flying gunner on a helicopter was enough action for anybody. When he first started it, he felt it was going to be a great adventure and his adrenaline was pumping. Later on, his adrenaline was pumping for another reason, knowing each mission could be his last. He was definitely glad when it was over.

Lieutenant Ludwell (Lud) McKay was another Bardstown native who was involved in helicopter duty. He had previously served four years as an enlisted man in the Air Force. When he got out, he went to college at a subsidiary of St. Louis University Parks College, where he participated in ROTC, and became a naval officer.[179] From there, he went to Pensacola Naval Air Station where he learned to fly in all types of naval aircraft, even off a carrier. Because of the great need for helicopter pilots, he was sent to Vietnam as an ensign. McKay initially flew out of Vung Tau (*Kentucky Standard*, June 20, 1968), which was a main port at the entrance to the Saigon River. He flew scouting missions along the coast, and down into the delta, trying to interdict Vietcong gunrunners and other activities in these areas. Much of the coast was still in Vietcong hands. He also flew other missions, carrying men and supplies for offensive actions, and evacuating the wounded.

McKay told his brother-in-law that after he had flown in men and supplies, he would slap a red cross on the nose of his helicopter and fly out the wounded. He was shot down and his helicopter destroyed. He was in a rice paddy, and was shot at while on the ground, but had good coverage by air. Within 25 to 30 minutes, he was rescued with only minor injuries by other helicopters. He wrote his parents that he would "probably be flying tomorrow. They say everyone has a crash sooner or later. So we've gotten our crash out of the way."[180]

He was later awarded the Distinguished Flying Cross when he served as a Seawolf commander on a gunship on a Vietnam combat support mission. In that situation, he guided his gunship into an action where American troops had been ambushed, and flew several treetop flights against a concerted hostile force. When his ship landed, he helped evacuate the wounded. McKay helped load the casualties aboard. He was in three helicopter crashes in rice paddies, but survived without serious injury. After Vietnam, he stayed in the navy and had an interesting tour of Europe and abroad.

According to articles in the *Kentucky Standard*, other Nelson County men were associated with helicopters in Vietnam.

Specialist Carl Lanham, a helicopter crewman, received an Air Medal for heroic action with the First Cavalry, Troop B near Di An (*Kentucky Standard*, September 25, 1969).

Private First Class Albert Terry Evans, with the 155th Assault Helicopter Company, was in combat within three days after arriving in Vietnam (*Kentucky Standard*, August 28, 1968). He flew missions with the Fourth Infantry Division in Operation Junction City and in the highlands close to the Cambodian border. He participated in operations Paul Revere and Sam Houston. While in Vietnam, he caught malaria and ended up in the hospital. After recuperating, he went back to his duties as a helicopter crewman.

David Forsee was with the 48th Assault Helicopter Company (*Kentucky Standard*, August 28, 1969). William C. Tichenor saved a captain's life in a medevac situation. The captain's father, Lieutenant General Conner, commended Tichenor.

CHAPTER 11

1967: FURTHER BUILDUP AND OFFENSIVE

By January 1967, General Westmoreland felt it was time to take the war to the enemy and destroy them. With his bolstered US Army and Marine units, his strategy was multi-fold. He wanted to clear Highway 1, the main highway north and south from Quang Tri to Saigon. He wanted to clear the area around Saigon from enemy threats. He wanted to thrust his army into the highlands west of Pleiku and Kon Tum, to drive the enemy out of that sanctuary. He wanted to gain control of the delta, another enemy bastion. Finally, in the northwest area of Vietnam, he wanted to stop the invasion routes through the A Shau Valley. It would be the year of the big battles.[181]

The Vietcong around Saigon had increased steadily. A sniper attack at Tan Son Nhut Air Base had almost succeeded. Roads in and out of Saigon were frequently under attack, and traffic with adjacent farmers was almost cut off. The VC even extracted tolls.

North of Saigon was a wedge of jungle and rice paddies known as the Iron Triangle. It was the center for terrorism in the Saigon area. It was a large area of concrete bunkers, supply depots, field hospitals, and connecting tunnels. An attempt to bomb it out with B-52s was largely unsuccessful. The American command decided to send in troops to clean it out. Operation Cedar Falls was designed to do that.

A force of 15,000 men was assigned the duty, including the 11th Armored Cavalry Regiment, the 173rd Airborne Brigade, and units from the First Division, the 196th Light Infantry Brigade, and the Fifth South Vietnamese Division, rated the best of the ARVN units.[182] The area was prepped with air and artillery bombardment throughout the whole triangle. A hammer and anvil maneuver was used. A coordinated sweep would be the hammer, and blocking troops the anvil, hoping to prevent any escape.

On the eve of the attack, helicopter units of the First Division forcibly evacuated and burned to the ground the village of Ben Suc, the reported hub of VC activity in Area C. Enemy defense was minimal. The VC skipped off into the jungle the night before.[183] The villagers were interrogated, and nearly 6,000 people were evacuated to a nearby refugee camp. Although most of the Vietcong had slipped away, 1,100 bunkers were destroyed. Five hundred tunnels were also found. Enough rice was found to feed 13,000 people for a year. A vast supply of weapons and equipment was found, plus a valuable cache of documents belonging to VC Intelligence. It was obviously a regional headquarters. It was later declared a free-fire zone. Seven hundred and seventy-five Vietcong were killed or captured. Cedar Falls destroyed enemy facilities, but failed to bag many enemy soldiers.

Operation Junction City was launched the following month. The failure to capture many of the enemy during Cedar Falls was thought to be due to the use of ARVN units, who seemed to lack aggressiveness and who may have forewarned the Vietcong. Operation Junction City would use only a few units of the ARVN in small numbers. The function of Junction City was to smash enemy power in War Zone C, an area where enemy had been since the separation of Vietnam. It was a flat marshy plain on the east and gradually changed going westward into forests and then mountainous jungle.

The plan of attack was complex. Units of the 25th Division would fly in to block the western front along the Cambodian border. The First Infantry would block the eastern side of the area, and the 173rd Brigade would seal off the northern portions, thus forming an inverted U. A brigade of the 25th Division and the 11th Armored Cavalry would then push up into the open end of the U, to trap the Ninth VC Division and destroy it. Bobby Lee, a Nelson County native, was with the 11th Armored Cavalry (Blackhorse) Regiment.

In the only major parachute jump of the war, a battalion of the 173rd parachuted down less than seven miles from Cambodia. Almost 250 helicopters flew in the rest of the brigade.[184]

A battalion of the First Division soon ran into the enemy. The leading unit was attacked by units of the 121st VC Regiment with machine-gun and rocket fire. Air support was called in. After 54 air strikes, the enemy broke off action. Air had won the day. Three days later, the 173rd discovered the VC information center with all sorts of documents.

An engineer battalion moved in to construct a Special Forces camp. For protection, the Second Mechanized Battalion of the Second Infantry Regiment surrounded the camp. At night, the 272nd VC Regiment attacked the camp. Wave after wave of attackers were mowed down by armor-mounted machine guns, artillery, and 100 air strikes. In the morning, the badly mauled VC broke off fighting.

On March 18, a brigade of the Ninth Infantry replaced the 173rd Brigade. Along Route 13 to An Loc, a firebase was posted by Troop A of the Third Squadron, with six tanks and 23 armored personnel carriers to help guard convoys using Route 13. On March 19, the 273rd VC Regiment attacked the unit. The assault was met by tank cannon fire, machine guns, and mortar fire. Despite that, the enemy got within the American lines, and swarmed over American vehicles. Artillery grapeshot was fired at the American vehicles, and dozens of Vietcong were blown off the vehicles. A sister squadron fought through prepared VC ambushes to come to the base's aid, and with assisting artillery and air support, they drove off the enemy with substantial losses.

On March 22, a small night patrol was returning to Firebase Gold, which had previously suffered 43 casualties during a sudden attack. The patrol was overrun by a VC attack after being blasted with mortars. Despite return fire and artillery, the firebase was partially overrun. There was close combat with entrenching tools, chain saws, and Bowie knives. Reinforcements came just in time in the form of units of the First Infantry and 34th Armored, and drove off the assaulting enemy.

The final large action of Junction City occurred on March 31. The First Battalion of the 26th Infantry air-landed on March 26 in tall grass near the Cambodian border, deep in War Zone C. Lieutenant Colonel Alexander Haig, who later served as secretary of state under Richard Nixon, commanded the battalion. They were obviously expected. VC warning signs had been put up.

On March 31, troops set out from the LZ to sweep the area. The reconnaissance platoon was hit hard and lost its lieutenant. Company B went off to its defense without artillery or air support, and became pinned down and unable to move. Haig was in a helicopter overhead, and seeing the desperate situation, landed in the middle of Company B to take command personally. Company A was directed to come to its aid. They were running out of ammunition, and its wounded commander was in shock. Late in the afternoon, the two companies were able to retreat to the battalion perimeter.

A First Division battalion supported the LZ. In the morning, they were attacked by a massive VC assault, resulting in hand-to-hand combat. Antipersonnel bombs, napalm, and helicopter gunships enabled the American command to beat the attackers. That was the last of the big actions in Junction City.

From April on, a "floating brigade" of the 25th Division swept through War Zone C, but had only small, infrequent contacts with the enemy. Junction City had been a great success. Three VC regiments were badly mauled. For the rest of the year, sweeps met only light actions. When the 25th Division reentered War Zone C in December, in Operation Yellowstone, it was met with frequent mortar barrages, but light ground contact.

At least five Nelson County natives were involved in Junction City. Two were involved in helicopters: Tommy Armstrong of the First Aviation Battalion of the First Division, and Private First Class Albert Terry Evans, who would participate in the highland battles later in the year.

E4 Gerald Bullock was in Operation Junction City. He entered the army in August 1966. After basic training, he went to Fort Polk, Louisiana, for airborne infantry training—rappelling out of helicopters. He didn't go overseas right away, because he had a brother serving in the navy on the USS *Roosevelt* off the Vietnam coast. After several months, however, he was sent to Vietnam where he joined Company A, Sixth Battalion, First Infantry Division. He served as a regular infantryman, but part of his platoon's job was supporting the mortar platoon. He went to Di An initially, one of the main bases for the First Infantry Division. He next went to Camps Bravo and Alpha, where his company did security duty outside of the Bien Hoa

Airbase. He was also at Phuoc Vinh for two short terms.

In Operation Junction City, Company A's job was to secure a vital intersection, and protect the MPs who directed traffic of tanks and other vehicles. The Vietcong didn't attack the company as they had other units of the First Division. His company was also in the less well-known Operation Thirteen.

Bullock's company occasionally helicoptered in where it was needed. The men stood up in their choppers all the way in. Their first mission was into a hot LZ. Everything happened so fast that Bullock didn't remember many details, but it was a good baptism of fire. In some of their missions, they rappelled into the LZ. On some of his patrol missions, he served as point man, and several times picked up trip wires for booby traps and disarmed them. He had a number of encounters with the enemy when on squad-sized patrols. When they met resistance of any size, they would pull back, and radio for air or artillery support. He was especially impressed by a plane called "Puff the Magic Dragon." He could see a continuous stream of fire from its guns into the enemy position. Every other round was a tracer.

As his company moved around in their area of operation, they would set up in camps surrounded by concertina wire and Claymore mines, and live in foxholes. Bullock recalled that they played a lot of poker in the foxholes to help pass the time. Once he lost $1,400 in army scrip in a foxhole game. Overall, though, he broke even.

They were attacked four times in their company perimeter. At one time or another, he used four different weapons, the M-16 rifle, the M79 grenade launcher, the 90-mm recoilless rifle, and a 45-caliber pistol. One time, he used his 90-mm recoilless rifle to kill a water buffalo that the Vietcong used to trample the concertina wire and set off Claymore mines. The recoilless rifle also had a ball-type charge that threw out a bunch of razor-sharp projectiles. It was very effective for close-in fighting, as close as 50 yards.

The worst attack that he remembered killed four of his unit. The enemy got close, in overwhelming numbers, but was repelled with airborne napalm. When the attack was over, the Americans counted more 200 Vietcong bodies, which they had to bury.

Bullock didn't know how many Vietcong he killed in firefights, but he remembered one confirmed kill. Two particular events stood out in his mind. One was when several men in his company were killed when they were digging a foxhole and inadvertently hit a buried mine. The second was when a sergeant and radioman were captured, killed, and mutilated. The sergeant had a big red one carved in his chest.

In addition to search-and-destroy missions, and patrolling around the company base, the men had to serve in two-men listening posts (LPs) outside the company perimeter to prevent surprise attacks. Although most of the company had to do such duty, frequently it was given to new men. (Men were constantly being rotated in to replace the sick, the wounded, and those whose time was up.)

Bullock's company had good duty in an area that served as a rest camp. It had an airstrip for helicopters and C-130s. The company was there for a month. The army rotated outfits to such places for stress control after severe battles and skirmishes. Bullock also had a week's R&R (rest and recuperation) in Singapore, which he really enjoyed.

Bullock put in 13 months, a month extra to get an easy out (easy duty when he returned to the states). He came back to Fort Campbell, where he was on light duty, except for two weeks when he had to guard prisoners on a work detail. He was discharged August 5, 1968. He received several medals, including a Combat Infantry Badge.

Other Nelson County natives served in Operation Junction City. Private First Class Joseph Essex was with the First Division, and Private First Class Albert Johnson and Sergeant First Class Joseph E. Newton were with the 25th Division (*Kentucky Standard*, May 11, 1967). Newton earned a Bronze Star when his squad was under VC fire; he exposed himself to enemy fire to give mortar fire and drive off the enemy.

MEKONG DELTA

The Ninth Division was deployed to the Mekong Delta area, bordering on Saigon. The Mekong Delta area included about one-fourth of all Vietnam. It was a very populated area, and the most productive agricultural area. Up until 1966, the Vietcong controlled about 90 percent the delta.

The Mekong River started branching up in Cambodia, and by the time it reached the South China Sea, it had many connecting branches, large and small, that eventually emptied into the sea. There were few roads and fewer bridges. Most transportation was by small boats called sampans and bigger ones called junks.

The Plain of Reeds, a flat, marshy area of shoulder-high reeds interlaced with canals, comprised much of the delta. There were also jungle-like areas and extensive fields of rice. Because of the delta's lack of roads and poor accessibility, it made an ideal haven for the Vietcong.

In an effort to dislodge the enemy from their sanctuary, the navy was called upon to develop boats to patrol the Mekong's branches, down to its smallest, and root the enemy out of its nests. Thus was born the Riverine Force of small, fast, well-armed and well-constructed boats. It was very dangerous work, since the boats could be ambushed from both banks, but they could give back as much as they got. They could not deal with large groups of enemy infantry and needed the help of the army.

The Ninth Division, called "The Old Reliables," was summoned to help drive out the Vietcong. General Westmoreland, the commander in chief of the Vietnam American Forces, served with the Ninth Division in World War II, and was a firm believer in its abilities.

The division had seen extensive action in WWII in North Africa (where it captured Bizerte to help end that campaign), in Sicily, and in France where it was instrumental in capturing the port of Cherbourg and in the breakout at Saint-Lô in Normandy, and many other battles culminating in the surrender of Germany. The division had also served in Korea. In late 1966, the division's 60th Regiment and part of the 47th Regiment participated in Operation Coronado, the first joint venture with the Navy's Riverine Force.[185] In early 1967, the 39th Regiment was brought in and the complete division became involved in delta operations.

Three Nelson Countians served in the Third Battalion of the 39th Regiment: Specialist Joseph Ronald (Ronnie) Greenwell in C Company, Eddie Gritton in B Company, and Donald Stivers in A Company.

The 39th slipped into Long An province, south of Saigon at Rach Kien. Long An had long been Vietcong territory. At first, any soldier who ventured 300 yards outside the base was subject to ambush. The 39th was there to stake its claim.

In Operation Enterprise, the regiment became involved in a 100-day campaign to roust the 506th VC Battalion, long in control of the area (*Kentucky Standard,* May 15, 1967). The operation started February 13 with small actions. On April 9, the Third Battalion was airlifted into battle outside of Rach Kien under heavy fire from the 506th VC Battalion. Two battalions from the 60th Regiment joined the Third Battalion in the battle along the Rach Dia River. Frequent airmobile assaults kept the Vietcong off balance. Company-sized American units conducted sweeps for three days. The Vietcong suffered considerable losses, but the bulk of the enemy battalion escaped. For the time being, their power in that part of Long An province was broken.

Eddie Gritton earned the Army Commendation Medal in Operation Enterprise. Private First Class Jerry Trent, a Nelson County native, was with Company A, Third Battalion, 60th Regiment, in Operation Enterprise. He and the others would continue to be involved in delta battles during the year.

The Ninth Division was involved in two major operations without the 39th Regiment. Both were unqualified successes, although the second was much more costly in American lives.

The first was Ap Bac II.[186] There were several Ap Bacs, but Ap Bac II was in the Mekong Delta, which was occupied by the 514th Main Force Vietcong Battalion. In the attack, three units of the Ninth attacked the VC from three different areas, attempting to bottle up the enemy and slowly compress them into an area where they could be eradicated. As usual, the Vietcong were well emplaced in camouflaged bunkers with machine guns, mortars, and recoilless rifles, but with artillery and aerial support, the enemy was slowly driven back. Armored vehicles were also used.

As the ring got smaller, the going got tougher. Firepower had to be limited for fear of hitting friendly troops coming in from the other direction. The last part of the operation had to be done by troopers crawling on their bellies along muddy dikes. There were numerous acts of bravery, and in the end, the infantry got to their feet and charged the Vietcong bunkers. The fighting was hand-to-hand. One Vietcong was killed, hit in the head by an American helmet, and another was stabbed to death. The enemy crawled out of their bunkers and tried to run away, but most were shot. As the battle ended, more than 200 of the 514th regular forces lay dead. Many who were wounded were assisted by comrades to escape in the fading light.

Fewer than 20 American soldiers were killed and about 70 were wounded. They were attended to by medics, and medevaced out. The 514th was destroyed as a unit. It had to slowly be built back, but for the time being, that part of the delta was relatively free of Vietcong.

Jerry Trent of the 60th Regiment was involved in a successful flanking action in the battle.

The other operation occurred in June 1967, and again was close to Ap Bac II village. The Fifth Nha Be Main Force Vietcong Battalion was operating close to Saigon, where it had been pushed back by the 199th Light Infantry Brigade to a safe haven to refit and rebuild. Operation Concordia planned to surround and destroy the battalion.[187] Using Riverine craft for deployment, the operation was carried out by three American and one South Vietnamese battalion. The forces were dropped off at three different places to form a triangle around where the enemy was thought to be.

The two northern legs started moving south hoping to squeeze the enemy in an enveloping attack. The Vietcong waited in dug-in defensive positions, in well-fortified and well-camouflaged bunkers. When the American troops moved close through a dry rice paddy, the enemy let loose with murderous fire at 40 feet. One American company was immediately mauled. Casualties rose swiftly and the injured could only lie flat on their faces, digging in as best as they could in the dirt. Another company was loading its mortar equipment in boats to cross a stream when the Vietcong sprung up all around them. Their 10 boats were sunk, and many men became casualties. Firefights burst out all over the area. Other American forces rushed with their firepower. Artillery was called in, but was tentative because the location of some friendly troops was not known. Another platoon was ambushed and its condition became critical. Several gunboats moved up and supplied heavy fire on the enemy strong points. There were numerous acts of bravery and self-sacrifice. Wounded were brought back and filled up the decks of the gunboats.

Artillery and aerial attacks got so close that their explosives bounced American soldiers off the ground. The bravery of the young draftees was amazing. They took the best the VC could give and seldom wavered, and took the fight to the enemy. Eventually, VC losses also took a toll. Naval gunboats brought in reinforcements, who charged the VC bunkers, and scattered some of their protectors. Other units that had been pinned down all day also moved forward. At dusk, the American units joined up, and while artillery was pounding the enemy bunkers, they went out into the paddies and pulled the wounded back into safe places. By the next morning, the enemy had moved out, leaving behind a rear guard. That was promptly disposed of. Friendly forces followed the VC trail. The enemy was finally pinned in from all sides, and pounded by artillery all night. By the next morning, the remaining enemy had snuck out, and the battle of the Can Giuoc complex was over.

During the battle, 268 bunkers were destroyed, and more than 255 enemies were killed. American losses included 42 killed and 150 wounded. The battle shattered the Fifth Nha Be Main Force Battalion. It would not return to combat efficiency for some time.

Sergeant First Class Frank Stephens, a Nelson County native, was with the Ninth Division at Long Binh.

Nelson Countian Ronnie Greenwell was promoted to sergeant and sent to the 47th Regiment at Dong Tam (*Kentucky Standard*, October 13, 1967). He was with that regiment on September 15 when it was involved in an operation to rout the enemy in the Cam Son Secret Zone. The boats carrying the soldiers came under intense fire from both sides of the river. One was badly damaged by rocket fire from heavily bunkered troops. The task force withdrew, regrouped, and returned downstream to realign and take off the wounded. They went upstream again under heavy fire, let off the soldiers in their assigned areas, and set up a naval blockade on the river, returning maximum fire. When the troops that had landed were pinned down, the boats returned under fire and extracted the Americans. Greenwell was involved in this and other actions. He stayed with the 47th until his tour was up.

Greenwell returned from Vietnam and took a job with the local newspaper, eventually becoming the sports editor. He wrote a book about his many years at the paper. He was often seen walking along the sidelines of local football games with his camera. He died in his 50s from a type of cancer sometimes caused by Agent Orange.

THE SPRING DMZ CAMPAIGN

In February 1967, the marine line south of the DMZ hinged on bases from Lang Vei in the west, past Khe Sanh, the Rockpile (a hill of solid rock that stood above the surrounding valley), Camp Carroll, Cam Lo, and their main command post in the east at Dong Ha.[188] They had two outposts closer to the DMZ—the firebases at Con Thien and Gio Linh. The area between the bases was manned by a mobile defense.

After the monsoons, there were increasing artillery barrages from both sides. A marine reconnaissance patrol bumped into the 812th NVA Regiment outside of Cam Lo. A marine company went to reinforce it. At dawn, after a mortar barrage, swarms of NVA soldiers stormed out of the jungle. They were thrown back with the assistance of heavy artillery support. Another reinforcing marine company ran into a perfectly camouflaged fortification as they came in. Still another reinforcing company was met by a large ambush, which tore the company to shreds, and killed the battalion commander. As other marine forces came in, the NVA left the battlefield.

A special marine landing force, assisted by the 11th Marine Engineers, of which Corporal James Barnes was a member, cleaned out a maze of enemy interconnecting tunnels and fortifications between Con Thien and Gio Linh (*Kentucky Standard*, June 15, 1967).

The "hill fight" around Khe Sanh followed. In April, it became evident that the enemy controlled several hills around the vital base. The effort to regain control of those hills lasted until mid-May, and required numerous battles. Hills 861 and 881 were the worst. Numerous units were involved, including a part of the Ninth Marines, and two battalions of the Third Marines. Repeated artillery bombardment was needed, but after substantial losses on both sides, the hills were in marine hands. The First and Second battalions of the 26th Marines assumed defense of Khe Sanh after that, and would stay through the siege of 1968.

Around Con Thien, intermittent artillery barrages went back and forth. In a month, the NVA fired approximately 3,100 shells at Con Thien. The NVA also made numerous attacks on Con Thien trying to isolate it. For a while, it looked as if Con Thien would become a small Dien Bien Phu. Marine patrols went out, met fierce resistance and took losses, but all NVA attacks were thrown back, sometimes with tremendous losses due to air and artillery bombardment.[189]

The Ninth Marines and the First Battalion of the Third Marine Regiment, of which Nelson County native Corporal John P. Coomes was a member, pushed around Con Thien. They were met with violent ground fighting. A mass NVA regiment attack was met by automatic weapons fire, artillery, and air strafing. The enemy losses were horrendous; a few of the enemy crossed into American lines, where they were shot or bayoneted.

In these grueling and deadly battles just south of the DMZ, casualties were high on both sides, and the marines considered Con Thien and Khe Sanh as some of the major battles in the Corps' long history.

Tommy Goben was another of Nelson County's sons who was at Con Thien. He joined the marines in late 1966, and did his boot training with Kenny Nevitt, also from Nelson County. Goben later had artillery training and was shipped to Vietnam. He flew to his battery's station in country in a C-130 that landed on a dirt airstrip. He was assigned to the 1/8s, firing eight-inch howitzers. Superior artillery helped the marines prevail. Goben was at Dong Ha, Cam Lo, and Con Thien.

Goben joined the marines with four buddies. Two of them signed up for two-year hitches, which almost guaranteed a tour in Vietnam. For most of Goben's tour, his unit was in a compound with an army unit that fired

175-mm cannon, and another marine battery that fired 155-mm howitzers. They were surrounded by a minefield and concertina wire, and protected by armored vehicles and infantry. The enemy got close, but never penetrated the compound.

Goben's outfit had flying forward observers who would call back coordinates for targets, and the big guns would fire several times every day. They packed a lot of firepower. An eight-inch cannon is the equivalent of 200-mm. The North Vietnamese frequently fired back across the DMZ with their heavy artillery. During the Tet Offensive, they would throw anywhere from 50 to 100 shells a day at the compound.

At one point, information came down that the compound was going to be under a big attack, and a unit of 105-mm howitzers was brought in for close-in support, but the attack never came. The big guns kept the enemy at bay, and in large part prevented the massing of any threat from the north.

Eventually the bombardment and attacks on Con Thien ended in mid October 1967, and the siege was lifted.

The last action of the year around the DMZ was when marines ran into a fortified village. The 716th NVA Regiment had snuck in behind the advancing Americans in a village called Thom Tham Khe. Fighting was intense, but confused, and the enemy managed to slip out. Lance Corporal Larry Greenwell's Ontos Unit of the First March Division was in the area.[190] They had been stationed at Dong Ha.

MARINE COASTAL CAMPAIGN

While the DMZ fighting was going on, the First Marine Division was sent to clean out the Phuoc Ha Valley, "Happy Valley," between Chu Lai and Da Nang. The First Regiment of that division was the first to push out.

Operation Union started when the Third NVA Regiment hit a hill outpost of Company F, First Marines, and the Fifth Marines came in.[191] The marines pushed north, and occasionally ran into stiff resistance. On April 15, the Third Battalion of the Fifth Marines ran into fortified NVA entrenchments. Through a 12-hour fight, the enemy was pushed out. The marines created a plan to trap and destroy the 21st NVA Regiment. Three American units helicoptered in from different directions. They met with the enemy at their main entrenchment on the hills. The Third Battalion of the Fifth Marines, of which Nelson Countian Private First Class Larry White was a member, charged up the fire-swept hill to overrun enemy lines at bayonet point.[192]

Operation Union I continued as Union II. In these operations, the Fifth Marine Regiment gutted a large part of the enemy's Second Division, and temporarily cleared out the Que Son Valley.

When additional US forces were thrown in, the beaten enemy withdrew. Corporal Ronald Greer of Nelson County participated in these battles in an air-to-ground team of the Second Battalion, First Marines. Three other Nelson Countians were involved in this campaign: Sergeant A.B. (Buddy) Grigsby, Sergeant Kenny Nevitt, and Lance Corporal Ronnie Coulter.

A.B. (Buddy) Grigsby was born and raised in Bardstown, where he was well liked, and a better-than-average football player at St. Joe Prep School. After high school, he decided to join the marines. Even though he signed up in 1963, he didn't go on active duty until January 1964. He first went to Parris Island, South Carolina, for boot camp, and then to Camp Lejeune, North Carolina, for advanced infantry training. His first duty assignment was on the aircraft carrier USS *Essex* in 1965. He then went to

Camp Pendleton, California, for overseas assignment. He flew to Da Nang, Vietnam, and was assigned to the Seventh Regiment of the First Marine Division, Second Battalion, Echo Company. The headquarters of the First Marine Division was just north of Chu Lai.

Grigsby's first action was Operation Arizona, out of Chu Lai sweeping north, battalion-wide over the shrub and forested coastal plain to Da Nang, and through a place ironically called Happy Valley. The Vietcong, and later the North Vietnamese Army, had long controlled the valley. They met with occasional stiff resistance and deadly firefights, but moved on.

Operation Arizona continued under other names. Eventually the area was cleared, but with time, the enemy moved back in, in squad and company numbers. Sometimes they would send recruiters into the villages by night, and impress villagers into the Vietcong and NVA units. There were frequent sweeps looking for enemy activity to prevent the enemy from coming back in large numbers or launching surprise attacks. Most patrols moved by day, and hunkered down at night so that they could conduct ambushes, and not be ambushed themselves. It was said that the army and marines controlled the land by day, and the enemy controlled it by night. Patrolling was a never-ending, necessary tactic.

When Grigsby first arrived, the marines were issued M-14 rifles. At the time, the army was using M-16 rifles. Grigsby said the army got the new equipment first, and the marines got the leftovers. Then they were given AR15s, a predecessor of the M-16, which had been discarded by the army. The AR15 and M-16 were notorious for misfiring and jamming, sometimes after only one clip. A marine patrol went out one night with AR15s, and was ambushed by an enemy platoon. Unfortunately, most of the AR15s malfunctioned. Fortunately, they had a good supply of grenades, and fought their way out of the ambush.

Grigsby's unit moved around from base to base in I Corps, wherever they were needed, such as Combat Base Esso, which was a major supply base that they had to patrol and defend. Most of their activities were in the southern part of I Corps. The northern part was under the jurisdiction of the Third Marine Division. Part of the function of Grigsby's unit was keeping Highway 1 open around a pass between Phu Bai and Da Nang. It was the main north-south artery. The highway snaked through a mountain range just north of Da Nang. It was a frequent site of enemy mines and roadside bombs. The enemy snuck in at night and placed the mines in the bed of the road. It was also a frequent site for ambushes.

Grigsby was on one of the hillsides, looking down on the road where his commanding officer was setting up defenses. The vehicle he was in was attacked by rocket-propelled grenades and machine-gun fire, killing everyone involved. Grigsby even saw the enemy sneak out on the road during the day to plant mines. When the enemy lived among the general population, it was hard to protect anything 100 percent of the time.

The continuous actions caused a steady rate of attrition in his outfit. His platoon was usually under strength. At full strength, it would have about 50 men, but most often operated at half that number. Disease, wounds, and death took their toll. At one time, they were down to about 15 men. There were seven men killed in his platoon, and more than 20 were wounded and medevaced out. According to Grigsby, more than 90 percent of his unit had wounds of some kind at some time. Many of the wounds were superficial, with pieces of shrapnel from mortars or fragments from shells. At one time, Grigsby had his back peppered with small pieces of shrapnel. Many others had similar wounds that they considered so small that they didn't even see a medic, unless the wounds became infected. Grigsby said it was funny that some wounds seemed severe and widespread over a man's body, and he would survive, whereas others had one little hole in their heads or chests, and died instantly. He saw others who died from seemingly minor wounds and shock. Grigsby was the right guard of his platoon, and was responsible for calling in the three B's: bread, bullets, and bandages.

Grigsby's outfit frequently flew into combat areas in helicopters—both Hueys and Chinooks, large two-rotor 'copters that could carry a full squad in and out of action.

In the last part of his year's rotation, he had the unenviable task of riding shotgun on supply columns of vehicles going to Khe Sanh in the northwest section of Vietnam, below the DMZ and close to the Laotian border. Their route was up Highway 1, and then over Highway 9 west.

Khe Sanh was kind of a stopper in a bottle that kept large numbers of enemy forces from entering South Vietnam through that natural passageway. The North Vietnamese army would later lay siege to it for several months, in what appeared possibly to be another Dien Bien Phu.

However, at the time Grigsby was there, the supply road was still open, although interdicted with frequent ambushes. No sizeable force attacked Grigsby's supply columns, but one time, just after they had arrived at Khe Sanh, they came under heavy enemy artillery bombardment. Grigsby recalled that there was a well-built bunker close by, and he and several of his fellow supply runners dove in it at the same time. They had faced heavy shelling before, and were pelted by several near misses.

At the beginning of Grigsby's stay, he had many friends in his outfit, and all were very close. When new men came in, they were often killed or wounded before he even knew their names. The closeness and camaraderie of many of his friends has lingered.

"We had many brave men and a number were decorated with Navy Crosses, Silver Stars, and Bronze Stars," he said in an interview. There was even a Medal of Honor winner in his battalion.

Grigsby has many memories, and keeps pictures of his outfit, maps, and computer printouts of one of the most defining times of his life. He is still loyal to the Corps, and frequently flies a marine "Semper Fidelis" flag in front of his home along with an American flag.

Kenny Nevitt was one of five Nelson County friends who joined the marines at approximately the same time. Nevitt and a friend, Tommy Goben, went active on the buddy system on October 31, 1966, for two-year tours. Three others went active two days later on four-year enlistments, where they could pick the school they wanted for specialty training. When interviewed, Nevitt recalled that, at the time, "Vietnam was not too big of a deal, and was far away." Much of American society felt the same way.

Nevitt and his buddy first went to boot camp at Parris Island, South Carolina. Boot camp lasted eight or nine weeks, and was one of the most memorable experiences of his life. It was tough and taught him a lot. It made him a marine, an identity he has been proud of ever since. After two years, he left the Marine Corps, but the Marine Corps never left him.

After boot camp, Nevitt was sent to Camp Geiger, close to Camp Lejeune in North Carolina, for more infantry training. From there, he went to Camp Pendleton in California for advanced infantry training for about two months. He was shipped overseas to Vietnam on March 6, 1967, where he became a member of Mike Company, Third Battalion, Seventh Regiment of the First Marine Division. His company was assigned to two hills just south of Da Nang. Two platoons occupied Hill 52, and one platoon occupied Hill 25.

Nevitt spent most of his time for the next 10 months operating off Hill 52. It was not a war of fronts. It was a war of enclaves held by American forces, which protected population centers, and from which offensive action could be sent. Hills 25 and 52 were outposts, so to speak, around an enclave to give it security. That enclave was Da Nang.

While on those two hills, Nevitt's unit ran ambushes, which usually lasted two days, and ranged several miles from the hills they occupied. The functions of the outposts were to notice any increased enemy activity in the area, and eradicate enemy patrols or personnel of any kind that they found. At night, they would frequently set up ambushes along trails with Claymore mines. The mines, which they could trigger, were pointed away from them. One morning, they found that the enemy had turned them around, and pointed the mines toward the marines. Ambushes would be alternated off different sides of the hill, alternating personnel. Nevitt would go out on them every other night. On other nights, he would go out to listening posts (LPs), which were two-man foxholes up to a half a mile from the base of the hill. LPs were scarier than ambushes because of their isolation, but they were necessary.

The ambushes were seldom successful, but they helped assure the safety of their hills. The area in front of the ambush was a free-fire zone. Anyone moving, friend or foe, could be a target. One night they killed three women carrying supplies to the Vietcong in the dark. On patrol, the squads always buried their C ration cans to prevent the enemy from using them for grenades and booby traps.

For the first six months, when they had to contend with only the Vietcong, their duty wasn't too bad, although it was always dangerous. When the North Vietnamese regular army troops (NVA) moved into their area, their duty was much more precarious. One time, when they were returning from an ambush, in what was supposed to be a friendly village controlled by the ARVN (South Vietnamese Army), the NVA ambushed them. They suffered several casualties including their corpsman. Nevitt's unit had thought highly of him. An estimated four out of five corpsmen became casualties during their tour. Corpsmen were actually naval pharmacy mates who gave battlefield medical treatment.

The NVA assaulted both hills, 25 and 52. On Nevitt's hill (52), enemy troops succeeded in penetrating the marine perimeter, but were driven off with heavy casualties. On another occasion, s, wearing only jock straps and equipped with wire cutters and satchel charges, made a break in the perimeter wire and overran Hill 25. (Sappers were troops specially trained to penetrate defenses, cut wire, plant explosives, and even clear minefields.) The marines called in anti-personnel artillery right on top of themselves. Even though they took casualties, they were able to push the enemy off the hill with the aid of the artillery, and regained control.

Nevitt frequently served as the point man on patrols—the first man in the formation. He recalled that it wasn't as bad as it sounded. The enemy would let the first two or three men through, and then close in behind them, making it difficult for them to fire backwards or for the other marines to fire forward for fear of hitting friendly troops. The NVA was particularly adept at doing that. As point man, Nevitt had to be particularly careful of deadly booby traps and punji sticks (sharpened bamboo sticks placed on trails and camouflaged with vegetation).

While on patrol, Nevitt's unit found several openings into tunnels. Rather than going down into them like tunnel rats sometimes did, his patrol would throw grenades into them, a much safer procedure. His group also had frequent short firefights, with the enemy firing from tree lines and other protected areas. It was hard to tell how many they killed, as the enemy often towed their dead and wounded away, but they left blood streaks behind. At that stage of the war, one of the main complaints of the marines was the unreliability of the M-16s, which often jammed during action, leaving them yearning for their old reliable M-14 rifles.

On two occasions, Nevitt had to go to China Beach to the hospital. Once he had malaria and was in the hospital for three weeks. He had been unable to take the malaria prevention pills because they made him sick. On the other occasion, he was wounded in the shoulder by grenade shrapnel. After the shrapnel was removed and the wound sutured, he was able to return to his outfit.

About two months before Nevitt's tour was up, his company had to give up their two hills. Intelligence indicated that the enemy had planned a big attack on his battalion headquarters hill, where marine fire support artillery was located. The outlying outposts were destroyed and the men were pulled back into the battalion base. The intelligence was wrong and the attack never came.

During his tour, Nevitt had two weeks of R&R: at Taipei on Taiwan and at Kuala Lumpur in Malaysia. Both were quite an experience for a young man from a small Kentucky town who hadn't seen much of the world. After a 13-month tour (marines had to serve an extra month), he returned home, and in a few months was discharged on October 28, 1968.

Nevitt has kept in touch with many members of his company, and has gone almost yearly to company reunions. The camaraderie engendered by his tour ran deep. He is proud of his marine service and said he would do it again.

Ronnie Coulter joined the Marine Corps on November 14, 1964, at the age of 19. He did his boot camp at Parris Island, and then went to Camp Lejeune for further training. He was sent to the Mediterranean Sea, where he served with the Sixth Fleet as a sea-going marine for nine months. Following that, he went to Guantanamo Bay in Cuba for five months, when Fidel Castro was making threats. After Cuba, he was sent to Vietnam by transport with 1,500 other marines. The bunks were stacked five high as they were on most transports. He never got seasick, but many did. Coulter recalled that the men avoided sleeping on the bottom bunk. The trip took a month.

When he reached Vietnam, he went in country right away. He had trained in artillery, but when he got to Vietnam, he was given a rifle, and became an infantryman in Mike Company, Third Battalion, Seventh Regiment, First Marine Division. Sergeant Kenny Nevitt was in the same company, and their tours overlapped for a few months.

Coulter's first assignment was with a platoon on Hill 10. It wasn't much of a hill, only 10 meters above sea level. He had been there only a few weeks when the North Vietnamese attacked and overran the hill. He was very fortunate, because he had been moved to another part of the perimeter. The enemy hit where he had been, and killed 10 to 15 men, two of whom he had served with since the beginning of his enlistment.

After heavy fighting, his unit drove the NVA off with heavy losses. He estimated that 100 of the enemy were killed. He was one of those with the unenviable task of getting rid of their bodies. He said they were put in a pile, doused with fuel oil, and burned. It was the most practical way to do it.

Coulter's duty was mostly search-and-destroy missions, setting up night ambushes, and serving on listening posts away from the unit perimeter. Every day they had some kind of duty. He never got used to night duty. One side or the other was always setting up ambushes, and the men never knew what was out there.

He remembered one particular search-and-destroy mission called Operation Dakota. They went out on several large operations, but he remembered Dakota particularly. The night before they went out, they were treated with extra beer rations. As they were sweeping out of Chu Lai, and moving over dikes and through rice paddies, they were hit with a fusillade of automatic weapons fire from a tree line. His corpsman, who was right in front of him, was hit in the forehead and died instantly. His company dropped down behind the dikes for cover. They were pinned down there for the better part of a day under heavy fire. When night came, they were able to fall back and regroup. The next morning when they attacked again, the enemy had slipped away.

When interviewed for this book, Coulter said that he never understood men saying that they weren't afraid under such circumstances. They were either liars or fools, probably the first. He thought anybody who was normal would be afraid. It was a sign of courage and training when you acknowledged fear, but didn't panic and went on and did your job anyway. Such was the feeling of most of those who served.

His unit walked almost everywhere they went, along jungle trails, through elephant grass 10 feet high, knee deep in muddy rice paddies, chest deep when wading streams, and in torrential rain during the monsoon seasons. Sometimes it rained so hard they couldn't see 10 feet in front of them. They discovered tunnels in hutches in villages and along trails.

Coulter was one of the smallest men in his platoon, and frequently became a tunnel rat. As he explored the tunnels, he was always leery of what he would find. Once he was startled by noise ahead of him in the tunnel. It turned out to be a pot-bellied pig. Otherwise, his explorations turned out to be fruitless. On their treks, they were always leery of booby traps, which could unexpectedly cause the loss of life or limb.

On two of their search-and-destroy missions, they went by helicopter. The helicopters often hovered off the ground to let their men off rather than touching down. The pilot of one of their helicopters leveled off at the top of 10-foot high elephant grass, thinking he was lower. The first man out fell 10 feet and broke his leg.

They never got hot meals, even on holidays. They existed on C rations.

For the first half of Coulter's tour, the marines used the M-14 rifle. Then they were issued the M-16, a lighter and more efficient rifle. According to Coulter, many of the marines preferred the M-14, and felt it was a more reliable weapon.

Coulter was wounded one time on ambush duty when he was hit in the arm and leg by shrapnel from a grenade. His corpsman fixed him up, cleaned the wounds, put on a dressing and an ace bandage, and he never missed a day from his company. He received the Purple Heart. He saw a lot of heavy action, and many people in his outfit, including some of his friends, were killed.

After his 13 months were up, he was sent back to the states to Camp Lejeune, and from there back to Cuba, where he finished his enlistment. He was proud to have been a marine. In his later life, he developed chronic lung disease. He was around Agent Orange and wondered if that had anything to do with his disease. There are many unanswered questions about the chemical.

THE HIGHLANDS

In early 1967, General Westmoreland decided it was time to destroy enemy power in the highlands of western Vietnam. Both the First and 10th North Vietnamese Divisions were there. The Ia Drang battles had been fought in this same general area and north of it. For this mission, Westmoreland picked the Fourth Division, whose motto, "Steadfast and Loyal," reflected a proud history from previous wars. In World War II, the division had landed at Normandy on D-Day and assisted in the breakthrough at Saint-Lô to start the drive across France. In 1967, the division would be sorely tested. Nelson Countians Mike Cornish, Robert Smith, Daniel Williams, and Sergeant Claude Brown were members of the division.

The Central Highlands comprised mostly heavy jungle, often triple-canopied, and rugged mountainous country, as well as rolling tropical plains around Pleiku and western Kon Tum province. The first part of the operation, called Sam Houston, swept through the plains, uncovering tunnel complexes and adjacent fortifications, removing caches of food and ammunition, and destroying them. This preceded the tougher part of the operation—pushing through the mountainous jungles close to the Cambodian border. This was the real lair of the North Vietnamese. The area contained trees 250 feet tall and seven feet in diameter, and peaks ranging up to 6,000 feet. The jungle floor, where light filtered through the canopy, was covered with thick vegetation; moving through it required arduous exertion.[193] Machetes had to be used, and visibility was often limited to only a few yards. The intensely humid heat that often rose to 105 degrees added to the difficulty of fighting in this country. Making way in this type of environment was fatiguing and debilitating.

In country such as the highlands, large-scale planned offenses using large units were impossible. Offense had to be broken down to small units of company and platoon size, and communication between these units was tenuous. The use of armor and mobility on which the army depended was impossible in such country. It was the land of the foot soldier and small unit action. Often a foot soldier's field of vision was only a few feet around him. It was a most difficult terrain for a soldier loaded down with a weapon, a supply of ammunition, several grenades, often a two-day supply of C rations, and several canteens of water. It required all of a man's energy to make headway in such a situation, much less to have to fight an enemy.

This was also ideal country for the enemy to set up ambushes. They had been there for a while and knew the lay of the land. Scouting patrols of the enemy sometimes shadowed American units, marching parallel to them. They gave advance notice to larger units that planned ambushes of the advancing American and any units that may come to reinforce them.[194]

Helicopters were useful in reinforcing and supplying Fourth Division soldiers, but finding and clearing landing zones was difficult. An intense action that was to typify the campaign of the Fourth Division broke out around one of these landing zones in mid-February. A patrol reconnoitering out from the perimeter of the LZ was cut off and almost decimated. Only the heroic action of a wounded private enabled the rest of the squad to escape. He was killed for his bravery.

Then the NVA attacked the LZ with automatic weapons. The advancing North Vietnamese were stopped by rifle and M60 machine-gun fire, but the LZ was surrounded and besieged. The American soldiers called in artillery fire and air support, but their usefulness in the thick jungle was limited. Company-size reinforcements arrived, but their helicopter landing was very hazardous due to enemy fire. Other American units, attempting overland relief, were attacked individually and besieged. Finally, they joined friendly forces, and moved out against the enemy.

Napalm and cluster bombs helped, but the main thrust had to be done by individual GIs carrying 40 to 60 pounds of ammunition, food, and water. Moving forward was a constant mental and physical drain. NVA reconnaissance teams and trail watchers dogged them. In the jungle, men could easily get lost from their unit and sometimes artillery blasts would be used to help them locate their comrades. Snipers often set up in trees along their route, adding to their soldiers' emotional strain. Their fighting ability was tried to the utmost by such strain and fatigue.

Intermittent firefights broke out when leading units were met with AK-47 fire, and the jungle would be shredded with fire from both sides. Such skirmishes would often last for several hours of violent action. The NVA would break off when the odds turned against them, and evaporate back into the jungle, carrying their dead and wounded with them. Enemy soldiers were more acclimated to the terrible heat and humidity, and they had to carry lighter loads for defensive actions.

The NVA knew about and guarded the few sites in the jungle where helicopters could land. The Americans could use the sites only with risk of losses. The locations were booby trapped with grenades that were thrown into the air when activated, sending fragments into machines and men.[195]

Terry Evans, of Nelson County, crewed helicopters into these areas.

In addition, the enemy could bring in companies from their sanctuary just across the Cambodian border to fight where and when they were needed, and when the action was over, sneak them back across the border.

At day's end, American troops dug into foxholes within their perimeter, using logs or sandbags where available to protect themselves against the inevitable night mortar attacks. The men slept between watches only because they were exhausted, and their sleep was often fitful.[196]

Bulldozers followed the advancing troops and built roads through the jungle for firebases. Supporting artillery, so necessary for the protection of isolated companies and platoons, used these bases.

After driving through the jungle and rough terrain, the Fourth Division approached the Cambodian border. They had driven out the NVA temporarily. They gave as good as they got, and showed bravery, often turning potentially disastrous situations into survival, if not success. Many men lost 10 to 20 pounds due to the ordeal. The men of the Fourth Division were thoroughly fatigued. It would take time to bulk up again for another fight. They had done what was asked of them. Most units were far from full strength. Unfortunately, after they pulled out, the NVA gradually infiltrated back. The big battles that American generals had counted on had not happened, although there were many small draining firefights. Operation

Sam Houston, as it was called, ended without the desired results, although successful in some respects.

The after-battle action report said, "The most difficult tactical problem in fighting the NVA in large areas of difficult terrain is finding the enemy. That is, finding him without having tactical units shot up and pinned down by automatic weapons and snipers, often at close range."[197]

Mike Cornish was a member of the Fourth Division when they went through the terrible fighting in the Central Highlands. Unfortunately, Cornish was in a motor vehicle accident after the war and suffered some head injury. His memory of the events of the Fourth Division's battles is poor, sketchy at best. He remembered the terrible conditions in which the battles were fought, and remembered that his buddy next to him was shot in the head and killed. When the movable Vietnam Wall came to Bardstown, Cornish found his buddy's name on the wall.

Cornish also served as a tunnel rat, going down into the serpentine tunnels that traversed much of Vietnam. It was an unenviable job. Tunnel rats took only a flashlight and a pistol into the darkness, and not only braved meeting the enemy, but snakes, rats, and other vermin. Most were amazed at what they found in the hiding places of the enemy—complete rooms used for hospital wards, dormitories, grenade and booby trap factories, and storage for food and ammunition. After the tunnels were explored, engineers were called in to destroy them, or they were exploded with grenades. However, it seemed there was no end of them.

After Operation Sam Houston, the Fourth Division started Operation Francis Marion. Two division brigades, weakened by casualties and sickness incurred during Sam Houston, pushed up against the Cambodian border, extending from the Ia Drang Valley up through Kon Tum province northward.[198] The main function of Francis Marion was to keep the NVA from crossing over the border in force into the central part of the country. Many fierce battles were fought with heavy casualties on both sides.

The operation started with an American platoon successfully ambushing an enemy platoon, but as the Americans followed up on their success, they were ambushed in turn, and pinned down in a paddy. As more American soldiers pushed forward to come to their aid, they, too, were ambushed, and two companies were fighting for their lives. One company was overrun and only a few were able to extricate themselves and make their way back to the perimeter of the second company. Later, 29 bodies were found at the site of the first company; 39 were wounded. The second company beat off several assaults with the aid of artillery and air support. Sometimes the fighting was hand-to-hand.

On another occasion, a firefight developed when an American platoon on patrol was assaulted from a tree line.[199] They called in artillery and napalm, but after the bombardment, when they tried to advance, even with a couple of armored personnel carriers, they were driven back by intensive automatic weapons fire. Finally, tanks were called in with their 50-caliber machine guns and 90-mm cannon that belched canister.

The NVA was relentless in their defense, and showed that they were some of the toughest and bravest fighters in the world, running out in front of the tanks, trying to disable them by throwing grenade under their tracks. They climbed up on them and tried to disable them, but were shot off by machine-gun fire from accompanying personnel carriers, and individual M-16s. Finally, the tanks and American infantry overran and crushed their bunkers and other fortifications.

On another occasion, two companies attempting to relieve a platoon ran into a buzz saw from the 66th NVA Regiment. They were driven back to their firebase and, with battalion aid, repelled the attack.

Perhaps the biggest action occurred toward the end of Francis Marion. A platoon was separated from its company, and assaulted by a battalion of the 32nd NVA Regiment south of Duc Co. The platoon was practically wiped out. The rest of the company established a perimeter, and hastily set up a ring of Claymore mines, which were detonated in the face of the charging NVA lines. Twice the NVA attacked, but the Americans drove them back. Two other American companies joined the battle. Air Force planes dropped bombs and napalm, not only destroying the attacking battalion, but with strafing also destroyed much of the enemy reinforcing battalion.[200] After that, the North Vietnamese pulled back across the Cambodian border, and made no further attempts to infiltrate that part of the Central Highlands.

DAK TO

As Operation Francis Marion wound down, a new battle was beginning in the northern part of the highlands. This battle would last off and on for more than four months. It occurred around the Special Forces camp of Dak To.

Dak To was in a valley surrounded by mountains and ridges; a road connected it to Kon Tum City a good distance away. The battle started in June when two battalions of the 173rd Airborne Brigade helicoptered into the stronghold of the North Vietnamese Army. While working their way down to the brigade base at Dak To, the forward elements of a company ran into a heavily fortified ridge. They were attacked and tried to pull back into a perimeter. Artillery and helicopter gunship support were difficult to bring into play because of the heavily canopied jungle. The paratroopers fought bravely, but were overwhelmed by large numbers of assaulting NVA troops.[201] Attempts to relieve the company were driven back, the company was overrun, and more than half of its men were killed. The relieving paratroopers fought bravely and finally drove off the attacking NVA. By the time they reached the site of the initial battle, however, it was too late. It was a foretaste of the grisly battles ahead.

The rest of the 173rd Brigade moved into Kon Tum City with the Third Brigade of the First Cavalry Division. They fought numerous small battles on heavily bunkered ridges fortified by the NVA, and took a steady stream of casualties for the next two months. Some ridges had been fortified for a long time. Heavy monsoon rains slowed the action and the rebuilding of the road from Kon Tum City to Dak To.

In October, the First Brigade of the Fourth Division air-landed at Dak To. The Fourth Battalion of the 173rd Airborne was attached to it. A South Vietnamese brigade attacked north out of Dak To, and the Americans attacked southwest of Dak To. Meanwhile, an enemy mortar attack scored a direct hit on the ammunition dump at Dak To, which slowed the attack. Emergency ammunition and supplies were helicoptered in. Progress over the fortified ridgelines was slow and costly. After attacking and taking Hill 823, the Fourth Battalion of the 173rd had to be relieved by a sounder battalion. Before the battle of Dak To was over, all three battalions of the 173rd that were involved had suffered heavily. One particularly heavy battle was fiercely fought hand to hand before the enemy withdrew. Six American bodies were found along one side of a log, and six NVA bodies were found on the other side.

The Fourth Division Brigade, moving alongside the 173rd, captured Hill 1223 after a furious fight. Moving from ridge to ridge, the American forces were almost up against the Cambodian border when they ran into

Hill 875.[202]

Hill 875 was one of the most grueling, prolonged battles of the Vietnam War. The hill had been fortified for six months previously with deep interconnecting tunnels and many rows of fortified lines.

A fresh battalion of the 173rd was set to assault the hill, but a brigade of veteran NVA troops assaulted them, throwing grenades and firing automatic weapons. Many platoons were chopped up and many more were surrounded. An air attack went awry. A 250-pound bomb landed right in the middle of the pinned down American men, killing many.[203] Another battalion of the 173rd came to their relief, joined by units of the Fourth Division. Slowly they made their way up the hill. Despite furious pounding, the defenders held on in their deep trenches and tunnels. Ordinary grenades, bombs, and rockets would not knock out their positions. Only aerial napalm or satchel charges thrown by brave men could get at the NVA in their deep, covered trenches and tortuous tunnels. Finally, after the top of the hill had been denuded and numerous previous assaults had failed, the last line of the trenches was assaulted. The soldiers found that the enemy had deserted the hill. It had been a bloody campaign, one of the bloodiest of the war, but Hill 875 ended the Dak To operation.

With this operation, some of the best light infantry troops in the world were driven from their intensely fortified positions, and forced to escape across the border into Cambodia. For a long time, the enemy wouldn't be able to use any of the Central Highlands for offensive operations.

Men from Nelson County were involved in these battles. Robert Smith fought in the highland battles with the First Battalion of the Eighth Infantry Regiment, Fourth Division. Daniel Williams fought with the Eighth Battalion of the Fourth Division. Private First Class Evans flew helicopter missions in the highlands battles, and Sergeant Claude M. Brown fought at Dak To with Third Battalion, Eighth Regiment, Fourth Division. Brown was wounded; he earned the Purple Heart, the Bronze Star, and Army Commendation Medal for Heroism.

OTHER COASTAL CAMPAIGNS

The marines had their hands full in the north. They were needed there against increasing enemy pressure. Consequently, MACV decided that army units should take over some of the marines' responsibility on the coast from below Chu Lai and upper Quang Ngai province up to Da Nang. A force, called Task Force Oregon, was patched together from several units.[204] It would initially include the First Brigade of the 101st Airborne Division, joined in April by the 196th Light Infantry Brigade, and the Third Brigade of the 25th Division.

The Second VC Division had roamed about freely in parts of Quang Ngai province. The Third Brigade of the 25th Division went after it, and after relentless pressure from mechanized troops, helicopters in surprise movements, naval gunfire, and B-52 raids, the VC withdrew in large part to their jungle lairs. Some VC-fortified villages continued to resist, such as An Thach, where a maze of trench lines wound through bamboo thickets and cactus hedgerows. Tanks and infantry moved in, supported by helicopter gunships. Other units flew in to surround the village. The VC tried to make a break for it, but they were cut into small groups and annihilated.[205] Only three surrendered. Meanwhile the 101st went out into the rain forests, some on weeklong patrols. Opposition was light, and the searches were relatively fruitless.

Task Force Oregon was reconstituted. The 101st was sent back to its base, and the 25th Division Brigade was switched to the Fourth Division for its highlands campaign. The 198th Light Infantry Brigade and the 11th Infantry Brigade joined the 196th Light Infantry, and Task Force Oregon became the Americal Division, in deference to the Americal Division of World War II.[206]

Late in the year, the Fourth Brigade of the Americal moved out against a coastal village island. Thick hedgerows and boulders covered a hill rising from rice paddies, and the entrenched Second NVA Regiment defended it. Machine-gun fire tore into the infantrymen, and tanks and armored personnel carriers moved forward. The fighting soon was a melee as more troops were thrown into the battle. Some tanks became mired. When the foot soldiers found a bunker, they fired tracer rounds into it, showing the tanks where it was. The tanks fired delayed-action shells into the bunkers to blow out the sides and kill the enemy. Recalcitrant foes in reinforced bunkers were blown out with satchel charges stuck into the bunker with long bamboo poles. The Americans also took fire from the surrounding rice paddies, which were bombed and strafed. Eventually, the NVA was pushed out of the area or destroyed.

In 1967, the enemy moved back into Binh Dinh province and the lower Quang Ngai province. The First Cavalry moved back in to roust them out. The Second Battalion of the Eighth Cavalry air assaulted into the Song Re Valley in Quang Ngai, and immediately ran into a ridgeline of camouflaged NVA fortifications. Machine-gun, mortar, and recoilless rifle fire knocked several helicopters out of the air. Close combat raged for four hours before they could pull back for fighter-bombers to come in for support. After 46 air sorties, the NVA withdrew.

The First Cavalry went back into the An Lao and Bong Son valleys, where numerous firefights erupted; one sizeable battle developed at Tam Quan village close to the coast. The hamlet was on a large paddy island, covered by bamboo thickets and hedges of cacti. An aerial platoon had reached the outskirts of the village, where it was pinned down by fire from trench lines and spider holes covered with logs and dirt. Another platoon was flown from another direction, but it, too, was pinned down by fire from trenches along the edges of the island. Reinforcements came in and perimeters were set up for the night.

The rest of the First Cavalry Battalion and an ARVN battalion surrounded the island. The next morning, helicopter gunships doused the island with tear gas, and sprayed the thickets with 40-mm fire. Artillery fire also pounded the enemy's positions, but when the cavalrymen and personnel carriers charged across the marshy rice paddies, they were met with heavy fire and repulsed. More artillery fire pounded the island entrenchments and with two additional flame-throwing armored personnel carriers, the cavalrymen went forward again. With a burst of flame, the Vietcong antitank gun was knocked out. This time, the assault was a success and armored vehicles crushed the bunkers and trenches. Combat engineers built a causeway to the island and buried the trenches.

The adjacent village at Dai Do was assaulted the next day, and fighting was fierce. The battle raged for several days, and the 12th Battalion of the Fifth Cavalry had to be flown in from Dak To before the village was finally overrun.

The battle of Tam Quan was costly to both sides. Hundreds of enemy bodies littered the battlefield; only a few of the enemy surrendered. The enemy soldiers were tough, indoctrinated fighters who would fight to the end, and it took a dogged, bloody offensive action to defeat them.[207]

The year ended with the Americans winning most of the big battles. Highway 1 wasn't completely open, but a lot of it was, and the Vietcong would no longer brazenly walk around in the open. Some of the major enemy strongholds had been overrun, and the enemy ferreted out. Sometimes the price was high, but it was paid. Prospects looked favorable for 1968.

Others from Nelson County who served in Vietnam in 1967 include:

Army

Specialist Joseph Frank Auberry: 577th Engineers

Private James Crume: Headquarters Battery, 517th Artillery

Phillip Metcalf: 47th Transportation Detachment

Sergeant First Class Frank Stephens: Army Commendation, Long Binh

Private First Class Phillip Trent: 577th Engineers

Private First Class Joseph C. Vittitow

John Hutchins served six months at Tan Son Nhut and six months at Long Binh with the 18th Engineer Battalion in the Headquarters Company. The 18th was over all engineer units in Vietnam.

Marines

Private First Class Joseph M. Brown: 11th Engineer Battalion, Dong Ha

Lance Corporal Ronnie Coulter

Private First Class Ronald Greer: Second Battalion, Seventh Regiment, First Division

Sergeant James B. Linton: Reconnaissance Company

Pharmacy Mate James M. Morton: HMS (corpsman), Da Nang

CHAPTER 12

1968: TURNING POINT

The year 1968 was probably the most momentous of the war as far
as America's attitude was concerned. Militarily, the US achieved its greatest
victories. Politically and psychologically, it was the worst year. Before that,
most Americans thought the United States could and was winning the war.
After 1968, there were many doubts and much dissension.

At the beginning of 1968, the American military command could
look back on a string of positive results. It had boosted army and marine
presence to more than 400,000 men.[208] It had destroyed the Iron Triangle
north of Saigon as a VC military base, had pushed most of the enemy out of
War Zone C up against the Cambodian border, and was sweeping it out in
Operation Yellowstone.

In the delta, the Ninth Division had made itself felt, and had
decimated two VC main force battalions. Together with the navy's Riverine
Force, they had cleared out large portions of the northern delta close to
Saigon. The First Cavalry Division had swept through the Vietcong-held
Binh Dinh province. The VC represented the biggest percent of the populace
there, and for the time being, their local power was crushed. The marines in
the north had several tough battles that were costly to both sides, but they
prevailed, and two North Vietnamese divisions that had been prowling there
had been pushed back across the DMZ. However, their presence loomed like
a threatening shadow.

The Fourth Division, in a continuous grueling battle, had forced the enemy out of the hot, humid jungle highlands up against Laos and Cambodia. In the bloody battles at Dak To, the 173rd Airborne Brigade had pushed the rest of the enemy in the Central Highlands back across the border. The marines and the reborn American Division cleared out much of the long coastal plain.

General Westmoreland had reason to feel good about the upcoming year, but he was concerned about the enemy's intentions in the north. The enemy was gathering around the northwest outpost of Khe Sanh. Westmoreland focused on Khe Sanh and the north. Fully half of his mobile army was in I Corps in the north.[209] Even though the American troops won the hill battles around the outpost, and controlled those dominating heights, there was evidence of two NVA divisions moving in the area. There was a danger that they could encircle Khe Sanh and put it under siege.[210]

The marines had recently inserted the fresh 26th Regiment of the Third Marine Division into the area as a garrison, but they would be in danger of facing artillery pounding and a massive number of enemy troops. To counter possible enemy intentions in that area, MACV moved the First Cavalry Division, "the first team," north to use as a fire brigade. MACV also relieved the First Marine Division of responsibilities in the Chu Lai area with the American Division, to allow the marines to face northward. A brigade of that division went to central Vietnam to take the place of the First Cavalry.

At the higher levels of the American command and the South Vietnamese army, there was a general feeling that the Vietcong in the south had been made ineffective as far as major operations were concerned, and that the real threat was with the NVA in the north.

At home, Americans increasingly had negative views about the Vietnam War. A 2,000-person anti-war rally, staged in Washington DC, became violent as protesters charged the Pentagon and had to be turned away at one of the entrances. Anti-war rallies happened in other cities and on college campuses. During some of them, the National Guard was called in to quiet things down and restore order. Occasionally, the army and marines were also called in.[211]

The situation in Korea heated up as the North Koreans became more combative. American patrols were ambushed outside their bases on the DMZ, and North Korean killer groups shot up American outposts. In January 1968, the spy ship *Pueblo* was captured in international waters with all of its crew. There was plenty to worry the four services without new trouble.

US forces were stretched to the limit, not only at home, but in Korea and Europe, and there was always the Russian menace.

Reserve and National Guard units were called up. The National Guard unit in Nelson County, Battery C of the 138th Artillery, was called up later in the year (*Kentucky Standard,* April 21, 1968).

The Tet Festival, the Vietnamese holiday celebrating the new year, was coming up in the last of January. There was tacit agreement between the two sides that war would take a holiday during the Tet Festival. Half of the South Vietnamese garrisons in all of the big cities were given a furlough, and the other half relaxed. The ARVN garrisoned most of the cities, and American forces kept peace in the fields outside of them. American MP units were in the cities to guard US military and non-military installations, and to keep GIs policed and out of trouble.

As the eve of Tet unfolded, units of Vietcong were quietly slipping into Saigon and most of the other major cities and capitals amid the celebrations.[212] Music, firecrackers, and all sorts of revelry were going on, and camouflaged their movements. Arms had been stashed in advantageous positions around the cities, and were distributed to the phantom armies moving in unnoticed and unsuspected. Some weapons were even stored in the basement of a Buddhist pagoda.[213]

The attack was well planned and squads were assigned certain objectives. One squad in cabs approached the US Embassy, and almost made it in. A marine guard suspected the movement and tried to stop it. He closed the gate and sounded the alarm, for which he paid with his life. The small contingent of marines held off the VC after they had blown an entrance in the wall until support arrived. None of the major embassy personnel were harmed. Ambassador Ellsworth Bunker was driven from his residence in an armored personnel carrier to the house of embassy security.[214]

Another squad seized the radio station to announce that the Vietcong had taken over the city. Unfortunately for them, they didn't have the technology to run the station, and they botched their opportunity and intentions. By the next morning, the South Vietnamese garrison had assaulted the radio station, and the station was back in friendly hands.

The "extravagances of the US military machine"[215] brought peasants seeking more money into the cities, altering the balance between rural and urban populations. Many refugees from farms could not be distinguished from the Vietcong, and this added to the success of the Tet Offensive.

Another large force attacked Tan Son Nhut Air Base and the associated MACV headquarters.[216] They broke through the hastily improvised cordon of defensive troops. More than 250 rockets hit the airfield and associated area. A number of planes and other structures, such as hangars, offices, supply buildings, and fuel storage depots, were destroyed or damaged. Air Force personnel, including Nelson County Sergeants Bobby Ballard and Gaylord Mattingly, who were stationed there at the time of the attack, went into sandbagged bunkers during the intense rocket fire. The Tan Son Nhut Air Base was so big that the part where Ballard and Mattingly were located did not come under direct fire and ground attack.

The Vietcong were driven off, but it was touch and go. MPs and other units kept the Vietcong from completely overrunning the base until a relief column of 25th Division armored vehicles broke through roadblocks and joined them, and pushed the enemy off the field. Ballard recalled that the VC tried to charge over a barrier in their part of the complex. Flares lit up the base, and artillery and helicopter gunships pounded it. The next morning, the men found hundreds of bodies there, so thick they had to be removed by bulldozers. When Mattingly returned to his barracks, which were close to MACV headquarters, he saw a big unexploded rocket half-buried in the ground.

The fighting in Saigon continued without letup, and lasted a week before most of the pockets of resistance were eradicated. South Vietnamese troops and American units (including mostly MPs early in the offensive), fought bravely. In many areas, the Vietcong dug in as if they meant to stay, particularly at the racetrack and Cho Lon, the Chinese sector.[217] The besieged VC fought viciously, and attacks by both Americans and ARVN troops to roust them were very costly.

A battalion of the 199th Infantry (of which Eddie D. Vittitow was a member) was called in to clear the racetrack and surrounding area, which seemed to be the center of enemy activity. A block-by-block battle was fought to get to the track. It was a fierce house-to-house battle, with recoilless rifles to blow holes in walls and supporting fire from armored personnel carriers. After six blocks were cleared to get there, they engaged the VC who had set up defenses behind concrete barriers within the track. After the track was bombed and strafed, the infantrymen directly assaulted it. They were driven off by intense fire. Later they attacked again after more shelling, and most of the surviving enemy withdrew. The next day the VC attacked the track again, but were driven off. Fighting went on around the track for seven days.

In Cho Lon, the South Vietnamese wanted to drive the enemy out by themselves. After a day, however, they called for American assistance, and units of the 199th went in and helped clear Cho Lon out. More fighting went on there for a week, but by that time, the VC were destroyed as a fighting force.

Sporadic fighting went on for 10 days. After much fighting and destruction, Saigon was in American and ARVN hands.

In addition to attacking Saigon, the VC attacked all up and down the country. The VC hit Long Binh, an important American base 17 miles from Saigon, with a vengeance. The 275th Vietcong Regiment attacked the northern perimeter, following a rocket and mortar barrage. The rest of the 199th counterattacked, assisted by helicopter gunships leading the way. Staff Sergeant William Stratton was in the area of the fighting.

A company of the 39th Infantry of the Ninth Division made a helicopter assault to protect the II Field Force headquarters, and cleared out that area after a day's fighting.[218]

The 274th VC Regiment rocketed Bien Hoa, another major airfield, and then attacked. They breached the east bunker line, but could not get further. After dawn, a battalion of the 503rd Airborne Regiment arrived to clear out the area.[219] A unit of armored personnel carriers arrived to link up with the 503rd.

Specialist Robert Earl Baldwin of the airborne infantry was killed on February 6. He was born in Bardstown, but raised elsewhere.[220]

Of the 12 critical central provinces, 10 were hit with major attacks, including several of the provincial capitals. One was the Pleiku area. This was in the province of the Fourth Division.

Three men with Nelson County connections were involved in these attacks. Sergeant Claude Brown, who had been wounded and decorated at Dak To, was wounded again with multiple shrapnel wounds. Sergeants Cale White and Robert Francis Ballard, with the Fourth Infantry Division, were at Pleiku (*Kentucky Standard*, October 31, 1968).

Da Lat and military towns, An Khe and Ninh Hoa, were also hit. Most were cleared within a week of heavy fighting, a lot of it by the ARVN. In the delta, 13 of 16 province headquarters were hit within the first three days of the offensive. The main highway of the delta, Highway 4, was interdicted in 60 places, and wasn't completely reopened for three months. ARVN and the Riverine Brigade of the Ninth Division had cleared most of the cities within a few days. The VC counterattacked, but after a vicious battle, were almost annihilated.[221]

In all, 36 of 44 provincial capitals, five of six autonomous cities, and 64 of 242 district capitals were hit.[222] In the north, Da Nang and the Marine

Air Base at Marble Mountain were hit. At Da Nang, a mixture of ARVN and military police troops initially held back the onslaught until two marine battalions hit the attackers from behind.

Marine Edwin Taylor (brother of Sergeant George Taylor and Corporal William Russell Taylor) was on his second tour in Vietnam. Taylor was sitting on a bunker outside Da Nang, having a drink of Jim Beam bourbon to celebrate the Tet, when rockets started coming in. The marines were used to having a few rockets hit them, but that night it was different—a barrage of rockets hit. Taylor knew something big was happening.

The cities of Quang Ngai, Tam Ky, and Quang Tri were well defended in the north, and Chu Lai was cleared after a daylong battle. In Hoi An, in Quang Nam province, seesaw battles lasted five days.

The main battle of the Tet Offensive in the north was at Hue, the old political and religious capital of Vietnam. Like Saigon, it was infiltrated in advance under the cover of darkness by large units with big caches of weapons and ammunition. By the time the battle officially started, large chunks of Hue, including the Imperial Palace, the old Imperial City, and the citadel, were in Vietcong and NVA hands.[223]

Much of the city south of the Perfume River was also taken, including the MACV compound, the university, and public utilities. The enemy was there to fight it out, and raised the Vietcong flag on the large flagpole at the compound's Midday gate. There they awaited further reinforcements. They intended to make a statement at Hue for the world to notice. In Hue, the Vietcong and the North Vietnamese intentionally killed 3,000 civilians in the first 48 hours, many without apparent reason.[224]

Initially, the ARVN airborne battalions and an armored squadron of two marine companies counterattacked. Despite heavy losses, they regained the MACV headquarters and the Truong Tien Bridge over the Perfume River by mid-afternoon the next day.[225] They returned to southern Hue at night. Another marine company from Phu Bai joined them in the next 24 hours, raising their numbers to a full battalion. In another 24 hours, the force doubled, and set about slowly clearing the southern part of Hue, house to house. It was a costly process in terms of lives lost.

In order to preserve the city's historic buildings, artillery wasn't used at first. Several battalions of ARVN troops attacked, but their progress was slow and ultimately they had to use artillery. Six- and eight-inch shells from naval ships slammed into heavily fortified areas. The marines also brought in their eight-inch artillery.

The Third Brigade of the First Cavalry Division flew in to block further enemy reinforcements from entering the city from the west. They ran into opposition five miles west of the city, and pushed forward anyway. Despite their best efforts, enemy reinforcements did get into the city. Private First Class David Royalty of Nelson County was a member of the Third Brigade (*Kentucky Standard*, October 31, 1968).

After nine days, the marines cleared the city south of the Perfume River, and the ARVN pushed into part of the citadel and the Imperial City. Every inch was contested. The First Battalion of the Fifth Marines was thrown into the battle on February 12—13 days after the onset of the Tet Offensive. After nine days, they had fought their way into the opposite side of the citadel from the ARVN. Only two lieutenants were left in 10 rifle platoons. They finished their part of capturing the citadel on February 22, and the ARVN theirs on February 24, when the elite Black Panther Company finally took the Imperial Palace, and raised the South Vietnamese flag.[226] Finally, the VC and NVA were pushed out, but the most historic and beautiful city in Vietnam was in ruins.[227]

Marine Corporal Roscoe Norris was present in the Da Nang area at the time of the Tet. He enlisted in June 1967, and went to Parris Island for basic training, Camp Lejeune for infantry training, and Camp Pendleton for jungle warfare training. Following that, he was sent to Vietnam via Okinawa. He landed at Da Nang on November 8, and was assigned to Charlie Company, First Battalion, Seventh Regiment of the First Marine Division. He went to Hill 55, which was the command post for the marines, and then on to Hill 10.

From there, Norris went out on patrols every day, and at night, the patrol set up ambushes. He was intermittently in a seven-man squad and a four-man fire team. At first, when they went out they faced only Vietcong, but gradually the VC were replaced by North Vietnamese hard-core regulars. The NVA posed more of a threat. However, the NVA were not familiar with the placement of VC booby traps, so these were removed, ultimately benefitting American troops. Norris recalled that the booby traps and grenades all seemed to be made out of Carling Black Label beer cans.

With the onset of the Tet, there was much more activity around their hill. Every day, mostly at night, for seven to 10 days, there was a lot of contact where either they ambushed the enemy or the enemy ambushed them. If the Americans spotted many of the enemy, they called in artillery. Two-man teams alternated two hours on and two off. One night while Norris was on watch, the marine with him, who was new, shook him awake, and asked if a man 15 feet away was the enemy. He was. Norris leaned against a dam in a rice paddy and shot him before he could react. Almost every night during the Tet, they saw groups of NVA crossing the paddies.

On one of his patrols, Norris found a six-foot rocket that he and another man retrieved. He also found a number of ditches dug in a T shape for firing the rockets. The rockets were simple. They could be ignited by a flashlight battery and had a primitive aiming device.

Norris served as leader for his fire team, and on occasion, had men who would not take orders. He reported them to his sergeant and the next day they were gone. He also had a man, who after a number of patrols and ambushes, asked Norris to shoot him in the leg so he could get out of action. Overall, though, Norris recalled that the men bonded quickly during combat. He said, "Combat was funny. Things happened so quickly, you didn't have time to think about death. You just did what you had to, and what you were trained to do. After it was over, then you worried." He said during an interview that you couldn't brood on it.

On February 13, his company went out on Operation Pursuit. The first day he was in the lead squad as they cut their way through thick bush and jungle up to the top of a big hill in a daylong trek. When they got to the top, they found an area with foxholes and slit trenches where the enemy had obviously bivouacked, probably in preparation for the Tet Offensive. After spending the night, they went down a trail on the other side of the hill. It was broader and made Norris worry. It looked too well used. Another squad was in the lead. Shortly afterward, the other squad was ambushed, and the whole squad killed or wounded. Norris's squad went to their rescue, pulled them back, and formed a perimeter with the rest of the company.

Medevacs came to take out the dead and wounded. While one of the helicopters was hovering over the perimeter area, the enemy fired a knee rocket at it, but missed. When it went off, it wounded five men on the ground, including Norris. He had a bad wound in his arm just below the elbow, and several minor ones. Another man was blinded. The rocket went off above them and if Norris hadn't been wearing his helmet, he might have been blinded, too.

They were medevaced out to Da Nang, where shrapnel was removed from Norris's arm, and the wound left open. He apparently had nerve damage since his hand felt numb and he couldn't move it. He was sent to Japan for more surgery, and back to the states for further therapy. Finally, after months, the feeling and motor ability came back to his hand. He concluded his service at Parris Island, Charleston, and Lejeune, and was discharged October 13, 1969.

Sergeant Joe Blanford, another soldier from Kentucky, arrived just in time to be involved in the Tet Offensive.

Blanford, now an accountant, was born and raised in Marion County, but has had his practice in Bardstown for 30 years. In his private office, he has a large picture of the Vietnam Wall. He is one of those who left Vietnam after his year tour, but Vietnam never left him. Many of the men in the platoon that Blanford was close to were lost in and around a small fortified outpost called Kham Duc in the northwest part of South Vietnam, close to the Laotian border.

Blanford first went to Vietnam on January 1, 1968, just before the Tet Offensive. He was assigned to the 196th Light Infantry Brigade of the Americal Division, close to Chu Lai. He was the radioman accompanying his platoon lieutenant. They normally did sweeps and reconnaissance missions, and set up ambushes for prowling Vietcong, who ordinarily traveled in groups of 15 to 30.

One night, a large group of Vietcong moved right in front of his unit, which was hunkered down in high bush. The Vietcong passed close by in an adjacent rice paddy. He didn't realize it then, but the VC were probably part of the Tet Offensive. His squad lay still as he radioed in artillery on the enemy. It was so close that it was almost like calling in artillery on their own position. With creeping rounds, the artillery was very effective, and shattered the attack. In the dark night, he could hear moans and movement as if the enemy soldiers were pulling out their dead and wounded. He could also hear gongs in the distance, which he presumed were rallying points for the enemy. It was a stark introduction to the Vietnam War.

The first casualties in Blanford's company, however, were two soldiers who were killed and several who were wounded when their amtrac detonated a roadside aviation bomb.

When Blanford was not on reconnaissance, a good bit of his time in Vietnam was spent clearing Highway 1, the main north-south road running the length of the narrow country. His unit guarded engineers with minesweepers who cleared the road of mines and bombs. Sometimes, innocent civilians were blown sky high when their carts or motorcycles detonated a bomb. Despite precautions, even army and marine vehicles suffered the same fate.

Blanford's unit went north of Da Nang during the Tet, but came back to a place called LZ Ross in Happy Valley, west and south of Da Nang. Blanford spent eight months of his tour around LZ Ross, which was a landing zone with an airstrip. It was used primarily as a supply base, and had an area of about five acres. He worked out of LZ Baldy, as well. His unit's job was to conduct sweeps to prevent surprise attacks. The unit was also used around the bottom of hills to protect outposts on the tops of the hills. None of his platoon were ever killed by booby traps, but they had to be constantly aware of punji stakes. For protection against them, the men had metal plates in their shoes.

Most of his time was boring, just waiting or on sweeps, but when action happened, it happened fast and was bad. The Vietcong would surprise them, have a sharp firefight, and then pull back. When the platoon was on guard at the base of a hill, they were probed five or six times, but never suffered any large-scale attack. After dark, they fired at anything that moved.

Blanford said he saw many brave guys in his tour. In particular, he remembered the helicopter pilots who would fly into a hot area, and stay there as an obvious target while the wounded men were loaded aboard, and then try to make it out.

In May of 1968, he got his week of R&R. He flew to Hawaii to be with his wife who was expecting. While he was gone, his platoon and its lieutenant, Fred Ransbottom, was overrun and wiped out at Kham Duc. Blanford had been close to the lieutenant and highly respected him.

Kham Duc was one of the first Special Forces bases founded in 1963. It was the last to close in the area. When intelligence came through that a large force of North Vietnamese, probably division size, was moving in on Kham Duc, General Westmoreland sent in a battalion of the 196th Light Infantry Brigade to man outposts around it. One of the platoons sent in was Blanford's.

However, Blanford was in Hawaii with his wife, and had no idea what was going on. Specialist Allen "Doc" Ho, a medic in Blanford's unit, was also in Hawaii on R&R. They were the only survivors of his outfit.

Seventeen of Blanford's fellow soldiers were killed trying to protect Kham Duc. The NVA came in overwhelming numbers (12,000 against a total of about 600 at the camp). The last word was from Ransbottom, saying that he was firing at North Vietnamese entering his bunker. Kham Duc was evacuated with considerable casualties.

In an interview, Blanford said of Lieutenant Ransbottom, "He was a hell of a good guy. I had been right there with him all of the time. He was a good man, a good leader, and he was courageous."

When Blanford came back from R&R, the rest of his stay in Vietnam was anticlimactic, much of it at landing zones Ross and Baldy. He saw no more serious action.

Blanford came home on Christmas Eve, 1968. When Lieutenant Ransbottom's remains were found in 2006, Blanford and Sergeant Ho communicated. They had had a defining moment in their lives.

Official ARVN history of the Tet showed 14,300 civilians were killed; 24,000 wounded; 7,200 homes destroyed; and 206,000 people left homeless.[228]

The overall effect of the Tet Offensive was to help turn the American public against the war. It was a psychological disaster for President Lyndon Johnson and his administration. It took the air out of the boasts that America was winning, and deflated General Westmoreland. The Tet Offensive exposed Westmoreland's war of attrition as fiction. The war was not going to be won.[229] The public had wondered before about all of Westmoreland's figures, body counts, and projections, but after Tet, they became highly skeptical, and felt they were being lied to.

The Tet Offensive was a actually military disaster for the enemy. The Vietcong was gutted. They lost more than 80,000 men, and weren't capable of any major offensive for a year. The majority of Vietcong company and battalion officers died in the Tet and Mini-Tet (also known as the May Offensive).[230]

American losses had been high, more than 10,000. American politicians and generals became timid, and very conscious of saving American lives rather than winning battles. Major offensive action was somewhat curtailed, and most of the American army was used to protect the big population centers. Tet was a decisive turning point in the war.

Another development would soon capture the attention of America and the world. Two North Vietnamese divisions encircled the marine outpost at Khe Sanh in the northwestern part of South Vietnam and placed it under siege. They blocked Highway 9, the east-west highway that was the overland supply route to Khe Sanh. They were deeply entrenched in the high hills on either side of the highway. They brought in big howitzers to bombard the outpost.

The 26th Marines garrisoned Khe Sanh. (The regiment had a proud World War II history. They had taken Mount Suribachi on Iwo Jima.) The First Battalion of the Ninth Marines and the 37th ARVN Ranger Battalion joined the 26th. The five battalions were stretched thin. They had to cover the hills overlooking Khe Sanh, which had been so dearly won a few months before. They had five tanks, three Ontos platoons, their artillery and mortars, and an airstrip for supply.[231]

E4 Donald Holbert of New Haven, Kentucky, served with the 26th, and kept a journal throughout his time in Vietnam. Holbert was drafted in

1967. He was inducted with 60 others. Of that number, seven—including Holbert—were picked to be marines. He went to Parris Island for boot training, Camp Lejeune for infantry training, and Camp Pendleton for five weeks of jungle training. After a leave, he was sent to Okinawa. From there he flew to Da Nang, and then by helicopter to Khe Sanh. He wrote in his journal:

ON THE MORNING OF DECEMBER 23, WE FOUND OUR COMPANY WAS GOING TO KHE SANH. SO CHRISTMAS EVE, I SPENT MY FIRST NIGHT IN KHE SANH. EVERYTHING WAS COOL. NOTHING WAS GOING ON YET. KHE SANH WAS ONLY SIX KLICKS [KILOMETERS] OR FOUR MILES FROM THE LAOTIAN BORDER, AND EIGHT KLICKS [FIVE AND A HALF MILES] FROM THE DMZ OF NORTH VIETNAM. WE WERE A LARGE AMMO AND FOOD SUPPLY BASE FOR EVERYONE IN THE NORTHWEST. THERE WERE RIGHT AT 5,000 MARINES GUARDING KHE SANH, AND ABOUT 2,000 OF THESE WERE AS GREEN AS THEY COME. WELL, FOR TWO WEEKS IT WENT FINE. HOWEVER, ON JANUARY 17, ALL CHANGED AND THE SIEGE OF KHE SANH BEGAN. IT STARTED WITH INCOMING ROCKETS, MOSTLY 105- AND 155-MM. IT WAS SOMEWHERE AROUND MIDNIGHT. WE WERE ALL IN OUR TENTS, AND HAD NO IDEA WHAT WAS GOING ON. I KNOW THAT FIRST NIGHT THERE WAS MASS CONFUSION EVERYWHERE. WE DID HAVE A PERIMETER SET UP. IT JUST WASN'T HEAVILY MANNED. DAYLIGHT WAS A WELCOMED SIGHT THAT MORNING. MOSTLY WE WERE GLAD TO BE ALIVE. IT SEEMED THAT THE WORLD WAS COMING TO AN END. ALL DAY LONG, WE KEPT GETTING INCOMING ROUNDS, JUST ROUND AFTER ROUND. YOU COULD HEAR THEM LEAVE THEIR GUNS, SO YOU HAD ABOUT THREE SECONDS TO GET DOWN. ANYWHERE WAS OK, JUST A DITCH WAS BETTER THAN NOWHERE, BUT NOWHERE WAS SAFE AGAINST A DIRECT HIT. KHE

SANH WAS ABOUT 20 ACRES, A LITTLE MORE OBLONG THAN ROUND. THAT FIRST 24 HOURS, IT TOOK ABOUT 1,700 ROUNDS. I WASN'T AWARE OF HOW MANY LIVES WERE LOST. I REMEMBER HELPING A LOT OF INJURED MARINES, AND SEEING A LOT OF DEAD MEN, BUT NOT AS MANY AS YOU WOULD THINK, CONSIDERING EVERYTHING.[232]

THE WORD ON THE LINE WAS THAT THE NORTH VIETNAMESE WOULD CONTINUE TO BOMB FOR TWO DAYS, AND THEN THEY WOULD TRY TO OVERRUN US BY SENDING IN THREE WAVES AT US, EACH WAVE GETTING CLOSER TO OUR LINES, AND FINALLY INSIDE IT. THEN IT WOULD BE ALL OVER FOR US AT THAT STAGE. OUR PLANES HAD ORDERS TO LEVEL KHE SANH.

DAY TWO CAME. EVERYONE WAS A LOT MORE DUG IN, AND A LOT MORE READY FOR A FIGHT. WE FELT WE HAD A CHANCE ANYWAY, EVEN THOUGH THEY ESTIMATED ABOUT 45,000 NORTH VIETNAMESE TO 5,000 MARINES. BUT WE HAD THE AIR FORCE THAT HAD PLANES IN THE AIR AROUND US 24 HOURS A DAY. NAPALM WAS THE BIG THING THEN. EVERYTHING WAS OVERWHELMING HERE. I'VE BEEN IN COUNTRY FOR THREE WEEKS, AND I WAS IN THE BIGGEST BATTLE OF THE WAR.

The fourth day came and nothing major happened. Holbert felt that the tide had perhaps shifted, that the marines were more able to repel an attack. They kept digging deeper.

In two weeks, they had dug a ditch or trench three feet wide and seven feet deep completely around the base, with a gun pit every 20 feet for a 30-caliber machine gun. Each pit had three or four men in it. They kept digging until they had a space of 12 by 12 by 8 feet deep. Then they covered it with runway matting from the airstrip, and put sandbags about two feet deep on top of that. It was like World War I trench warfare, with bunkers connected by a deep trench. Holbert said:

THE DOOR OUT OF OUR HOME OPENED RIGHT INTO THE DITCH, SO YOU NEVER HAD TO GO ABOVE GROUND. THAT WAS GOOD BECAUSE WE WERE STILL TAKING 800 TO 1,200 ROUNDS A DAY. OUR NEW HOMES WERE BUILT REAL GOOD, BUT WOULDN'T WITHSTAND A DIRECT HIT FROM A 105-MM OR 155-MM. BUT THEY WOULD A 60- TO 90-MM MORTAR ROUND."

THE ONE THING WE FEARED THE MOST WAS A DIRECT HIT. THE SHELL ITSELF WOULDN'T PENETRATE THE TOP AND GET YOU, BUT IT WAS THE CONCUSSION THAT GOT YOU. I KNEW THIS FIRSTHAND, FOR THE BUNKER NEXT DOOR TOOK A DIRECT HIT AND EVERYONE DIED THAT WAS INSIDE. I KNEW ALL OF THEM A LITTLE BIT. BUT YOU DIDN'T WANT TO GET TOO CLOSE TO ANYONE, BECAUSE IT MADE IT EASIER WHEN THEY LEFT. THE NIGHTS WERE THE HARDEST TIME. EVERY NIGHT, YOU HAD TO STAND GUARD FOR TWO HOURS AT A TIME. THERE WERE FOUR OF US, SO IT WORKED OUT, STARTING AT 10 P.M. TO 12, 12 TO 2 A.M., 2 TO 4 A.M., AND ON TO DAYLIGHT. IT NEVER MATTERED WHAT TIME MY SHIFT WAS, IT SEEMED LIKE IT WAS NEVER A GOOD TIME TO SLEEP.

AFTER THE FIRST MONTH, NO ONE KNEW WHAT CHARLIE [THE ENEMY] WAS GOING TO DO. BY NOW, OUR PERIMETER WAS WELL FORTIFIED. ROLLS AND ROLLS OF CONCERTINA WIRE, AND ROLL AFTER ROLL OF TANGLE FOOT (THAT WAS BARB WIRE PUT ON METAL STAKES ONE FOOT OFF THE GROUND IN ONE FOOT BLOCKS—20 FEET OF IT IN FRONT), PLUS ALL OF THE CONCERTINA WIRE.

Holbert catnapped a lot, and averaged about four hours sleep out of 24. He recalled his sister company, Charlie Company, whose job it was to secure Hill 861. They would send out marines every day, and bring back their dead and wounded. The hill was an estimated 1,000 yards away, and the enemy could send in mortar rounds from it every night onto Khe Sanh. It often cost the lives of three or four marines daily and a dozen more wounded to keep it secure. The backside of the hill was only about 2,000 meters from the Ho Chi Minh Trail.

Holbert was free to roam around outside if he desired. He remembered one time he went out to the runway and saw 26 body bags.

"I was asked to help load them on a C-130," he said. "We got done loading the dead marines, and as I was going back to my hooch, about halfway back, I heard about 12 rounds leave Charlie's tubes. Well, it so happened I was right in the middle of a bunch of 155-mm rounds; I just laid down and prayed that nothing got close. I waited for them to hit, and I moved out. I got almost to the ditch, when I heard some more coming. Before I could lay down, one hit only 10 feet away. It blew me down, and my helmet went flying off of my head. Luckily, I didn't get no scrap metal from it, but did get some little rocks in my arms. But the biggest thing was the ringing in my ears, which lasted for weeks. The ringing eventually stopped, but it caused lasting damage. So, after that little adventure, I stayed close to my hooch, just to go out to the head when needed, and back to the hooch. Very few men were killed by rifle fire. Most were killed by mortar fire when out in the open, or shell fire."

The air over Khe Sanh was crowded despite the cloudy monsoon season. In addition to transports dropping supplies, there were Skyraiders, jet aircraft, and spooky aircraft. There were frequent thunderous bombings by B-52s, unloading monstrous deadly loads on the NVA trenches. Bodies of NVA soldiers flew through the air during B-52 attacks.

Captain John Finn Hurst was in one of the B-52s.[233] Hurst was born in Bardstown and spent his early years there. In Vietnam, he flew 115 missions out of Okinawa, and earned the Air Medal with four oak leaf clusters. (He was later promoted to lieutenant colonel.)

Donald Holbert felt the air protection was very good. The jets, usually F4 Phantoms, dropped bombs and napalm off and on all day and night. He could hear the B-52s, but could very seldom see them. They would often drop firecracker rounds or anti-personnel bombs. They would go off before they hit the ground, and each round had thousands of little metal darts, which dispersed over a large area. They would be dropped where any large group of enemy troops were spotted by observation planes, from the DMZ on down. The B-52s were in the air day or night. Practically all of the countryside around Khe Sanh was denuded of vegetation and the ground pulverized, due to the bombing.

Despite the frequent shelling, the air runway was kept open. Men were constantly being shuttled in, as men left when their enlistment time ran out, and the wounded and dead were taken out. Helicopters stayed on the ground for as short a time as possible.

Holbert was taken out for a three-day, in-country R&R in Da Nang after two months.

C-123s and C-130s would often drop supplies without landing. They came in 20 feet off the ground and dropped supplies on skids out of compartments in their bellies. They would skid, but most often stopped within the compound perimeter.

The marines had to go out beyond the wire on outpost duty, usually 150 yards outside the perimeter, and about 50 yards beyond the wire to pick up enemy movements at night. They had to pick their way carefully through the wire, and had a radio to call in suspicious movement. The radio could also be used to call them back if they were in imminent danger. Frequently, flares helped their visibility. It was scary and seemed a lot farther out than 150 yards. To a great extent, their situation was like World War I trench warfare.

The shelling flattened almost everything above ground. Ammunition dumps were spread around and, one time, one of them exploded with a loud roar. North Vietnamese troops made frequent small probes against the perimeter, but were easily driven off. One large attack hit the perimeter about a quarter ways around from Holbert's sector. The fighting was fierce, but the attack was driven off with severe losses. A few of the enemy got within the perimeter, but were killed or driven off.

Toward the end of the siege, things quieted down, and the bombardments lessened. The nightly anxiety that the men had felt for the first few weeks about imminent attacks was gone. Life became complacent except for outpost duty and hill duty as the men got used to living underground. Patrols later went out through the wire, to see what the enemy was up to, but met little opposition.

The psychological impact on the men varied. Holbert was so busy the first half of the siege and concerned about staying alive, that he didn't have time to get depressed. Toward the end of the siege, he did get a little down. After the first day of his three-day R&R in Da Nang, he didn't feel right.

Things just didn't feel comfortable to him until he got back to his company. The siege bonded the men closely.

In March, the monsoons ended, and with good weather and diminishing NVA pressure, the outlook of the defenders of Khe Sanh improved. They began sweeping the perimeter. As the pressure on the outpost lessened and the enemy was subdued, the upper echelons decided that the time had come to break the siege and relieve Khe Sanh.

The relief, Operation Pegasus, started April 1. Battalions of the First and Third Marines marched up either side of Highway 9. Marine dozers and Seabees followed them to open the road with culverts and bridges. Three battalions of the First Calvary Division flew in by helicopter and landed about halfway to Khe Sanh. They were unopposed. Then three more battalions flew in southwest of Khe Sanh, again meeting little opposition. On April 4, the marines assaulted Hill 1417; the hill overlooked Khe Sanh, and had been in NVA possession since January. They reached the top by noon and ran off a counterattack. The only major opposition was from the old French fort, which the First Cavalry captured in a series of running battles. The 26th Marines cleared the area between Hills 861 and 881. Two days later, the 12th Cavalry swept overland to the ruins of Lang Vei. The NVA launched only one major attack, but they were beaten off. On April 8, the First Cavalry helicoptered into Khe Sanh. The siege was officially declared over.[234]

At the end of the siege, Americans battalions got word to pull out and leave everything they had built with so much labor. Khe Sanh was going to be abandoned.

Holbert said, "I just couldn't believe it."

They left on April 19, 1968. They marched north and saw dozens of charred North Vietnamese, burned by napalm in foxholes and against trees. After they left, Khe Sanh was abandoned and destroyed by American forces.[235]

When the 26th Regiment left, it joined the 101st Airborne Division in a sweep that was called Operation Kentucky. They marched north to the DMZ, meeting very little opposition.

"It was spooky," Holbert said in this journal. "There were graves everywhere, like an ancient burial ground."

The night they spent there was a long one. At the DMZ, they turned right for about 1,000 meters. They proceeded south through a village and met no opposition. Only the aged and the babies were there. They continued south until they reached Da Nang, passing through Phu Bai, where Holbert met Milburn Howard from New Haven, Kentucky, who was serving in a navy construction battalion.

At Da Nang, Holbert got the first warm food, cold beer, and a shower that he'd had in four months. They were there for two weeks, and then they were put on standby for Operation Sparrow Hawk.

In that operation, a spotter plane would fly over the country around Da Nang. If the pilot spotted any of the enemy, he would call standby troops, who would take off in helicopters in pursuit. The choppers would put down as close as possible to the enemy.

"We'd get out firing and looking for cover," Holbert said.

They chased the VC 100 to 150 yards, and then returned to the helicopters and base. The function of Sparrow Hawk was to keep the enemy off balance. After that, the 26th went north to Operation Scotland.

In Operation Scotland, Holbert and the 26th Regiment went north to the A Shau Valley. The valley had tall elephant grass.

Holbert recalls, "[It was] like big palm leaves, an inch and a quarter wide and six to eight feet tall, mixed with three- to four-foot bushes—real tough terrain to fight through."

Each man carried a belt of 100 machine-gun rounds, a 60-mm mortar round, five or six hand grenades, a canteen, a M-16 rifle with anywhere from 100 rounds up, and C rations for several days carried in a sock around his neck. They ran into increasing opposition for a week. Every day was hectic. They started in line for a frontal assault for 200 to 300 yards and met opposition. The vegetation was so thick that it was hard to see the enemy, who were hard-core North Vietnamese. The fighting was vicious.

Holbert would fire 50 or 60 magazines every day. In addition, they had artillery support. Some days they would fight all day and not gain any ground. A lot of their time was spent taking care of the wounded. All the men had first aid kits, and they'd help bandage the wounded, and drag them back to a medevac chopper. The corpsmen couldn't take care of all of the wounded. Many of them died.

Holbert said, "One thing you learned was when one of your men got hit and had to leave the field, you got his rifle and ammo, and anything else you needed. The reason was, most rifles wouldn't last long in a firefight. Some days you would shoot 500 to 600 rounds. You see, if you had two or three M-16s handy, when one quit, you just picked up another one. I tried to keep 50 to 60 loaded magazines all of the time. I carried them around in a haversack."

Both sides seemed to enjoy nighttime. Before dark, they would regroup and pull back into a perimeter. Each man dug his own foxhole, and prepared for the worst, being overrun.

"That never happened to us, but did to some," Holbert said. His company lost its captain, gunnery sergeant, and many foot soldiers. Some were taken out in body bags and others on stretchers.

One day after being in heavy fighting all day, they were starting to set up for the night. Holbert walked across a little clearing and stopped to look back.

"I took a round in my left chest," he said. "I hollered for a corpsman two or three times. Meanwhile I was taking off my flak jacket and shirt. I remember three men coming up to me."

They laid down a field of covering fire, laid him on a poncho, and dragged him to cover. A corpsman patched him up, and an emergency chopper was called in. A sniper had hit him. The wound was only an inch from his heart, and had exited below his left shoulder blade. The medevac got there quickly, and on the flight back to Da Nang, Holbert became increasingly short of breath. Each breath made it worse. He had a sucking wound; his lung had collapsed and his chest cavity filled with blood. He felt like he was going to die.

He remembers that when they arrived at the Da Nang hospital, the doctor said, "This will hurt a little," as he poked a large, double-edged scalpel into his chest.

Holbert said, "It looked like a gallon of blood came out, but I could breathe again."

The next week his condition got worse, despite having a chest tube inserted and needle aspirations. Finally, the surgeons opened up his chest, and did definitive surgery on him. After that, his course was all uphill. He was sent to a hospital in New York for convalescence. From there, he was sent to Fort Belvoir, where he served out his time in the marines doing security duty in Washington, DC.

General Westmoreland and MACV decided on a counter offensive. The A Shau Valley in the northwest was one of the areas hit. It was one of the main corridors that the NVA used for infiltration into the First Corps region, threatening Hue and the other cities. The A Shau Valley had long been considered a threat.

The Third Brigade helicoptered into the northern end of the valley and set up an LZ. Private First Class David Royalty of Nelson County was a member of the Third Brigade (*Kentucky Standard*, Oct. 31, 1968).

Succeeding flights, however, ran into severe NVA anti-aircraft fire, and 10 were shot down. The monsoon season had set in, and fog and mist often encased the valley. Reinforcing helicopters were somewhat protected from anti-aircraft fire by the fog, but their pilots had to make difficult, dangerous instrument landings. However, they successfully brought in the brigade. Later, they brought in an ARVN brigade and the First Brigade of the First Cavalry. [236]

Sergeant Thomas Cecil was a member of the First Brigade, and helicopter crewman Specialist Carl Lanham received an Air Medal for heroic action with troop B, First Cavalry (*Kentucky Standard*, August 22, 1968).

The First Cavalry swept the valley, but the enemy withdrew and refused to fight. Large caches of food, arms, ammunition, and other supplies were found. One PT light tank was also found. Finally, frustrated without bringing the enemy to bear, they withdrew.

In late April after Khe Sanh, while the marines were preparing an offense into the DMZ, the 320th NVA division struck first and moved within two miles of Dong Ha, the major marine base in the north. The NVA took Dai Do, a nearby village. The marines attacked them, but the first battalion was caught in an ambush and hurled back. Another battalion from the Fourth Marines made better progress, and after a rolling barrage, retook the village. Then the NVA counterattacked using mortar and artillery coverage. They broke through the marine artillery and air strikes into the marine lines. A ferocious hand-to-hand fight lasted for four hours and the NVA were repelled. The NVA wasn't defeated, however. They made two more attacks with desperately fighting units again, but both were repelled. The NVA desisted for two weeks, but made another approach toward Dong Ha. On May 26, the Third and Ninth Marines drove against each flank of the NVA thrust, forcing the enemy to discontinue attacks on Dong Ha.[237]

As part of the counteroffensive, the marines swept Thua Thien and Quang Nam provinces, and another Nelson County soldier died in action (*Kentucky Standard*, July 4, 1968). Marine Private First Class Albert Hawkins had moved with his family to New Haven, Kentucky, 20 years before (*Kentucky Standard*, June 6, 1968). He had gone to school at St. Francis and St. Catherine's. After high school, he worked as a groom at Kentucky's racetracks. He enlisted in the marines in August 1967. His brother, Larry, had enlisted in the marines two days before him. Larry was stationed at Dong Ha at the time of Albert's death. Albert Hawkins was killed by hostile fire at Quang Nam on May 17, 1968, 20 days after coming in the country.

The Americal Division was also making sweeps in the area around Chu Lai. Sergeant Joe Blanford (mentioned in chapter 12) was with the Americal Division, the 196th Light Infantry Brigade. There were mostly only short firefights, and artillery was called in when necessary, but even the short firefights were associated with adrenalin-pumping action. A soldier never knew when his number would be up. Frequently, artillery preparation was called in on an area before the Americans went in, because of enemy ambushes.

Early in the year, engineers rebuilt the road from Dak To to Kon Tum for resupply to Dak To. Occasionally, the enemy attacked them. During one of these attacks, Private William D. Price was killed (*Kentucky Standard,* March 21, 1968).

Price was born December 9, 1947. Six months after graduating from high school, he volunteered for the army on January 3, 1966. His early training was at Fort Knox and Fort Leonard Wood. He trained to serve in the engineers, and was assigned to 76th Engineer Maintenance Company at Fort Lee. From there, he was sent to a replacement base in Oakland, California, and then to Vietnam after a 15-day leave. He served there for a year. Little is known of his first tour of duty, although his unit was intermittently involved in combat. Engineer duty in Vietnam was often hazardous, searching for and defusing mines and booby traps, and even going into Vietcong tunnels to destroy them. While in Vietnam, Price wrote a poignant letter in response to a Christmas card.

Dear Friends:

Thought I would drop you a few lines, and show my appreciation for the beautiful Christmas card and note I received from you today. I really and truly appreciated it very much. Thanks a million.

Some people never know how lonesome it is to be 10 miles from home, and here I am, like many other lonesome, homesick GIs, 10,000 miles from home and our loved ones. It will be a happy day when we get word to pull out of Vietnam.

I know you and your husband, relatives, and friends love freedom. That is why we are here, to stop Communists from entering our United States. When I entered the United States Army in 1966, we took a pledge to defend our country, and if we must die to keep the pledge, we will. We have many, many Americans depending on us.

We need your support, and if you can, help with your prayers. The good Lord has a great deal to do with this war. He watches over every one of us each and every night, and I can say he has done a great deal for me and many other soldiers, not only in Vietnam, but all over the world today.

Again I want to thank you for the beautiful card.
Yours truly,
Private Wm. D. Price

Price finished his first tour in August 1967, and returned to the states. He was stationed at Fort Meade, Maryland, until December, when he re-enlisted for a second tour in Vietnam. Three months later, while serving with the 289th Engineers, he was killed in action. A telegram from Major General Kenneth Wickham stated that he "died of metal fragment wounds while on a combat operation, when his unit engaged hostile fire in a firefight."

Price died March 18, 1968, in Kon Tum Province. He was brought home and buried at Little Union Baptist Church in Deatsville, Kentucky.

He had served his country as he saw fit, and served it well. He died in one of the many little firefights not written up in books.

Beginning in early May, the VC, though only a shadow of its former self, attempted another offensive, mostly around Saigon. It was called the Mini-Tet. On May 4, a taxi loaded with TNT exploded and signaled the onset of the Mini-Tet. There was an attack on the main bridge between Saigon and Bien Hoa, but South Vietnamese marines repelled it. There also was an attempt by the VC to take two small villages close to Tan Son Nhut Air Base, but the 25th Division stopped them before they got started. Two VC battalions attacked the critical Chu Y Bridge in Saigon over the inter-city canals, and two armored battalions of the Ninth Division took several days of house-to-house fighting to drive them out.[238] They also returned to the old Tet Offensive battle sites of the racetrack and the Chinese district, Cho Lon.

ARVN Ranger troops fought them off and on for several weeks, but finally defeated them. By the first week of June, quiet had returned and Saigon would have no further serious attacks during the war. Like the Tet, the Mini-Tet was a bad defeat for the VC and NVA militarily.[239]

Various other VC-initiated attacks occurred in mid-1968, but none was of serious consequence. One was at Dau Tieng, west of Saigon, a base of the 22nd Infantry Regiment of the 25th Division. A rocket bombardment was followed by a ground attack that was driven off without any serious damage or casualties.

Private First Class Joseph Leslie, Thomas Boone, and Travis Evans of Nelson County served with the 22nd Regiment.

In August, the 101st Airborne First Brigade went back into the A Shau

Valley, some of the world's toughest tropical terrain. Sergeant Ed Greathouse was a member of the 101st.

Greathouse went to Vietnam on April 16, 1968. He was drafted at the age of 22 in November 1967. He first went to Fort Knox for basic, and stayed there for a radio repair course at the Armored School. He next went to Fort Campbell to become part of the 101st Airborne Division, Second 327 Company. From there, he went to Vietnam with his company. Following a 20-day course of "in-country" training, he was sent to Phu Bai, and from there on up close to the A Shau Valley.

Greathouse was first sent to a pathfinders unit. Their job was to search for information about the enemy's movements, and return with that information so that bigger units could destroy the enemy. They kept in contact with air liaison and helicopters. Sometimes Greathouse flew in helicopters as a radioman, usually in Hueys, but also in Chinooks, and even C-130s. C-130s would fly at treetop level to prevent early detection. One time, he flew over the Laotian border on a C-130 mission. Another time, when he was with the pathfinders, they came up on small group of Vietcong when his unit rappelled down toward them. They fled and left a large cache of SKS rifles, grenades, and food.

Later, Greathouse went out with his old company, Second 327 Airborne, on search-and-destroy missions. He laughed when he talked about "humping the boonies." He had to carry six fragmentation grenades, four smoke grenades, two bandoliers and 20 clips of M-16 ammunition, four canteens of water, a case of C rations, two bottles of MSI grease for machine guns and rifles, insect repellant, three packs of MREs ("meals ready to eat"), his personal kit, and his M-16 rifle. He put much of this in his backpack. Often he had to be helped up, and when he walked, he had to lean forward. In addition, he had to carry a 15-pound radio. They had to have enough supplies to last for two weeks and sometimes longer on patrol, and enough ammo to fight a sustained battle. All of this in a steaming hot jungle. Fortunately, his load got lighter as the patrol progressed.

On one of his patrols, he ripped open his hand. A medic sewed it up on the spot, but the next day it was swollen and exuding pus. He was sent back to a base hospital, and loaded up with penicillin for three weeks before it healed.

Later, Greathouse went back to the A Shau Valley. He was on a hill that was assaulted by the NVA and almost overrun. His company was off-lifted by helicopters.

He again returned to the A Shau Valley. They came in by helicopter under fire. They were let off in high elephant grass. They had people directing them which way to go in the grass, which was sometimes over their heads, and had communicating lines to follow. The NVA had teams in the elephant grass, cutting the lines. It was there that Greathouse came face to face with an enemy patrol 12 feet away. They looked at each other, but passed on, neither one taking a shot. The Americans found a cave nearby with hospital equipment and supplies.

The second day, Greathouse took the point with a scout dog in front. Contact was light, but on the third day, they moved up towards three hills, with the enemy dug into the third hill. His unit moved up the second hill and set up a perimeter. Jets came in, and bombed and napalmed the third hill, but when the paratroopers moved out against it, they were met with withering fire. Another air assault was called in against the hill, but because of drifting smoke from a marking smoke grenade, eight bombs were dropped short, right on his company. The second flight with napalm was called off. As it was, friendly fire caused 60 casualties.

Greathouse said that he had never seen such carnage. He had a minor elbow wound which he bandaged to stop the bleeding, and then went around helping bandage and care for the others. He saw horrible scenes of men disemboweled and blown apart. One man with his face blown off was still alive.

A similar episode had happened at Dak To the year before with worse results. One medic whose tour was up the next day, and who was supposed to go home to his pregnant wife, didn't make it. Only three people in his squad were uninjured.

Greathouse's unit was brought out, brought up to strength with raw recruits, and sent back to the A Shau Valley. He received a field promotion to platoon sergeant. They set up a perimeter the first day out, and moved up on the second day. They inflicted and received casualties from the enemy who popped up out of holes. They were led the next day by harassing artillery fire in front of them. He was told to move up to the front of the column, and pop a smoke grenade for helicopters to come and pick them up. While there, a mortar shell came in and exploded near him. He had a wound in his right arm that was spurting blood; he remembers standing there in shock, and then he fell over in a ditch of water. He was bleeding badly and colored the ditch water red.

When he got up, he was very weak and his buddies laid him down to render first aid. One of them told him he had a chest wound, which he hadn't noticed, but he could see bubbles coming out of it. For the first time, he thought he might die. His wounds were bound up, and the bleeding stopped. He, other wounded men, and the scout dog were picked up by a helicopter and transferred to a hospital. All the while, he felt very thirsty and weak, which accompanies blood loss. Finally, he was X-rayed, given IV fluids and blood, and taken to an operating room. He was afraid his arm might have to be amputated, but when he woke up from surgery, his arm was still there, in a sling, and he had a chest tube in to keep his lung inflated. For about a week, he was in severe pain, mostly from his chest tube, and required repeated shots of pain relievers. When the chest tube was removed, he felt much better. He was told he was going home. While in Cam Ranh Bay, where he was moved before coming home, he met Father James Litchfield from Bardstown.

Greathouse was sent to Walter Reed Hospital for further care, where he also received psychiatric clearance. He understood why. He had seen a number of soldiers go berserk under fire. One even offered him money to shoot him in the leg to get him out of Vietnam, and another ran into concertina wire and cut himself badly to get out. Greathouse eventually came home. He got medical retirement with a 70 percent disability. He later had further surgery on his arm at the Robley Rex Veteran's Administration Hospital in Louisville. He had a tendon transplant to make his hand more useable.

Greathouse received the Air Medal, the Combat Infantry Badge, the Purple Heart, and many other medals. He now works as a maintenance man at a local hospital, and does part-time work as a stonemason. He has overcome his disability and gone on with his life.

As the year wound down, numerous small actions occurred. Although small, they were as deadly as the big ones. In November, the firebase of Battery C, Eighth Battalion, Sixth Artillery of the First Division was attacked. It was there that Nelson County's last Vietnam death of 1968 occurred.

It was Staff Sergeant James Raphael Norris (*Kentucky Standard*, November 3, 1968). Norris was born May 19, 1946, in New Haven, Kentucky. He enlisted in the army in March 1965 at the age of 18, and steadily rose to the rank of staff sergeant. He had reenlisted in 1967 for a six-year term. He started his last Vietnam tour on January 28, 1968, as a howitzer section chief. On the night of November 3, his battery was in their night defensive position close to Loc Ninh. Following an initial mortar, rocket, and recoilless rifle barrage, the enemy attacked and penetrated a sector of the perimeter.

With complete disregard for his personal safety, Norris left his protected position and rushed through a hail of incoming rounds to assist in halting the enemy's advance. He found that all members of the howitzer crew nearest the onrushing insurgents were severely wounded. Norris started firing the howitzer in an effort to stop the enemy's penetration. After putting forth accurate, close-range fire on the hostile assailants, he realized that the enemy was about to overrun his emplacement.

Norris started running to another howitzer position in order to continue his devastating fire, but was wounded by an enemy rocket. His extraordinary example of selfless courage and initiative inspired his men to continue fighting vigorously, and the enemy was repelled. Norris had multiple serious wounds. He was taken to the hospital where his arm was amputated. Despite the best of surgical care, he died two days later.

Norris earned the Silver Star for gallantry. He left behind a wife and an eight-month-old son. His brother had been wounded while serving with the marines less than a year before.

The year ended with a continuation of small battles and firefights. Even though the year's end was not as dramatic as the beginning, the war remained a deadly possibility for everyone involved. The year 1968 had a greater mortality rate than any other. About one in four Americans deaths in Vietnam occurred in 1968. The death rate for the enemy was much worse, but like the boxer who keeps getting up, they kept coming back and had a sting to their blows.

Nelson Countians or those colosely associated who served in 1968 in other actions and were not previously mentioned include:

Marines

Private First Class Larry Bennett: Third Marine Amphibious Force Reconnaissance Pathfinder. Wounded by a booby trap in body and extremities; required several operations and grafting.

Private First Class Kenneth Brown: Second Battalion, Third Marines

Sergeant Michael Brown: Marine Fighter Attack Squadron, First Marines

Corporal Ronald Greer: awarded a Bronze Star

Lance Corporal Kerwin Kerr: First Marine Air Wing; awarded a Bronze Star

Lieutenant Daniel Kurtz: First Marines Motor Battalion, Da Nang

Corporal Samuel Lawrence: Marine Intelligence

Sergeant William S. Lawrence: Headquarters, First Marine Division

Sergeant Charles Phillips: First Marine Aviation Wing, Third Marines

Sergeant Joe Louis Phillips: reenlisted

Private First Class Joseph F. Price: First Amtrac Battalion, A Company

Private First Class Danny Taylor: Headquarters Battalion, First Marine Division

Private Jerry Wheatley: hospitalized with hand wound

Robert J. Williams: 11th Battalion, First Reconnaissance Company, Sniper Second Platoon; wounded

Private First Class Bobby Wood: Second Battalion, Seventh Marines; served a second tour

Army

Specialist Joseph Auberry: Engineer Battalion

Private First Class Travis Barnes: 25th Division, radio operator, Dau Tieng

Specialist Charles Berry: C Battery, Fourth Battalion, 77th Artillery

Private John Calbert: Headquarters Battery, 32nd Artillery, Sixth Battalion, Tuy Hoa

Private First Class Louis B. Cecil: Battery B, 2135 Artillery

Private First Class Gary D. Downs

Specialist Robert E. Durbin: Bearcat base, east of Saigon, Ninth Division Transportation

Specialist Larry Goode: First Aviation Battalion, First Division

Private First Class Robert E. Gribbons: Company A, First Battalion, First Division; near Quan Loi

Specialist Matt Gross: heavy equipment operator, 289th Engineers at Pleiku

Private First Class Henry Hayden: 57th Transportation Battalion

Specialist Loy Haynes: Long Binh

Staff Sergeant Marvin Littlejohn: 27th Transportation Battalion, Qui Nhon

Private First Class Kenneth Mattingly: 363rd Transportation Battalion

Private Norman Metcalf: Fourth Division, near Du Lui

Specialist Clifford Morley: First Cavalry, helicopter machinist, 288th Aviation Battalion

Private First Class William C. O'Bryan: 617th Engineers

Specialist Bennie Eugene Smith

Staff Sergeant Johnsie Brown Stanley: 16th Infantry, First Division. Awarded Bronze Star, Gallantry Cross, Silver Star; platoon leader.

Specialist John R. Thompson

Steve Tolliver: served from March 1968 to January 1969 with the engineers, operating heavy equipment and building roads

Corporal Robert Upshaw: 10th Cavalry, tank commander, Fourth Division, Pleiku

Sergeant Joseph Patrick Vittitow: Wounded and awarded Purple Heart; died in motor vehicle accident after returning to the United States

Sergeant Cale White: Fourth Division, Pleiku

Specialist Joseph F. Willett: Artillery; wounded near Cambodia and at Chu Lau

CHAPTER 13

AIR WARFARE

After the patrol boat attack on the destroyer USS *Maddox* in the Tonkin Gulf, and what was thought to be a second attack on the *Maddox* and the *Turner Joy*, President Johnson approved a retaliatory attack by naval air planes on North Vietnamese patrol boat and oil facilities.[240] The attack was a success, destroying half of the patrol boats and 10 percent of the oil supply. Only two planes and one pilot were lost. In addition, air force planes were sent to Da Nang and Tan Son Nhut air bases, the latter just outside of Saigon.

A few days later, a U2 pilot noticed that 30 MiG-17 fighters had been moved from China to Hanoi. The United States sent two squadrons of B-57 Canberras to the poorly guarded Bien Hoa Air Base. The communist reply was to bombard the base with mortars.[241] Five of the B-57s were destroyed and 13 damaged. Johnson was urged to bomb Hanoi, but he demurred and instead sent replacement B-57s.

In February 1965, Vietcong sappers blew up a number of US aircraft, and mortared the barracks of American advisors at Camp Holloway at Pleiku.[242] They also raided the US advisers' compound at II Corps headquarters. Eight Americans died and 128 were wounded. In a second raid, 23 were killed and 22 wounded. After conferring with the Joint Chiefs of Staff and other advisors, President Johnson targeted for bombardment four areas identified as infiltration staging areas. Within four hours after the decision, navy jets were being warmed up and armed. Shortly, 83 planes were in the air. Three of the four flights aborted because of bad weather, but the fourth plastered Dong Hoi, a major staging area. Johnson also sent a detachment of marines to defend the Da Nang Airfield. Lastly, he ordered home all American dependents in Vietnam.[243]

Worried about the situation in the south, and America's image in defending it, after much thought and discussion, the powers that be in Washington decided upon a gradually increasing air campaign against the north. It was to be called Rolling Thunder.[244] F-100 Super Sabres out of Da Nang led the first Rolling Thunder mission on March 22, 1965. It was to continue for more than three years.

Rolling Thunder was carried out in large part by F-105s from Thailand and South Vietnam bases, and navy planes flying from three carriers on Yankee Station off the coast of North Vietnam. Initially, they weren't to bomb past the 19th parallel, but that later changed. The first attack was on Xom Bang, which had a large ammunition dump. F-100s suppressed anti-aircraft fire. They were followed by two waves of F-105s. Then a wave of B-57s dropped their loads. At the same time, 19 South Vietnamese Skyraiders bombed the Quang Khe Naval Base 30 miles further north. Seventy to 80 percent of both targets was obliterated.

Various air wings rotated in and out from the Pacific every six months. The bases in Thailand were kept secret at the wishes of the Thai government. Initially, South Vietnamese planes accompanied the strikes. Later that was relaxed. A list of targets was sent to the Joint Chiefs of Staff and then to President Johnson's office for final approval from a political angle, but flexibility was given in the choice of weapons and the timing of the strikes. There were two primary groups of targets. The first was along railroad, highway, and coastal sites. The second group of targets was nine radar sites below the 19th parallel. The week became known as Radar Busting Week.[245] All nine targets were knocked out.

The purpose of Rolling Thunder was to influence the leaders in Hanoi to consider a truce, but they were intransigent. President Johnson even offered a billion dollars economic inducement to get them to the peace table, but they wouldn't be bought. His military advisers advised him to bomb all of North Vietnam, but Johnson was concerned about starting a wider war, and possibly bringing China and Russia into the conflict. Because the enemy wasn't moved by the initial phase of Rolling Thunder, it was expanded up to the 20th parallel, and primarily aimed at bridges, tunnels, and all checkpoints of the transportation system. Targets were picked more for their military than psychological or political value.

Key bridges bristled with anti-aircraft batteries, and MiG-17s were used intermittently, but in four weeks, 26 bridges and seven ferries were destroyed.[246] Armed reconnaissance missions expanded to 24 hours a day, and destroyed hundreds of trucks and train rolling stock.

As the bombing increased, so did world criticism and protests in the United States. After two months to see if the Communists would consider peace talks, President Johnson decided on a bombing pause.[247] He sent a secret message to Hanoi about the pause. If it was not met by a lessening of Vietcong activity, the president warned of escalation. If nothing happened, then he would tell the world of Hanoi's intransigence.

Bombing did increase, and the number of sorties escalated to 4,000 by May. However, the bombing was becoming less effective as fixed military bases were moved north of the 20th parallel and supplies were moved along small roads and paths through jungles. By mid-summer, it was obvious that Rolling Thunder was not going to get the desired quick results. It also became obvious that more aircraft were going to be needed in South Vietnam to help defeat the Vietcong and infiltrating North Vietnamese Army troops.

Airfields were enlarged and new ones were built. New squadrons of all types of aircraft flew in. Tactical air command came under the command of General Westmoreland. Even though Rolling Thunder continued and expanded, air power played a bigger part in the battles and life-and-death land struggles in the south. Each battalion had a small observation plane that could help with and plan aerial support. Units of any size had ground-to-air radiomen to call for help. Smoke grenades were used to locate the friendlies and the enemies for air strikes.

Rolling Thunder started again and gradually expanded to involve more of North Vietnam. By mid-1966, it encompassed all of the North except a 30-mile ring around Hanoi and Hai Phong. Continued efforts were aimed to interdict the supply routes in Laos and Cambodia on the Ho Chi Minh Trail, but that was difficult as the targets were spread out and largely covered by jungle canopy. As Rolling Thunder increased, North Vietnamese air defense improved proportionately. Russian and Chinese anti-aircraft guns of 80- and 100-mm were installed around most populated areas, around targets such as bridges, military, and industrial sites, and particularly around Hanoi and Hai Phong. Starting in 1968, Russia supplied sophisticated surface-to-air missiles (SAMS); these increased in number over time. Not only were MiG-17s used, but the much faster and more sophisticated MiG-21s were added in defense of the North.[248] The MiG-21 was equal to the F-4 Phantom in most capabilities.

American countermeasures were used, such as converting F-105s into

"Wild Weasels." These homed in on SAM radar and followed the beam to destroy the SAM sites. This effort would prove only partially successful, but helped cut the SAM destruction rate to only 20 percent of American planes lost. Seventy percent of American losses were due to conventional anti-aircraft weapons and 10 percent were due to air-to-air combat. F-4s were used to take on the MiGs and, for a while, had a four-to-one kill rate, but as the Vietnamese pilots became more seasoned, it dropped to two-to-one.

In addition to the anti-aircraft defenses, Rolling Thunder suffered from an insufficient number of bombs for six months. The Department of Defense had to buy back a number of bombs it had practically given away from 1962 to 1964. In all, Rolling Thunder dropped a greater tonnage of bombs than was dropped in the whole European theater in World War II. By August 1968, American planes had dropped almost 2.6 million tons of bombs and rockets in Indochina, more than were dropped in World War II. That would be tripled by the end of the US engagement in Vietnam.[249]

From December 31 until the last of January 1966, President Johnson tried another bombing pause, but it was as unsuccessful as the previous one. Rolling Thunder had a number of successes. It knocked out critical bridges and rolling stock. It destroyed 70 to 80 percent of North Vietnam's oil supply at Hai Phong, Hanoi's main port. It knocked out North Vietnam's main industry, its steel-producing plants. For a while, it knocked out Hanoi's power plant[250], but for all of the damage it did, it didn't reduce Communist activity in the south.

Oil and gas could be brought in in 50-gallon drums rather than being stored in large tanks. Power was brought in on another grid and bridges were rebuilt. Willing peasants transported goods to the south. The Ho Chi Minh Trail, despite occasional bombing, remained usable.

It appeared that Rolling Thunder was not achieving its objectives. It cost America over 700 highly sophisticated planes, and resources for their backup. Most of the pilots of those planes were lost to death or imprisonment in North Vietnamese prisons. It exhausted the best of American airmen, both air force and naval. It caused much protest worldwide, and on American streets and campuses. It had not brought the North Vietnamese and Vietcong to the table for peace talks. On March 31, President Johnson announced he would not run for reelection. On October 31, he announced the end of Rolling Thunder.

Aside from Rolling Thunder, a great amount of credit has to be given to the ground support given by the air force and naval air arm. They were never lacking when needed if the weather would allow flying. When word went out for help, they were quick to answer. Time and time again, they helped tilt the balance of battle in favor of American troops. When Colonel Hal Moore's battalion sent out the message, "Broken arrow" (meaning, "we're about to be run over"), planes flew in and were stacked five high waiting for their turn to wreak destruction on the enemy and repel them. General DePuy of the First Division said that air support proved to be the deciding factor in Srok Dong.[251] It happened repeatedly.

Many different types of planes were used for tactical support. The old reliable was the propeller-driven A-1 Skyraider.[252] It was a powerful, single-engine plane that could carry almost any kind of ordnance, and the same amount that a WWII B-17 could carry. It was slow and could stay over the target longer. It could be a little more selective of its targets than faster planes. F-100 jets, F-105s, and F-4 Phantoms were used, as well as the navy's A-6. They could deliver an assortment of weaponry. Napalm or jellied gasoline could incinerate a large area with a ball of fire; these weapons were most feared. One hundred, 250- and 500-pound high-explosive bombs were probably the most frequently used. Anti-personnel bombs, which spread hundreds of pellets over an area, could be devastating to enemy troops out in the open. In addition, machine-gun strafing and the use of rockets could be very punitive to the enemy.[253]

Rarely, bombs fell short, such as at Dak To and on Ed Greathouse's 101st Airborne Battalion, with dire results. Like errant artillery fire, they were responsible for deaths from friendly fire, but the American ground forces would take that risk any time when weighed against the great benefits of tactical air support.

Air support was also used to soften up an area before helicopter assault landings of troops to help avoid dropping troops into hot landing zones.

The air force's transport and supply planes, the C-123s and C-130s, were another great benefit during combat in Vietnam. They were necessary to maintain outposts and outlying bases not accessible by roads or in ambush country, where overland supply was treacherous. Sometimes they had to fly in under fire, particularly when an outpost was about to be overrun and they were needed to evacuate threatened troops. Sometimes they were shot down.

They were so valuable that when the Tet Offensive threatened their main maintenance base at Tan Son Nhut Air Base, the mechanics were all moved to another air base.

Lastly, the war saw the use of strategic bombers for tactical purposes. B-52s were used in support of ground troops to good effect. In the Ia Drang battle, they blasted the Chu Pong Massif, where the enemy troops were staging, and then were used repeatedly.[254] They would obliterate an area with their massive bomb loads. They bombed from 30,000 feet, so the enemy didn't know they were there. They bombed wherever there was any suspected concentration of troops.

One of their classic attacks was on the enemy besieging Khe Sanh. Siege lines were destroyed, and North Vietnamese bodies could be seen flying through the air. The siege was broken after repeated attacks.

Nelson County had a number of people involved in the air war. One was Lieutenant Colonel James Bean.

James Bean, called "Jimmy" by his friends, had been a hero most of his life. In high school in 1942, he was the star of a team that went undefeated and untied. No other team had ever even scored against his team. He got a college football scholarship, but left at mid-term to join the Army Air Corps. An accomplished pilot, he flew P-47 Thunderbolts in World War II. After the war, he stayed in the service and soon graduated to jets. He did some of the testing of the new F-84 Thunderjets. His post-war service was spent in Europe as part of the shield against a Russian invasion.

In the 1960s, he switched to F-105 fighter bombers, and later transferred to Vietnam. He flew out of Korat Air Base in Thailand, and was part of Rolling Thunder. He was credited with knocking out two SAM sites close to Hanoi. In 1968, his plane was hit by a missile and caught fire; he was forced to eject (*Kentucky Standard*, January 4, 1968). He suffered burns, but landed safely in North Vietnamese territory. He was soon captured. His burned arms were tied tightly behind him, and he was marched to captivity.

He was kept in a local jail, and was tortured by having his burned arms tied to his feet behind him over a wood frame, and left in that position off and on for days. Despite this and other torture, he refused to sign a confession, or give any military information. The food was meager. He lost 30 pounds. He was moved from prison to prison, and finally ended up in the infamous "Hanoi Hilton." There he was placed in solitary confinement for two years, communicating with other prisoners only by tapping. Torture continued, but he refused to confess to lies. The prisoners were fed only cabbage soup and sweet potato soup with a little rice. Finally, the prisoners were allowed to mingle some.

The North Vietnamese used prisoners as pawns to extract concessions from the United States. Peace talks dragged. Bean said what finally convinced North Vietnam to sign the peace agreement and release the prisoners were the Christmas bombings of 1972, when B-52s bombed Hanoi with thousands of tons of bombs over a two-week period. During one of the bombings, he stood in a concrete doorway with John McCain. Both felt President Nixon was right in ordering the bombing. Finally, they were all released, and each came home to a hero's welcome.

John Finn (Jack) Hurst, Jr. is another airman who had his roots in Bardstown, Kentucky.[255] Hurst's family moved to Louisville when he was seven, but later moved back to Bardstown.

Hurst served in the Marine Corps from 1946 to 1948, and entered the air force in 1951. He finished pilot training in 1953. He was assigned to air force bases in Okinawa, Nebraska, Oklahoma, Montana, Texas, and Thailand. He flew bomber aircraft in the Strategic Air Command, including B-29s (heavy bombers), B-47s (medium bombers), B-52s (heavy bombers), and EB-66s (electronic warfare). From 1966 to 1971, during the Vietnam War, Hurst flew B-52s out of Guam and Thailand on 119 combat missions. Generally, the B-52s flew 12-hour, high-level missions, and dropped 108 500-pound bombs. Hurst said that the B-52s were especially effective against enemy tunnel areas and troop placement bombings. They flew so high that troops on the ground could not see or hear them. The enemy was only aware of them when massive explosions began erupting around them.

In 1968, Hurst's unit of B-52s was sent to Okinawa to prepare for a retaliation strike at North Korea for capturing the USS *Pueblo* and its crew. The navy crew was later released (the North Koreans still hold the *Pueblo*). Hurst logged over 4,600 hours in the B-52.

From 1972 to 1973, Jack was reassigned to EB-66 aircraft stationed at Korat Air Base in Thailand. The EB-66 was a highly effective unarmed, electronic warfare platform aircraft that flew in unison with the F-4, F-105, and C-130 gunships, and B-52s during their strike phase, confusing the enemy radar and jamming their signals. At Korat AB, Hurst commanded the 42nd Tactical Warfare Squadron as a lieutenant colonel, and flew on 81 combat missions. Many of these missions, particularly the ones that flew in the Hanoi and Hai Phong areas, provided exciting moments for the crews as they dodged North Vietnamese surface-to-air missiles.

The EB-66 was instrumental in Linebacker II, the Christmas bombings of Hanoi and Hai Phong. During the Christmas season of 1972, B-52s from Guam and Thailand bombed targets in the cities of Hanoi and Hai Phong for 11 nights, and brought the enemy to the peace treaty table.

During this tour of duty, Hurst was awarded two Distinguished Flying Crosses and a Bronze Star. He said that war is generally a long trudge, interrupted on occasion by periods of terror, horror, and even worse, death and disability. He received numerous Air Medals for his 209 combat missions. He retired as a lieutenant colonel.

Patrick Johnson of New Haven, Kentucky, has a most unusual and interesting story. He started college at Bellarmine University in Louisville, but lost interest in school and joined the air force in June 1963. He went to survivor school in Florida, and then to avionics school, a field in which he became very adept and expert. He was assigned to the new F-4 Phantom jet, a superior, high-performance plane. He soon rose to crew chief, and went on a world tour with the Phantoms to display their ability and versatility. He was sent to Thailand, where he served at both Ubon and Udon Royal Air Force Bases. He served with the 555 Squadron of F4C Phantoms. In 1964, before America was officially at war, the squadrons flew support missions for the Army of the Republic of South Vietnam. Although Johnson didn't fly Phantoms in combat, he did frequently fly them to check out their avionics.

After the US officially went to war and Operation Rolling Thunder started, Johnson's squadron started flying bombing missions over North Vietnam. Rescue missions were carried out when planes went down and their pilots ejected into the jungle. Johnson had survivor training, and became involved in these missions. Helicopters would fly to the jungle sites where aircrews had ejected, and try to pluck them out of enemy territory. Johnson was on a number of these missions, some successful. On one, he was wounded, but not too seriously.

On his last mission, however, after he was lowered to pick up a downed pilot, he was hit in the arm by a poison dart from one of the North Vietnamese tribesmen. On the way back to safety, his arm started swelling, and he started developing systemic symptoms. When he arrived back at Udon AFB, he was flown to the hospital at Bangkok, where it was felt that his condition was hopeless, that he was going to die. He was loaded up and flown to the naval hospital at Subic Bay in the Philippines. There he was rushed to the hospital, and received an exchange transfusion and dialysis. It was touch and go for a long while, but he survived. After his convalescence, he was discharged. When he got back, he had lost 40 pounds. After he recuperated, he went to the University of Kentucky. He earned a degree in mechanical engineering, and led his class. Johnson received the Air Force Commendation Medal, the Vietnam Medal, and others.

Sergeant Bobby Ballard was another airman from Nelson County. Ballard joined the air force in April 1966 at the age of 21. After basic and specialized training, he became an aircraft electrician. He went to Vietnam in December 1967, landing at the Tan Son Nhut Air Base, where he was stationed during most of his stay.

Tan Son Nhut was a massive airfield, a large part of which was used for civilian and non-military purposes. It was also America's largest air base in Vietnam. Tan Son Nhut was rocketed sporadically, but airplanes and hangars were rarely hit. The rockets were fired more or less blindly, but had a great nuisance value. Most of the personnel would just jump in a bunker, (many were spread around the base close to working spaces), and wait it out. Only a few rockets were fired at a time.

Ballard had been there only a few weeks when the Tet Offensive of January 1968 shook the whole area. The civilian part of Tan Son Nhut and even part of the military sector of the air base were overrun by a massive Vietcong attack. A number of aircraft, sheds, and hangars were destroyed, and some American military killed, mostly MPs guarding the base. Three-sided metal walls, reinforced by sandbags, protected most of the aircraft. The attack was a disaster for the Vietcong. There was a killing zone of about one-half mile of cleared area outside of the walled-in areas, and the Vietcong were mowed down there by helicopter gunships, and "spookies" or "Puff, the Magic Dragon" C-47s with double Gatling guns firing out of both side of the low-flying planes. Ballard said there were so many Vietcong killed there that, after the battle, it took a bulldozer to pile them up and dig a ditch to bury them.

Because of the Tet battle and disruption of operations at Tan Son Nhut, Ballard's unit was sent to Phan Rang, a base further up the coast that was guarded by a South Korean battalion. This was necessary to keep the cargo planes, C-123s and C-130s, flying. They supported and resupplied all of the outlying bases and outposts that had dirt and gravel runways, and that were under constant threat of attack. Cargo planes were tough and serviceable, and could land on short airstrips.

After four weeks, Ballard's unit went back to Tan Son Nhut to continue their systematic servicing and repair of air force planes. They repaired all sorts of planes in addition to C-123s and C-130s: F-4 Phantoms, F-105 fighter-bombers, F-101 Voodoo aircraft that flew anti-aircraft suppression missions, helicopters, and Canberras, which were painted black for night reconnaissance missions.

Although most of Ballard's time was spent at Saigon and Tan Son Nhut, his unit was moved occasionally to other airfields, such as Bien Hoa, to help with maintenance problems. His unit was made up of all types of repairmen: hydraulics, instrument, engine, and structural specialists, in addition to electricians. They were capable of fixing almost any problem.

Occasionally, they went to Saigon on day passes, and he considered it fairly safe. There was a curfew, and they were not allowed on the streets at night. The streets were well patrolled by MPs. Saigon was considered mostly Third World, with primarily bicycle and motorbike traffic. During the war, their economy was bolstered by the influx of American servicemen and money.

After his year was up in Vietnam, Ballard came back to the states, and was stationed at McClellan Field, close to Sacramento, California. The duty was good, and he was situated between San Francisco, Lake Tahoe, Las Vegas, Reno, and the Sierra Nevada Mountains. From there, he was sent to other airfields in Hawaii, Texas, and Las Vegas for special repair duty. They worked on F-101 Voodoos in Las Vegas, and had to redo a whole squadron of new F4Ds with cannon in their noses, after one of them caught fire on takeoff. Ballard was discharged in 1970 after four years of sometimes dangerous, but interesting duty.

Sergeant Gaylord Mattingly was another Nelson County airman. He joined the air force in December 1965 at the age of 18, and went to Lackland Air Force Base in San Antonio, Texas, for basic training. He trained in communication, writing and decoding encrypted messages. He then went to Thomasville AFB in Alabama, where he did further communication work.

After four months, he was sent to Tan Son Nhut Air Base in Vietnam, which was the biggest airfield in Vietnam and just outside of Saigon. Part of it was used for commercial flights, but much of it was used as the headquarters of MACV and the Seventh Air Force.

While he was there, Mattingly saw General Westmoreland and other high-ranking officers. For the last nine months of his tour, Mattingly was in charge of a sandbag-filling detail. Such is the operation of the service. They put people where they are needed and not necessarily in positions for which they are trained. Tan Son Nhut was rocketed frequently, and was in constant need of sandbags to protect planes and their backup personnel, equipment, and hangars. This was particularly true during the Tet Offensive.

Tan Son Nhut was often hit by 10 or so rockets each night, but at the outset of the Tet Offensive, Mattingly estimated that 250 rockets or more hit the base. Before that, he had spent most of his nights in the air force barracks, but from then on, if there was any doubt, he slept in a sandbagged bunker. The Vietcong had "walked in" rockets (used explosions from previous rockets to guide in subsequent ones) to destroy as many planes as possible. They pushed through the perimeter of the base, but were thrown out. The only thing most airmen could do was stay in their bunkers during the first few days of the offensive. Some planes were destroyed, but most were saved by encircling sandbags. When Mattingly returned to his barracks, there was an unexploded rocket sticking in the ground about 100 yards from where he normally slept.

Before the Tet Offensive, Mattingly would go with friends into Saigon almost weekly, where they toured around in motorized rickshaws. Even then, there were certain areas of the city that were off-limits to American servicemen, such as Cho Lon, the Chinese sector. Mattingly had never felt in danger, but after the Tet, he chose to not go back.

He remembered the monsoon season, when it rained almost every day with a constant steady drizzle, and he remembered the steamy oppressive heat, but overall, his tour wasn't too bad. He got a week of R&R and spent it in Hawaii. After his year in Vietnam, he returned to the states where he finished his service at Charleston AFB.

Other Nelson Countians or those closely associated who served in the air force in Vietnam include:

1966
Airman Second Class James E. Brown

Airman First Class James G. Burba:
earned an Air Force Commendation Medal at Bien Hoa
Airman Ralph Hawkins: Da Nang
Airman Ray Wilson

1967
Airman First Class James Bartley: Ubon Air Force Base, Thailand
Airman First Class William R. Falls: Thailand
Airman First Class James Parker
Airman Second Class Marshall Simpson

1968
Sergeant Robert B. Ballard: Thailand
Airman Charles Brewer
Airman Kenny Lear
Sergeant Arnold Lyvers: Thailand

CHAPTER 14

1969: First Five Months

After the VC and NVA took a beating in 1968, it would have been logical to expect that they would be cowed and hesitant in 1969. They weren't. They kept on pushing and shoving, always trying to find an opening or a weak spot, trying to find a base camp they could smash, or a city they could rocket with impunity. They weren't about to show any weakness. They couldn't appear to be any less potent and threatening.

With the new American policy aimed at saving lives—attacking areas of entry into South Vietnam to keep the enemy off balance and guarding enclaves—the VC were freer to move about the country. The Americans weren't going to pursue them as forcefully and avidly as before. They could and would attack whenever and wherever they saw an opportunity for success. With the Vietcong numbers down to less than an estimated 50,000, the NVA moved in to take over. In 1969, NVA troops moved into the delta for the first time.

On the American side, things were also happening. The policy of Vietnamization was being implemented, i.e. the training and equipping of the South Vietnamese Army to take over the fighting. They had an army of roughly 750,000 soldiers, and the United States gave them the latest equipment. By mid-March, their army would all have M-16s. By mid-year, they would have 60 boats of the Riverine Force, tanks, armed personnel carriers, small arms, and even some artillery. Richard Nixon had become

US president and his policy—dictated to General Creighton Abrams, who had taken over from General Westmoreland—was the gradual drawdown of American troops. The policy also included provincial protection for pacification efforts.

On January 1, 1969, there were 360,000 army personnel and 80,000 marines in Vietnam.[256] On July 8, the first army unit, the Third Battalion of the Fourth Division, flew home. In October, the Third Marine Division would start the process of pulling out and coming home, and by the end of the year, all of that division would be home. The Fifth Mechanized Infantry Division would take its place guarding the DMZ, and Quang Tri Province.[257] A brigade of the 82nd Airborne Division was sent in to help ease the losses.

Unfortunately, Vietnamization of the war did not adequately take the place of American combat forces. A study done by MACV found that "the South Vietnamese army's fighting spirit was low, a fact reflected in the devastating desertion rates. Lack of aggressive leadership remained prevalent and combat staff support, planning, and coordination was practically non-existent."[258] Experienced generals openly expressed skepticism over South Vietnam's chances of survival without substantial American combat support.

The results were mixed. Some of the ARVN units fought well, and others poorly. The much fought-over Kon Tum province was almost completely in their hands, as was the protection of Saigon. In general, in much of the country, the American army was to be in supporting roles.

After cessation of Rolling Thunder, the NVA brought in more men, equipment, and supplies to the south. They started what was called the post-Tet Offensive, which consisted mostly of rocket and mortar shelling, all up and down the long reach of South Vietnam. There were few large attacks.

Two at Long Binh and Bien Hoa were easily driven off. In March, a large tank-supported enemy attack hit Ben Het, a Special Forces camp. Most of the fighting was done by the South Vietnamese troops, with some American support. In the end, the enemy withdrew.

The enemy also tried hit-and-run attacks on infrastructure, including attacking truck convoys and pipelines, and conducting shipping and ground sapper attacks, and rocket and mortar shellings. As the army withdrew, service units became responsible for their own protection, and had crash courses in firing all sorts of weapons for their own survival.

In the delta, the US Navy announced that it had established the final link interlocking water patrols along a 150-mile stretch of the Cambodian border, and Operation Rice Farmer started.[259] It would last for months, and the South Vietnamese would take over more and more of the operation as the Ninth Division gradually withdrew.

Charles Dickerson was one of the first casualties from Nelson County in 1969. He had come in country in late December 1968 as a member of B Company, 47th Regiment of the Ninth Division, serving in the delta. On January 7, 1969, while Dickerson was on patrol, the point man in front of him tripped a booby trap. Dickerson was hit by shrapnel in the neck and almost killed. A large blood vessel was severed and the cervical nerve plexus damaged. Only timely first aid saved his life. He also lost his voice. After local intervention, he was sent to Walter Reed Hospital in Washington, where radical surgery of a vein-to-artery graft restored circulation, and physical therapy helped him compensate for nerve damage. It took him six months to get his voice back, by forcing air up out of his lungs. By sheer determination, he was able to go to college and get a teaching degree.

Gunner's Mate Stewart Wade Maddox served with an advisory group for the River Patrol Group.

Private First Class Marshall Huff earned an Army Commendation Medal for action against a hostile force in the delta. He was with the Ninth Division's 11th Engineer Battalion.

Private First Class William Linton received the Soldier's Medal for bravery and valorous action (*Kentucky Standard*, May 20, 1969). He was with Company D, Fourth Battalion, 47th Regiment. The commendation noted that, while Linton was retiring from a combat mission by boat, the boat capsized. He saved two men from the swift current, endangering his own life. He continued his rescue work until exhausted.

Robert Durbin earned a Bronze Star against hostile forces at Bearcat base, close to Long Binh (*Kentucky Standard*, February 13, 1969).

In Quang Ngai province, the Ninth Marines started a sweep to clear the Cape Batangan area. A group of 1,800 Americans finally succeeded in occupying a village against the resistance of 200 enemy troops. American forces found 52 Vietcong and 100 women hidden in a tunnel.[260]

In the north, the Ninth Marines started Operation Dewey Canyon in the Da Krong Valley and the adjacent A Shau Valley. It was hot, steamy, and wet. Extensive NVA anti-aircraft deployment made helicopter use dangerous and inadvisable, so marine movement had to be overland through the jungle.[261] They would advance to the limit of their artillery coverage, build a new artillery firebase, and move on. They slowly swept the valley, running into occasional opposition, but overcame it. There were numerous cases of heat stroke and heat exhaustion, but they overcame the terrible climate undeterred. In the campaign, they uncovered large caches of enemy equipment—525 tons of enemy weapons and ammunition, including 12 large 122-mm howitzers. These were the results of enemy stockpiling after the end of Rolling Thunder. It was a major loss for the enemy. Following the enemy across the Laotian border, marine elements bushwhacked a supply column. They stayed in Laos for about a month interdicting the Ho Chi Minh Trail.

Private First Class Frank Hayden, from an old Nelson County family, was wounded February 13 on Tiger Mountain. He was a machine gunner, I company, Third Battalion, Third Marine Division; he earned a Purple Heart.[262] He ended up in a hospital in Japan.

Gunnery Sergeant George M. Taylor was awarded a Bronze Star (*Kentucky Standard*, April 10, 1969).

Air protection was associated with practically all marine and army action. A native of Bardstown was part of that support. Rick Molohan, an excellent athlete in high school, enlisted in the marines with several of his friends in November 1966. He went to Parris Island for his basic training, and from there to Memphis, Tennessee, for training in aviation electronics, radar, and navigation. He was there from February to November 1967. Then he was transferred to Cherry Point Marine Air Station, where he worked on planes, mostly A-6A Intruders. The A-6A had a very sophisticated radar and navigational system. Programmable instrumentation, which guided the plane on its mission, was enclosed in a 75-pound box that could be removed from the plane. Molohan was trained in this highly complicated system of avionics. In October 1968, he was sent to Camp Pendleton, California.

In December, he went to Vietnam to be stationed at Da Nang Air

Base (*Kentucky Standard*, January 2, 1969). The squadron had 22 planes for which Molohan was responsible. His barracks were about 10 miles from the air base workstation, bordering on Visual Mountain, across the base from the sea. During his year's rotation in Vietnam, he spent the whole time at the base.

While Molohan was there, the base was rocketed daily, mostly at night. Sometimes there were only a few rockets, but at other times, there were many more. Since the rockets didn't have good guidance systems, the rocketeers would use their first shot to aim successive shots. Sometimes they would "walk" their rockets right up to their targets. There were a number of concrete hangars on the base. During Molohan's stint there, the hangars had to be repaired six or seven times, and some had to be rebuilt. Molohan's wooden workshop was hit three or four times a month and had to be repaired. One time, high winds blew the workshop over onto a plane. Six planes were lost to rockets. The ammunition dump and the oil storage areas were hit. Sappers also hit the base. The area became known as "Rocket Alley."

Molohan's squadron lost four planes to combat while he was there. The planes flew almost every day. They could take off at night and fly in all kinds of weather because of their advanced avionics. They usually flew combat support missions for marine ground units, but sometimes flew bombing missions over Cambodia, Laos, and North Vietnam. Molohan's only contact with the pilots was discussion of electronic problems. There was no discussion of missions. The planes were kept ready all of the time. In addition to their plane repair work, Molohan and his peers became experts at repairing their workshop.

One of his most vivid Vietnam memories was of unexpectedly meeting a group of National Guard soldiers from Bardstown one day. One of the biggest post exchanges in the area was at Da Nang, and the Bardstown men had come down to visit the PX.

Molohan's Vietnam tour left him unscathed, but he was always in danger from rocket attacks. He returned from Vietnam in December 1969, first to the El Toro Marine Base near San Francisco, and then back to Cherry Point, North Carolina, where he stayed until his discharge in August 1970.

In the early spring, Task Force Remagen, of the 77th Armor of the Fifth Division, made a sweep through Quang Tri province over the old Khe Sanh and Lang Vei battlefields. They were subjected to intermittent rifle and mortar fire.

Platoon Sergeant Albert Cotton, a Nelson County native, received a Bronze Star for meritorious action in the operation, as they cleared the area of the enemy on the northern flank of the A Shau Valley.[263]

In April, the 101st Airborne Division attacked the southern part of the A Shau Valley in Operation Massachusetts Striker. The division later joined the Ninth Marines in Operation Apache Snow to attack the northern part again. On May 10, the 101st helicoptered into jungle-covered hills north of the valley close to Laos. Rising above them was a prominent hill—Hill 937 or Ap Bia. It would later be called Hamburger Hill. As the men of the Third Battalion of the 187th Infantry Brigade started pushing forward up the hill on May 11, they were met with a fusillade of machine-gun and small-arms fire coming from unseen locations in the heavy jungle. The fire cut down the lead elements of Company B. The battle of Hamburger Hill had begun.

Heavy artillery and air support bombing pounded the hill for two days. On May 13, two companies of the 187th stormed the hill, but were driven back by heavy automatic and rocket fire. The NVA had built almost indestructible deep bunkers, flush to the ground with overhead cover, built to give mutual crossfire coverage.

After more artillery and air pounding the next day, the whole battalion charged forward up the hill, but again made no progress. For 36 hours, further pounding by air and artillery obliterated the surface coverage of the hill. By May 18, two other battalions of the 101st and an ARVN battalion were thrown into the battle. Some encircled the hill base, while two battalions assaulted the hill, one on the south face and one on the north slope. It was Dak To all over. After taking severe losses, some platoons reached the summit, but a cloudburst hit the area. With most of the vegetation blown off, the hill became so muddy that the men couldn't stand, and the lead platoons were forced to withdraw. After a massive bombardment two days later (on May 20), all four battalions attacked, and the North Vietnamese were driven off the hill. After 10 days, Hamburger Hill was taken with heavy losses. Questions were raised about why one hill should cost so many lives, when US troops would shortly withdraw from it, and the enemy would move back in.

Charles A. Downs was with the 101st Division (*Kentucky Standard*, November 17, 1968 and April 10, 1969).

North of that action, the NVA began attacking across the DMZ in late March. They were met by elements of the "Red Devil" Brigade of the Fifth Division in a three-day battle. Temperatures reached 105 degrees. In a fierce struggle of assault and counter-assault, the American forces won and drove the enemy back at bayonet point.

South of there, the American Division was engaged in coming to the relief of the Special Forces detachment's A102 Compound. It had come under attack by the Third NVA Regiment. Bitter fighting lasted off and on for eight days, with American troops charging well-bunkered NVA troops, backing off for artillery and air support, and then charging again.

Three Nelson County soldiers participated as part of the artillery support. Two received Bronze Stars, and another the Army Commendation Medal. They were Sergeant Louis Thompson, Sergeant Charles T. (Tommy) Riggs, and Private First Class Danny Cheatham (later promoted to corporal), who had been transferred from Bardstown's Battery C of the 138th Artillery to the 82nd Artillery (*Kentucky Standard*, October 6, 1969).

Finally, the Americal Division took bunker after bunker with flamethrowers, and drove out the NVA. The same unit was involved in retaking a critical militia hill site. The artillery literally blew the top off the mountain.

The First Marine Division was involved in battles at An Hoa and the Que Son Valley, and in sweeps of the "Rocket Belt," from which the enemy was bombarding the Da Nang facilities with rockets. This extensive area of booby-trapped fields and villages caused an inordinate number of casualties.

Staff Sergeant Raymond Phillips of the First Battalion, Fifth Marines, earned the Navy Achievement Award with a V for valor in these sweeps and in the valley fighting. Lance Corporal David Ball, with a reconnaissance group, was wounded and suffered second-degree burns over his body. He was sent to a hospital in Japan (*Kentucky Standard*, April 10, 1969).

On May 28, the marines, with a Korean battalion, attacked Go Noi Island, long a haven for the Vietcong. They ended up using bulldozers to clean the vegetation off the whole island, depriving the VC of their hiding places.

In the south, the First Cavalry Division and the 25th Division guarded the Cambodian border and tried to prevent attacks from bases across the border. Many firefights erupted from ambushes on both sides. On April 28, the First Cavalry started Operation Montana Rancher in War Zone C and extended it into War Zone D. These attacks were to follow massed B-52 bombings. The cavalry air-hopped from landing zone to landing zone, but the enemy pulled back into thick jungle and bamboo thickets. The VC were difficult to see. They often allowed American patrols to bypass them and then fired upon them from behind. Helicopter gunship, artillery, and air force rockets, napalm, and bombs allowed units to back out and charge again knowing where the enemy was. After the operation, many remaining pockets of the enemy had to taken out one by one.

Warrant Officer Francis T. Hagan was a helicopter pilot with the First Cavalry near Tay Ninh.

The 25th Division was in position south and west of the First Cavalry. They built a number of patrol bases along the frontiers and near some branches of the Mekong River. With listening devices, they were able to detect enemy movements prior to attacks, and bombarded these movement areas with marked success. Sometimes the conditions required touch-and-go sweeps through the area.

Sergeant Richard Hicks earned an Army Commendation Medal: "While on a sweep operation, a troop came in contact with a large enemy force. Although he was subjected to deadly enemy shelling, Hicks, with complete disregard for his own safety, moved through the enemy kill zone, and began placing devastating fire on the insurgents. His heroic action contributed immensely to the success of the mission."

Sergeant Joseph W. Brown was with A Battery of the Sixth Artillery, transferred from Battery C of the 138th Artillery (*Kentucky Standard,* May 20, 1969).

In the area around Saigon, the First Division activity was relatively quiet, and combat relatively light. The division's energy was spent mostly in pacification efforts and training ARVN units. The division also cleared and widened the road from their base to Phuoc Vinh and Song Be. The narrow jungle road had been the site of many Vietcong ambushes. With the clearing of a 250-foot swath, ambushes became infrequent. Firefights did occur.

Corporal James K. Strange, with the First Division, received an Army Commendation Medal for heroism (*Kentucky Standard,* March 6, 1969). He directed artillery fire on numerically superior enemy forces and helped defend Firebase Rita.

Sergeant Joseph Nalley, a Nelson County native, was a gunner with the First Division.

In the same area, the 11th Armored Cavalry Regiment had a three-day battle on the Michelin rubber plantation. They lost several tanks against a tenacious 320th NVA Regiment as they advanced through a bunker-studded forest. With one remaining tank in the company, armored personnel carriers lined up on either side of it, and with troops marching in a battle line, they cleaned out a group of bunkers. Another squadron took over the next day, and continued cleaning out the plantation. The regiment was under the command of Colonel George Patton, son of the famed World War II leader.

Specialist Tommy Lanham was with the 11th Armored Cavalry (*Kentucky Standard*, April 10, 1969).

The first five months of 1969 had been a time of fewer large battles and operations, such as Hamburger Hill, and more small-scale fights. These fights involved squads and platoons more than massed formations. Nelson Countians were involved in most of the actions north to south.

June 1969 was a terrible month as far as combat deaths from Bardstown and the surrounding county were concerned. Over half of the local deaths occurred that month. From June 11 until July 2, there were eight local men who would not return alive from the war.

On June 11, Staff Sergeant Harold Brown was killed by rocket fire in a bunker near Chu Lai. He had been in the local National Guard unit for five years and in Vietnam for eight months. He had only a short time left before being transferred to a regular army unit in support of the Americal Division.

On June 25, Barry Neal Thompson was killed by shrapnel close to the Cambodian border.[264] He made it to the hospital, but died later in the day. He was wounded while on one of the always-necessary ambush patrols. He was a member of Company B, First Battalion, 28th Infantry, First Division. It was a famous outfit—the "Lions of Cantigny"—who were in one of the first battles of World War I.

On July 2, Jim Wray was killed (*Kentucky Standard*, July 24, 1969). He had been with the local guard unit, but had been transferred out several months before. He was with the First Battalion, 40th Artillery Regiment. Wray was killed by friendly fire, when a supporting artillery shell fell short. He was the only one killed in the mishap. Death in war is always a tragedy, but being killed by friendly fire is most difficult for the family to accept. Unfortunately, it happened all too often.

However, Nelson County's night of trial was to occur on Tomahawk Hill and would involve the National Guard Battery C, 138th Artillery.

CHAPTER 15

1969: THE WORST MONTH

Specialist Donald Parrish contributed this chapter about Charlie Battery, Second Battalion, 138th Field Artillery, Kentucky Army National Guard. Parrish was chief of section for the battery's fire direction center in the Republic of Vietnam in 1968 and 1969.

During summer camp at Fort Campbell, Kentucky, in 1967, I remember speaking at the end of a day's training with First Sergeant Pat Simpson about combat experience. We agreed it would feel good to have some under our belts, but we also agreed we did not want to invest in this experience just to have it under our belts. Neither of us could imagine that we were in direct line to go to a war zone and collect that experience. We were just completing that year's training, only to find we were again one of the top-firing artillery battalions in all of the US Army. That made us a target for the insatiable appetite of a country determined to change the government in a foreign land.

Most of the men in the National Guard had joined for various reasons. I, for example, joined in order to avoid the draft and be able to remain with my family business with the least amount of time spent away fulfilling my commitment to the military. Several others did the same thing. Still others wanted to serve in a unit with friends and relatives rather than volunteer for two years and spend that time with strangers. There were various reasons for others, but the eventual result was that our unit was very close knit and worked well as a military unit, whatever the underlying reasons for having joined.

TRAINING

National Guard units across the nation were trained in similar fashion as other branches of the military—basic training of eight weeks at an army post, followed by advanced individual training (AIT) in whatever field the soldier was to be employed. For artillery soldiers, AIT was at Fort Sill, Oklahoma. Just as in the regular army, most of these jobs required classroom training followed by training in the field. In other cases, individual soldiers were placed into existing units of artillery battalions and had on-the-job training. This is how many of us were trained, including me; that is, we simply went to work and paid attention to what was going on around us. At the conclusion of six months, the training was considered complete and the soldier was allowed to go back home to his daily life, but now he was a trained part-time soldier serving God and nation. From that point, the military obligation was to complete six years, including the aforementioned training as National Guard troops.

We met to train one weekend per month through those six years and went to a two-week summer camp on an army post with a large artillery range. At summer camp and during many of the weekends, we were in the field, firing howitzers and honing our skills. Weekends were spent at Fort Knox, and most summer camps were spent at Fort Campbell in southwest Kentucky.

While we did not train nearly as much as regular army soldiers did, we were just as good as any of the full-time soldiers and better than most. This was partially because we knew each other quite well and worked well together.

RIOT CONTROL TRAINING

In 1967, this nation faced racial tension like nothing I have seen before or since in the form of intense violence, primarily in large cities in the South and West. In order to maintain peace and protect life and property, governors of many of the states ordered their respective National Guard units be trained as quasi-military police for the purpose of riot control. We were issued batons, which resembled a nightstick about three feet long, and we were trained in their use.

During winter and spring of 1967 and 1968, we trained for riot control. We were pressed into service, for example, to provide additional security during the events of Derby Day at Churchill Downs Racetrack. For the entire day, many of us were in the infield along the rail on the track, facing the infield crowd. Our duty was to keep the crowd under control. This we did with little contact, as there were few problems while we were on duty.

There was a situation in the Cincinnati area that grew daily in intensity, and we were concerned our unit was going to be activated for service there. On a Wednesday around noon, my dad returned to work at Ray Parrish & Sons, telling me that he understood from the news reports that the Bardstown unit was to be activated right away for service in Vietnam. I thought he might have made an error, and we were really to be sent to Cincinnati for riot control duty. I was the one thinking wrong, and I reported to the armory on Monday morning, and soon learned our destination in I Corps, South Vietnam—a small town called Phu Bai. Our battery consisted of 106 officers and men, mostly residents of Nelson County, a few from surrounding counties. There was general disbelief that this was even possible. Many of us thought that this was only an alert that would surely never end in a trip into war, but it was indeed true and we were destined to go to war.

The Bardstown National Guard unit has a long history of going to war in times of great need and this time was no different. During World War II, the unit was an ordnance company that was activated, sent to Mississippi for extensive training in the then-new equipment and updated techniques of war. These men then went to war principally in the South Pacific, serving on Guadalcanal and other islands fighting the Japanese. During the Korean conflict, the unit was once again activated, trained, and sent to war. While Vietnam was a continuation of this tradition, there was more yet to come. The unit, now a self-propelled 155 howitzer firing battery, would go to Iraq and be retrained in military police duty.

War is unpredictable. The National Guard can be called upon because these warriors are available, willing, and ready to tend to the needs of this nation's first line of defense. We were ready for our turn to come to the aid of our country.

Captain Tom McClure was our battery commander and had been in that position only a few weeks before we were called up. Second Lieutenant Thomas Raymond Ice was executive officer, and Second Lieutenant Jack Doyle had just graduated from Officer's Candidate School at about that time. Our first sergeant was Pat Simpson of Fairfield, Kentucky, and chief of firing battery was Staff Sergeant Buck Harned of Boston, Kentucky. These men were all highly respected leaders and provided a chain of command that would see our eventual success as a fighting unit.

Captain McClure was the first to join Pat Simpson in arriving at active duty. I was activated early, on April 20, in an effort to speed preparations. Soon others followed and the entire battery was present by May 13. While Buck Harned's enlistment was to be up in a short time, he rejoined so he would be able to go with his longtime friends and serve his country with distinction. This decision was to become traumatic for him. (After our tour of duty in Vietnam, our three officers would remain with the National Guard; one would retire as a full colonel, the other two as brigadier generals. Our first sergeant would also remain and finish his career as an outstanding leader.)

Following about four weeks of exercise, training, and bodybuilding at the armory, we inventoried all of our equipment, and loaded gear in vehicles for transport. We received immunizations, had our physicals, and tended to other paperwork, including making wills and filling out next-of-kin papers. By then, I, along with a handful of cadre, knew our eventual location in Vietnam. All of us would have to explain to our employers what was going on, and hope that our jobs would be available once we returned to civilian life. At that time, there were no guarantees that job openings would be available upon our return home, but as it turned out, jobs were kept available for virtually all of us. Many of us were self-employed in family businesses, mostly farmers, and the loss of men in this capacity became a major burden to the livelihood of that business. When men are deployed to war, many sacrifices are made, not only by the men and their families, but also by others who are left behind.

We flew to Fort Hood, Texas, where we were issued new equipment, including six of the newest 155 self-propelled howitzers, M-109 and other track vehicles, as well as the M-16 rifle, M79 grenade launcher, new radios, and other modern items of war. I believe it was when we received the then-new M-16 rifle and jungle fatigues that most of the men in Charlie Battery concluded we were, in fact, going to war. Up to that point, there had been a little bit of doubt left in the minds of some about our eventual destination.

In the past, we had used the towed 155 howitzer, which was towed by a five-ton truck.[265] The truck also carried the crew who muscled the gun into firing position, and performed the duties of a gun crew, loading, firing, and maintaining the gun. This howitzer has a long history of service to the US Army and Marines dating to before World War II. The newest generation of weaponry was in our hands and we had to retrain in the use of this weapon. Being self-propelled, this gun was more versatile and could more quickly be set up and prepared. We could also fire more quickly with this gun, thanks to the electrical and hydraulic systems.

We trained at Fort Hood until September, when we were allowed a 30-day furlough at home. During that time, we were able to obtain several used refrigerators, washing machines, and ice-makers, thanks to the generosity of Bardstown residents. These were sent to our final destination and were a vital help in making our experience more comfortable than that of many other soldiers in a war zone. These items were left to those who followed us in that war-torn region. Bardstown residents deserve a major "thank you" for their support during this very trying time.

While home, both before Fort Hood and afterward, several of the men hurriedly completed plans to marry their sweethearts and make other long-term decisions regarding their futures, including making wills and other arrangements that were indicated by this intrusion in their lives. Newspapers were full of wedding stories and photographs, as well as other stories related to our imminent departure. Several of the new brides relocated to Killeen, Texas, to live with their husbands who were training on new equipment. They, too, had returned home during the furlough, and would remain there for the long year ahead while their loved ones went to war.

DESTINATION VIETNAM

Once we returned to Fort Hood, we soon were in the air, destination

Da Nang, South Vietnam. Our purpose was to provide artillery support to various infantry units, mostly of the 101st Airborne Division. Many thoughts were going through the men's minds and they let these thoughts be known. A few said that we were probably going to fly out a short distance and return home, part of a great training exercise showing we really could be used in a war. Others thought we might be deployed to Korea or Japan in reserve. Our mission, however, was to be in the thick of an unpopular war.

Several planes were used to transport the battalion to Vietnam. They included Air Force C-141s, and private commercial contract carriers. Our battalion consisted of three firing batteries, A Battery from Carrollton, B Battery from Elizabethtown, and C Battery of Bardstown, along with Headquarters Battery and Service Battery, both of Louisville. Each battery boarded a plane, and included portions of C Battery, such that five batteries of more than 100 men flew in four planes, along with their personal gear including rifles and ammunition. I was in the last plane, an Air Force C-141, an enormous plane with only four tiny windows. We were on our way. The flight was 26 hours long with one stop in California and a second one at Midway, the island made famous during World War II.

When we landed at Da Nang at about four in the morning, there had been a rocket attack and we were all told to get off the plane, load our weapons, disperse in all directions, and take cover. Welcome to the war.

Later in the morning, we were on another plane on our way to Phu Bai, just south of Hue, and from there by trucks to Gia Le, a large facility known as Camp Eagle, where the 101st was headquartered. Once there, we started getting organized as a firing battery. It was mid October, and we were in for the real training for war, under fire with human lives at stake on both sides. This, our first combat position, was to be the safest position we were to occupy in Southeast Asia.

SETTLING IN

Artillery consists of firing batteries, three per battalion, and each battery usually has the same size or caliber howitzer. In our case, it was the M109 self-propelled 155-mm howitzer, firing a projectile weighing 98 pounds. It was fired using as many as seven bags of powder, each about two or so pounds. These guns could fire a high explosive round with great accuracy to a target 14,400 meters, or about 10 miles distant. Each battery had six howitzers, or guns, each with a crew of about nine men, consisting of the chief of section, gunner, assistant gunner, and others responsible for activities needed for efficient firing. These men were the ones who did the enormous work of getting the rounds out. Imagine two men carrying 98-pound projectiles for each of six guns, and doing this at night. On more than one occasion, more than 2,000 rounds were fired at night, equaling over 100 tons of ordnance.

There was also the fire direction section, consisting of chief computer (also serving as chief of section), assistant chief computer (who led half of the men so we could function around the clock), chart operators, map readers, and radio operators. I was chief computer and chief of section. Fire direction had communication with virtually everyone involved in the area of our capability, a circle approximately 20 miles in diameter.

If troops had need of artillery support, a forward observer would call the firing battery and speak immediately with the chief computer on duty, giving him the details. This was frequently while the observer was under fire, and activities at this point were frantic. It was our responsibility to get rounds of illumination or high explosives on the way as soon as possible. While we were considering the situation and calculating the needed data, we were in contact with our battalion headquarters. Although they might be 50 miles away, they would calculate the same data to check our work, insuring that there were no shootouts or friendly-fire incidents. We were fortunate to have not had a mistake in our firing for the entire stay, during which we fired many thousands of these rounds.

Other weaponry in our battery included M-16 rifles, M-79 grenade launchers, 45-caliber pistols, 50-caliber heavy machine guns, and M-60 light machine guns. We also had some Claymore anti-personnel mines, and there were always grenades.

We were well supplied for our entire stay in country. Other equipment in our personal gear included a bayonet, the one implement of war that no one ever wanted to be forced to use. In order to make good use of the refrigerators and washing machines given by the folks back home, we had to acquire generators for the electric supply. While there were many such machines in country, none was authorized to us, but that did not keep us from obtaining them and putting them to good use. Several generators were located quickly once we learned the lay of the land, and we were in business. Some were acquired through bargaining and others were simply acquired. They were among the most valuable assets we had during the entire time.

Artillery involves shooting heavy rounds in a large arc; the round goes high into the air on its way to the assigned destination. However, a howitzer can also fire much as a tank does, using direct fire. This is where the gun barrel is leveled at a target less than a mile away, and either bore-sighted (by looking through the bore of the gun barrel), or using a scope alongside the gun barrel. This sort of firing is quite impressive since there is no need for a fire direction center (FDC), and the exploding rounds could be observed from our position on the firebase. It was quite exciting. We had twice observed this sort of firepower.

One afternoon, a VC sniper was shooting at vehicles traveling along Highway 1 just off Hill 88. Once we learned of the situation, we told all guns to train on the sniper's position on the side of the mountain just across Highway 1 from our position. I do not recall how many rounds were fired, but shooting from that sniper was not heard again. The demonstration was simply awesome. Enough smoke from the explosive rounds covered the area that nothing could be seen on the ground for a few minutes. On yet another occasion, this action was repeated at the same location, but I am sure it was a different sniper. This time, air force jets joined us; they delivered a dozen or so 500-pound bombs, which made a deafening sound and made the earth tremble.

Artillery also can fire at either low angle or high angle. Low-angle fire requires that the gun barrel not rise above 45 degrees. High-angle fire calls for the barrel to rise beyond 45 degrees, and is used to place rounds on the backsides of hills and mountains. Once the round is fired, more than two minutes often passes before that round hits the target. Artillery is a very accurate means of delivering devastating consequences to the enemy, and is quite valuable to the infantry in the field as a defensive or offensive weapon.

Little has changed in centuries of wars where groups of men try to outdo each other to see who can inflict the greater damage to his opponent. The principal difference is that when soldiers from a few centuries ago entered battle, weapons consisted of edged weapons, swords and spears. All battle was up-close and personal, and the swinging of swords separated a head, arm, leg, or other body part from the body of an enemy. Now this service is performed in similar fashion; however, there is no blood left on our clothing. Artillerymen provide the same services as swordsmen of centuries ago; we just do it from a distance.

FIREBASE DENISE (HILL 88)

On Thanksgiving Day, we moved about 40 miles south to Firebase Denise, otherwise known as Hill 88, where we remained for about five months and had very good experiences on a hill that was easily defended. Located on Highway 1, we could see the South China Sea off to our north where the Gulf of Tonkin begins. At one point, we witnessed the battleship *New Jersey* firing her 16-inch guns, all nine of them, over our heads. Our safe location on a defensible hill caused us to feel safer than we perhaps should have. The approaches to this position were very steep, and we and the 101st occupied the high ground, which gave us the upper hand in warfare. There were no spots higher than ours anywhere close for an enemy unit to use.

Upon our arrival, our first efforts were to clean up after the 155 towed battery that had moved out on the same day, and position the guns and ready the fire direction center so we could declare ourselves open for business. We were in position very quickly, and within less than an hour or so, we were actually firing missions. We were soon firing something called a registration mission that establishes base data for future missions, allowing for accurate fire at a moment's notice. While one battery was moving out— actually, while they were completing a mission—we were replacing them and firing within minutes.

We built new bunkers for living quarters, since the ones left by our predecessors were insufficient, and soon life was good for a war zone. We built our bunkers using 12-inch square timbers as posts and beams. We then added a deck of scattered three-inch timbers followed by a perforated steel deck plate called PSP. In order to make the bunker water resistant, plastic sheathing was added on top of the steel deck and then layers of sandbags, weighing perhaps 70 to 100 pounds each, were packed tightly to provide protection from the tools of war, including bullets and high-explosive devices, RPGs, satchel charges, and the like. We added a tent to the top of our position in anticipation of winter rains that would not cease for months at a time. Our future locations would not require such protection from rain, but they did require additional sandbags.

Other sections prepared their own spaces. Maintenance located a large tent to provide shelter from the weather for service to vehicles; communication located inside a bunker; the exec post was erected for the chief of firing battery, and so on. Our mess section built a portable building, using lumber, sheet metal, and wire screen for their kitchen and serving area. This included a new upright freezer bought by our friends in Bardstown that was powered by a large generator found somewhere in country. This was a major benefit to the ingenious men of the mess section, for they were able to acquire various supplies of foods that kept all of us well fed throughout our stay in Vietnam. Our reputation for having good meals most of the time brought many visitors to our locations wherever we were.

On Firebase Denise, we were able to build our bunkers into a hillside and required fewer sandbags for the wall sections than if we had built on flat ground. This was a definite advantage in being able to build a home in a short time to provide protection from enemy fire and the weather. Comfort and amenities were added as time permitted, including a shower that was heated, some of the refrigerators from Bardstown, and other amenities. Within a few weeks of arrival, we were pretty well fixed for protection and comfort considering we were in a war zone.

A three-legged dog wandered in from somewhere. Sergeant Ronnie Simpson adopted it and we had a pet. The dog was well cared for, and as time went on, other members of the unit adopted a couple of other dogs, providing a little bit of home for many of us. Throughout our stay in country, there was a constant attempt to maintain contact with wives, girlfriends, and families back home. Some men wrote daily, others perhaps two or three letters a week. During off times, there was always a little basketball or softball activity as weather and duties allowed.

Mail call was probably the happiest time on the hill because it provided contact from back home. No one knows loneliness quite like a soldier far from home for extended periods of time; Christmas and other holidays were the worst. For those men whose wives were delivering babies, loneliness became only more agonizing.

We established a perimeter defense system using barrels of jellied gasoline, referred to as phu gas, with Claymore mines set behind the barrels. Controlled by an electric charge, the Claymore mine would blast the jellied gasoline, igniting it out in a devastating arc of fiery death, consuming any of the enemy unlucky enough to be in its deadly path. Several of these devices were positioned in key points throughout our location. Guard bunkers were also constructed using sandbags, culvert pipe sections, and other items, providing protection as well as a good defensive shooting position. There were coils of razor wire or concertina wire arranged in some of the most vulnerable locations. Once in position, this coiled wire would make entry into the protected area virtually impossible. It would snag the intruder's clothing and trap him. Our enemy, usually the Vietcong, or VC, also known as Charlie, would thwart this protection by stripping off their clothing down to their shorts or even less, so they could feel the sharp wire points and worm their way inside our perimeter.

Artillery supports infantry units, and usually occupies an easier location to defend, unlike the infantry themselves who are in the greatest danger at all times. This danger is mitigated somewhat when artillery from a nearby fire support base can be called in to destroy or chase off a threatening enemy unit.

In addition to high-explosive rounds, called HE, we fired many illumination rounds, giving the infantry the advantage of sight during hours of darkness, and taking the advantage of fighting in the dark away from the enemy. These illumination rounds were canisters containing a flare that, once deployed out of the canister, would ignite and burn brightly for about two minutes. This flare was held high in the air by a silken parachute. The resulting light enabled infantry and the enemy to see nearly as well as they could in daylight. However, the advantage was virtually always for friendly forces.

Another round we fired was filled with white phosphorus; it was known as WP, or Willie Peter. This round was usually used as a marker round so a forward observer would easily see white smoke from the first round and could then adjust subsequent rounds. White phosphorus burned at a very high temperature and was used to incinerate villages and other targets.

I remember one village we burned to the ground with these rounds, not a pretty sight. When people were the intended target, it was impossible to get the burning fuel off, and survival of these injuries was not likely.

Artillery rounds were infinitely adjustable in terms of where we were able to put them inside a range of about 10 miles. That is a circle 20 miles in diameter. A call from a forward observer would let us know his exact location, and he would give coordinates for his target. We would calculate the needed data to send to the guns and they would commence firing. Since the first round was seldom right on target, the observer would let us know from his perspective how we needed to adjust fire. We would then recalculate and move the rounds as needed, continuing this process until we reached end of mission and the enemy had been satisfactorily thwarted or destroyed. We even could and did chase some enemy troops by following adjustments from forward observers and continuing to fire as best we could. This resulted in destruction of some enemy targets on the move.

Sometimes we had multiple fire missions at the same time. There might be a couple of firefights underway along Highway 1, needing "light bulbs" (as the illumination rounds were sometimes called), and then one of these firefights might ask for HE at the same time. These missions were always carried out, as needed. One night, there were several of these firefights underway requiring light bulbs, and then HE rounds were called for at the same time. On this occasion, the other shift of workers was called upon to assist in the FDC and each of these missions was carried out without a flaw. At one point, there were five fire missions going at the same time, and we met the infantry's every need. That was simply a remarkable accomplishment.

One of the more boring duties we performed was the harassment and interdiction missions, known as H&Is. We were given coded targets each night that required us to fire on the targets during the night at specified times, maybe as many as four or five times per night. Some nights, there were in excess of 100 targets requiring accurate data be calculated and sent to the guns. No one looked forward to this long, boring work, but as it turned out, several of these missions were quite helpful in attacking known paths and trails used by the enemy, ammunition stashes, and other targets. There were a number of successes in these missions and some American troops were saved as a direct result.

Firebase Denise was the site of a great deal of firing, mostly at night. We fired many illumination rounds, providing light of nearly daytime quality for infantry engaged in firefights at night along Highway 1. A few nights we fired in excess of 2,000 rounds of illumination and high explosive. That is a lot of work for the gun crews since each round weighs 98 pounds, exceeding 200,000 pounds of shells and powder in one night, handled by about 24 men, serving six guns. The hard work in a firing battery such as ours was mostly in the hands of the gun crews who handled a lot of ammunition, none of it light.

Various elements of the 101st noted our performance. Whenever any of these units were within our range and we had capability to provide fire support for them, we got the job. We were very accurate and fast in getting rounds out, saving many of the infantry from a horrible fate. In fact, the reason our unit was activated in the first place was that we were the top firing unit in all of the reserve units in the nation, and we continued that tradition as long as we were in Vietnam. The enemy also noted our proficiency, because they suffered many casualties and lost a great deal of ammunition and other supplies to our constant pounding of their positions and caches of munitions.

Highway 1 is the principal north-south road running the entire length of Vietnam. Consequently, that route was the principal road for supplies moving north to American troops in I Corps, the northernmost quarter of South Vietnam. Many infantry units guarded bridges and other areas of this road because of its importance to US troops. Each morning, there were minesweepers walking up and down Highway 1, clearing mines installed the night before by the Vietcong.

A narrow-gauge railroad ran parallel to this main artery for most of its length and it was guarded as zealously as the highway. The railroad was harder to guard because of the jungle, and rough terrain, numerous tunnels, and other reasons, and it was the subject of many mine explosions. Either a diesel or steam locomotive pulled the train while pushing a flat car in front. The flat car usually took the brunt of explosions from the nightly deposited mines. One morning, there was an explosion on the railroad that blew a flat car off the tracks and derailed the locomotive. This happened on the railroad just adjacent to Highway 1 directly across from our position on Firebase Denise. While there was little or no activity in the area, several of us went down to the railroad and looked at the wreckage, walking all around the area, including the track in front of the wrecked train.

After a while, we returned to our firebase and continued to watch the scene from atop the hill, about 800 yards or so away. Another train arrived from the opposite direction to aid the wrecked string of equipment and get the track open again. Just a few feet away from the blasted flat car, another mine exploded, and then there were two trains disabled and blocking access to the north. This mine exploded right where several of us had been standing only minutes before. Good fortune was with us that day. Within a few days, the wreckage was removed, repairs to the track made, and train traffic resumed. We collectively determined we would not investigate any further train wrecks or mine locations.

Travel on Highway 1 was not the same sort of routine as is found anywhere else in the world. At dark, this highway and others in Vietnam belonged to the enemy. The next morning, the US Army would take the highway back and use it again that day until evening. This scenario was repeated again and again. I do not recall there being very many incidents where mines exploded upon contact with army vehicles, but the psychological effect was there nonetheless. Danger lurked everywhere in Vietnam, but travel was especially dangerous. Bridges were frequently the targets for Charlie since repairs to a bombed-out bridge took considerable time, during which time the bridge was unavailable to American and South Vietnamese forces. Several Bailey bridges, an engineering marvel still used today, were always in use beside bombed-out bridges while permanent repairs were made to the original bridge.

The United States Army Engineers rebuilt Highway 1, and I'm sure others as well, and ultimately paved the entire highway throughout I Corps. I do not know if this highway was completed to Saigon or not. In any event, the newly paved surface resulted in higher speeds for travelers, less dust and mud, and fewer potholes. It was more difficult for Charlie to install mines in the paved surface although these mines still appeared in lower numbers. This work was completed a few months after we had arrived at Firebase Denise, and was a welcome relief.

Firebase Denise was located on a hill that was 88 meters or 289 feet above sea level, adjacent to Highway 1. The base stood on a sandy flat plain with some rice paddies and a few huts scattered to the north and east, and a small village to the immediate south. Further south was Highway 1 and the railroad. Immediately south and west stood mountains reaching a height of nearly 4,000 feet, running for hundreds of miles north and south. It was in these mountains that many of our enemy lived during the day, coming down at night, bringing death and destruction. Many of our artillery targets were in these mountains, including bivouac sites, trails used by the enemy resupplying the VC and NVA soldiers, and ammunition storage areas.

There were three other firebases within range of our position, providing us with additional security. One of these locations, Firebase Roy, had a self-propelled, eight-inch howitzer battery with six guns. Another,

Los Banos, had a 105-howitzer battery, also with six guns. The third one, Firebase Tomahawk, had many units coming and going throughout our stay in Vietnam. A platoon of 101st infantry on the very top of Hill 88 had 81-mm mortars and 4.2-inch mortars.

These infantry soldiers served in the jungle and on the road for a week or more at a time, but there was always a significant group of infantry on the hill with us, providing more security. I never envied their role in this war, watching them pick leeches off one another as they walked back up the hill after a week or so in the jungle, exhausted from their toil.

Firebase Denise was located at the extreme east end of a very straight portion of Highway 1 called the bowling alley. At the other end of this straight 12,000-meter, or nearly eight-mile stretch of road, stood Firebase Tomahawk, where we were to relocate later. This firebase stood in a shallow, saddle-like hill with higher ground on three sides of its position, and was nearly impossible to defend. There had been a long history of tragedy on this hill. Once a truck ran off the hill, killing the driver. There were several casualties from enemy contact, and one accident that killed one or more American soldiers when a guard bunker collapsed during heavy rain. This was no place for any military unit to take up a position, yet the US Army continued to station units at this position until an enormous disaster occurred. We were to play a pivotal role.

THE UNUSUAL

While many successful fire missions were carried out daily, there were various unusual events marking our stay in that location. I received a radio contact from a forward observer flying a LOH (light observation helicopter), claiming there was a squad of enemy moving up a hillside. He requested we fire one gun, one round of high explosive in an effort to stop this squad.

Once we fired the one round, the observer called corrections, and asked for another round to be placed nearby. This continued for about a half hour, while we fired 16 rounds, moving each one further up the slope of the hill in an effort to kill the enemy. Finally, the forward observer called back "end of mission," signaling there was no further shooting to be done. He told me he would get back with me a little later.

A few hours later, this same helicopter landed on our chopper pad and the lieutenant got out and headed for FDC, where I was still on duty. He told me this story. As it turned out, the target was not a squad of infantry, but an adult tiger. The 16th round landed close enough to the animal that the concussion killed the beast. The tiger had only one small wound in its side where a tiny piece of shrapnel entered his body. The lieutenant had been a taxidermist before entering the army, and he had just bagged a prime trophy with a 155-mm howitzer. He promised to bring some photos to me, and sure enough, he did so, a few photos of him with the tiger showing the small wound in its side.

On another occasion, we received a fire mission during the night. The target was two elephants. The Vietcong were using elephants to haul munitions through a railroad tunnel, and it was up to us to stop them. It only took a couple of rounds to kill the hapless animals. On yet another occasion, we had a target that turned out to be a deer. We never knowingly fired at an animal unless there was a clear military objective, as was the case with the two elephants. When a forward observer called a target to us, we fired based on his description of the target, but a few of those targets turned out to be something other than what we were told.

On at least one occasion, we conducted two fire missions simultaneously while each of the forward observers corrected our firing, walking rounds nearer and nearer to their respective targets. We learned later that these two observers were playing a game, walking the rounds nearer their own positions in a game of "chicken." This incident was called into higher headquarters once the ruse was learned, and I hope these two forward observers were taken out of action. Unfortunately, not all American soldiers were fit to serve our country in an admirable fashion.

On one beautiful morning, I was walking from the FDC bunker to our living quarters. I was roughly 12 to 15 feet away, and I heard a very loud gunshot and almost at the same time heard a bullet crash through the ridgepole of the tent used to weatherproof our bunker. In a split second, a 50-caliber round went off and over my head about three or four feet. A soldier was cleaning his 50-caliber machine gun and didn't clear the weapon first or double check. The incident resulted in disciplining the soldier, followed by a proper training exercise. I could have been killed if the weapon had been aimed a little lower. That was one memorable occasion. I never heard of another occurrence anything like that the rest of our tour.

SOME OF THE GOOD TIMES

Not all of our time in Vietnam was work in the firing battery. While all of us were expected to work 12 hours every day, seven days a week, we usually had 12 hours off, although not always. During this time, the off-duty personnel would take care of personal items, writing letters to loved ones back home, doing laundry, getting haircuts, taking occasional trips to the rear (our headquarters in Phu Bai), and sleeping in preparation for another 12 hours on duty.

There were times when the off-duty men could entertain themselves with softballs and gloves, pitching and catching for extended periods. One of the most beautiful beaches in the world was located only a few miles away where men would go for a swim and float on their air mattresses. A few of the men, armed to the teeth, remained ever vigilant, watching for the enemy to appear. They hoped there would be no incidents, and there weren't. We also had the advantage, while at the beach, of having our very own artillery battery we could call upon should there be an enemy attack. We frequently used this time to wash our vehicles, as well. Phu Bai, where we returned for the last several weeks in Vietnam, had a volleyball court on a concrete slab, and we played many vicious games there. Basketball goals were available, and there was a small library. Frequently, movies were shown using a sheet for a screen. We saw some really good movies, but had no popcorn.

Shortly after arriving in country, the maintenance section discovered the whereabouts of a marine vehicle called a mule, and learned that it might be available for trade. A deal was consummated and without knowing all of the details, Charlie Battery maintenance section had a mule, and somewhere there was one fewer typewriter. This vehicle provided many hours of entertainment for the entire battery, and for a few of the Vietnamese children nearby.

One of these children greeted us on our return trip some 35 years later, and that young man had a very good visit with Joey Keeling; each of them remembered the other all these years later. Keeling is a native of Nelson County who lives east of town on the family farm. He was a specialist 4 and one of the better mechanics in the US Army. Not all of our experiences in that part of the world were bad.

I had purchased a tape recorder that included an FM radio and a wireless microphone. One day, while nothing of note was going on, several of us planned a ruse on one of our friends. There had been talk ever since we had arrived that the National Guard units would go home early instead of remaining a full year. A lot of this was simply a time-killing exercise, but there were those who actually thought there was a chance we would return to the states early.

The ruse went something like this. I had purchased a radio shortly after arriving in country and kept it tuned to Armed Forces Radio Vietnam. We decided to use the wireless microphone and two radios, using one to transmit the radio station signal to the second through the microphone, everything seeming to be normal. Then one fellow "interrupted" the broadcast, relating a late and breaking news story about the National Guard going home early. We managed to lure one soldier up to FDC telling him of the news bulletin we had heard. Once he heard the "bulletin," he was certain we would go home soon and left FDC shouting the good news all over the hill. Not long afterward, we heard from him again after he learned of the trickery. I must say he was quite good-natured about the whole thing. I do not remember hearing any further conversation about going home early.

Several of our men brought many talents with them. Certainly, our maintenance section was well prepared when educated by the army, but their knowledge of equipment, engines, and mechanics went way beyond their training. These skills were invaluable to us in Vietnam.

Corporal John Rizer was a butcher by trade, a gun chief in our battery, and he was a good barber. He not only cut hair, but was a good conversationalist while cutting hair and collecting his 50 cents.

Weather was always an issue, with a great deal of heat during the summer season, and cold and rain during the winter monsoon season. Relief during the heat of summer came only at night, while during the monsoon season, relief from cold damp weather was found only in our sleeping bags. Toward the end of our tour of duty, a typhoon brought enormous winds carrying dust and later rain; it made operations outside the shelter of our bunkers quite difficult. However hot it was in I Corps, I know that further south was even hotter, and the monsoon season was much wetter, and therefore was more miserable as well, although those people did not have to deal with the awful cold and wet conditions at the same time.

There were a lot of good times on our firebases, as well as the bad times. Our mail delivery was usually only three or so days from home to the hill. Mail call was one of the biggest lifts I recall while on our tour of duty. Our rear element, consisting of our Supply Sergeant Kent Bischoff, a farmer close to Bardstown, and Specialists Pat Duffy of Louisville, and Private First Class Ronnie Rexroat of Lebanon Junction, Kentucky, always got our mail and supplies to us in a timely fashion.

Christmas brought some special packages from home and the boxes frequently included items made by mom and others—cakes, cookies, and the like. There were packages that were somewhat fragile, and popcorn was used as a packing material. The person receiving the parcel enjoyed the main contents, but his friends usually devoured the popcorn (which had been salted in anticipation of its being eaten). In my case, a package sent to me by my mother that included a jam cake, never arrived because the plane carrying my parcel and many others destined to the soldiers in Vietnam was lost somewhere in Alaska. However, another parcel sent to me by a business friend in Louisville did arrive. My friend was known for his ability to make wonderful fudge. His parcel contained a large amount of this fudge, but buried in the center of the box of homemade candy was a bottle of Maker's Mark, wax seal and all. Little did I know just how many friends I really had.

THINGS CHANGE

Sometime after our arrival at Firebase Denise, we were introduced to something called the infusion program, established to break up units like ours that originated from small towns with virtually all of the members being from a relatively small geographic area. The reason is obvious. Small towns should not suffer out-of-proportion losses to their young men if there were to be a catastrophic event such as an overrun of our firebase, or an errant artillery round or bomb that might kill and maim many individuals. The intention was to replace various members of the battery with other personnel transferred in from other units in country.

In doing this, the unit lost much of the original manpower, men who were used to the work and methods used in Charlie Battery, as well as the camaraderie we had enjoyed for several months. The replacement men were in some cases, but not all, ready for service in an artillery firing battery. Others were misfits that regular army units simply rid themselves of.

This program, while well intentioned, probably offered as many negatives as it did positives. Some of the men who moved to other locations included Corporal Tommy Riggs (later promoted to sergeant), Privates First Class Danny Cheatham, Specialist Bruce King, Privates First Class Teddy Marshall, and David Unseld; Specialist Jim Wray, Specialists Jimmy McGee and Teddy Collins; Staff Sergeant Harold Brown and Sergeant Louis Thompson; and others. While there were certainly advantages to not having so many men from one small community exposed to a catastrophic event, there were certain disadvantages. The work did not flow as well, and accuracy and timing suffered somewhat. The overall result was that our unit— originally among the best firing batteries in Vietnam—was compromised into something closer to an average battery. Our reputation was tarnished. However, we soon were able to make adjustments that resulted in our becoming a highly effective firing battery again.

Some of the men who infused out of our battery into some other army units in Vietnam said that they went to units whose purpose was not held as high as it had been in their original unit. For example, there was a great deal more drug and alcohol abuse, and there was less concern for doing the job right. Cleanliness and order were frequently below the standards set out in our unit, and esprit de corps was, in many cases, lacking. This is not to say the regular army batteries were not doing their jobs, but in some cases, there were individuals in these units who pulled the overall quality down to below the army's normal standards.

Some soldiers were able to return home before the rest of the battery because their obligation was complete, having served their six-year term. First Sergeant Pat Simpson of Fairfield, Kentucky, was one of these, along with Staff Sergeant Kenny (Big) Ice, a gun chief; Staff Sergeant Gary Taylor, our chief of mess section; and Sergeant Kent Bischoff, our supply sergeant, all of Bardstown. While these men and others were happy to return home, it was obvious they also did not want to leave their brothers in arms.

BROTHERS IN COMBAT

There were seven pairs of brothers in Charlie Battery. That had to be a real shock to the regular army units we contacted. There were also many other friends and relatives, including Stewart McClaskey, my second cousin. These relatives and many others who had been lifelong friends and schoolmates were beneficial to the mission of our unit. These relationships provided a second sense as to what was expected in day-to-day activities and our efficiency was enhanced as a result. This is something unavailable to most military organizations anywhere else. On the other hand, new friendships that continue throughout life are frequently started in regular military service. While this is certainly a positive for these units, we feel we had a genuine advantage, and that close relationships served us well.

The seven pairs of brothers included the following men. Ray Ice was a lieutenant at the time, and his older brother Staff Sergeant Kenny Ice, was a gun chief. Staff Sergeant Charles "Skippy" Stone was a gun chief, and served with his brother, Specialist William D. Stone. Their cousins, Sergeant David Stone, and another gun chief, Private First Class Stanley Stone, were in the battery. First Sergeant Pat Simpson and his brother, Sergeant Mike Simpson, were both from the Bloomfield/Fairfield area of Kentucky. Specialist David Collins and his brother, Specialist Wayne Collins, were on gun crews; David lost his life and Wayne was critically wounded at Firebase Tomahawk. Their cousin, Specialist Teddy Collins, was also in our battery. Corporal James D. Simpson and his brother, Private John R. Simpson, were both on gun crews. Specialist Joe Shelburne and his brother, Specialist Kenneth Shelburne, and Private Gary Lewis and his brother, Private Wayne Lewis, were all in Charlie Battery.

The battery was made up of men from many walks of life—factory workers, professional men, managers, business owners, and farmers. However, the many pairs of brothers, plus cousins, in-laws, and other relatives, made the battery unique. It was of great concern should there be a large loss of life affecting families back home, but there were advantages, as well. With such close relationships, communication was easy and efficiency was at a maximum. Some of these qualities resulted from the long-standing relationships that occurred beyond family. Many of our group went to school together, played together, and were sometimes on either the same teams or opposing teams in organized sports.

While the United States Army's average age was, and still is 19, our average age was closer to 24. This brought an immense amount of experience and maturity to our battery. We also had many who were college graduates, and we were better educated in general than the average army unit. All of this positively affected our unit, and it showed.

Our mess section consisted of several very good cooks, capable of preparing food fit for almost anyone, frequently under quite an array of difficult circumstances, but we always ate well. Many times, we ate food that was better than that which was scheduled for us because our cooks managed to "acquire" some finer foodstuffs.

The generosity of the people of Bardstown brought many things of value to support our cause, such as refrigerators and washing machines. However, we also had to be ingenious to make life better while away from home. One item acquired at home for our use was a large freezer, which we managed to take with us wherever we went. In Vietnam, we located a generator, and was always power for the freezer. The cooks kept that freezer filled with great food.

Early on, someone in our battery located a wing tank off an air force jet, acquired it, and next thing we knew, we had a shower available. We hauled water from an army purification plant located close to one of the many local streams. Plumbing supplies appeared and a hot shower was in place. We heated water with a gasoline garbage-can water heater. The shower was a welcome addition, especially during the hot, dry season. We found it much easier to sleep once we had a hot shower. Ingenuity was our best friend.

All over South Vietnam, American forces were required to burn human waste in an effort to control disease. That job was not very popular among our troops, but it happened every day or so anyway. There was a door in the rear of the outhouses found on every firebase or other area under the command of US forces. We would open the door, drag out the half barrels, add diesel fuel, and light them. This job would last for an hour or so. A clean up was performed at the same time, and the outhouse was ready for use for another day or two. It did not smell so good while this was going on, but the result was a clean facility for all to use and everyone benefited.

While we supported the 101st Airborne Division, we shot many fire missions using an enormous amount of munitions. Some of these munitions were secret and somewhat experimental, and we were among the first to use them in combat. We had some rounds that were referred to simply as special munitions. This round carried about 60 small bomblets that, once deployed overhead, would disperse and cover a large area with anti-personnel, grenade-like explosions. These same munitions were used in some bombs carried by air force and navy planes. Although we were also qualified to fire other sensitive weapons, we were never called upon to use them.

War is such nasty business, with no winners. There really is little difference in warfare over the centuries, only a difference in the technologies used. Maiming and death is the same, only the safety to those inflicting the carnage has improved; or has it?

THE FIRST OF OUR LOSSES

In the spring of 1969, we conducted something called a "hip-shoot." We packed up the entire firing battery and fire direction, left the firebase, and went to another location. Once there, we went through the process of "laying the guns," and otherwise setting up shop so we could fire on targets that we couldn't hit from our regular firebase. This exercise took place on Firebase Tomahawk, and was to last for only a few hours, at the conclusion of which we would pack up again and return to our regular base, Firebase Denise. On the morning of this move, March 6, 1969, a very dense fog limited visibility to 50 feet or so. Our mission was to fire on enemy targets—I suppose in a surprise attack—in an effort to render them less able to continue the fight.

A light observation combat helicopter (LOCH) arrived, accompanied by one or two Cobra gunships, riding shotgun with the smaller chopper. The helicopter picked up our battery commander, Captain Lyle Thompson, a career army officer who had taken command a few months earlier. He was to be the observer calling for fire from our now relocated firing battery. First Sergeant Pat Simpson of Bloomfield, Kentucky, was to ride with Captain Thompson, but there was not enough room for him in the chopper—luckily for Pat.

The helicopters flew out in the dense fog and soon Captain Thompson started calling grid coordinates to us, and the battery started firing the missions. Very soon after the firing commenced, there was no further radio contact with the captain. We found out several days later that all of the helicopters had been shot down or involved in mid-air collisions, and there were no survivors. A squad of long-range patrol from the 101st Airborne Division located the wreckage and recovered the remains of those who died. This was the first time Charlie Battery lost one of its men, but it certainly was not the last.

It was questionable at the time and even today, why we relocated for this mission, since the target area was within reach of our home base. With the dense fog, it was certainly a hazardous move to fly into enemy-controlled country.

When an American soldier dies in combat, there is always a reason he died, and that usually is distilled down to a set of circumstances that were to lead to a bad conclusion. Some of these deaths are not preventable, because it's not possible to avoid every single set of circumstances. In the case of Captain Thompson, those circumstances that led to his death were at least somewhat predictable, and there was even discussion among some of us that the chance he took in going into that heavy fog was a bad decision. Does this mean he never had a chance of emerging with his life? Not so. We cannot always predict the outcome of our actions, but surely it is prudent to consider all of the possibilities one might face, and the potential of meeting death or great harm. In this case, Thompson went ahead with his mission in the face of terrible flying conditions, and it cost him and others their lives. Lieutenant Tom Eatmon, our executive officer, was promoted to battery commander.

MOVE, SHOOT, AND COMMUNICATE

In April 1969, we closed Firebase Denise, destroyed all of our bunkers and defensive positions, and moved the battery to Firebase Tomahawk. We stayed there a short time, and then moved to a point about 40 or so miles away to a village called Roung Roung, in the Elephant Valley, a part of the A Shau Valley. The infamous Hamburger Hill, where many American lives were lost, was not far away. It was one of the most notorious sites of disaster during the entire war.

We did not dismiss knowledge of this sort. We feared that we would be in this same level of danger. This was quite an adventure. The entire battery and elements of the 101st traveled on what had once been a one-lane road, but had been washed out and bombed to the point of needing a complete rebuild. An army engineer outfit was in the lead with bulldozers and crews opening a path that would allow us entry into the valley. The trip took about a day and a half. We set up in a low, flat area to stay the night.

Then it rained—boy, did it rain—flooding our position and creating general chaos. Fire direction had pulled the armored personnel carrier into a pit created by one of the bulldozers, and water filled the hole, chasing us out in the middle of the night. Next morning, we gathered up wet belongings and continued our trek.

At our destination, we were expecting a great deal of firing in support of a large operation in that area. As it turned out, the tour in this area was of little consequence and not much shooting occurred. This operation lasted about two weeks, and the greatest excitement was in the two-day adventure getting there: making the trip through the jungle, traveling non-existent roads, clinging to the sides of mountains, and fording streams. The greatest amount of time was spent waiting for engineers to make a road in front of us, while we all took up guard positions, hoping the enemy would not attack us while we were stopped, and they didn't. Overall, it was quite an adventure with little to show as a result.

However, before we arrived in this new valley in anticipation of a large battle, Sergeant Jerry Janes and Staff Sergeant Buck Harned went out by helicopter to pick out a location and organize the battery's position. Their arrival was non-eventful, and they completed their job and simply waited for the rest of the battery to arrive. As it turned out, travel to this position was far more difficult, and consequently took much longer to accomplish. The road snaked up the sides of mountains, and crossed streams, resulting in equipment breakdowns. Engineers, moving ahead of us, had to rebuild the roadway. This delay resulted in a 40-mile or so adventure becoming a two-day event instead of one day. We had to set up a defensive position in an otherwise unknown spot on the map, and then it rained heavily during the night. The mess of the following morning delayed progress further, but we arrived in the afternoon of the following day. Harned and Janes unexpectedly spent a night with no support, and only the rest of their meager C rations to eat. We were in a position to fire artillery for them if needed, but that is of little comfort for men caught unexpectedly in "Indian Country" with a rifle and little else. Janes recalled how dark it was that night and how brightly Harned's cigarette glowed.

A South Vietnamese 105 artillery battery flew in and set up next to us as part of the overall plan of attack. We liked to observe this battery and watch how they performed as an operating unit.

Their mess section, or meal preparation area, consisted of a large iron pot located under a single tree. Water and other mystery ingredients seemed to be always boiling over a fire built from wood scraps and other firewood. I recall that a whole chicken, featherless, but otherwise pretty much unmolested, with a piece of wire tied around its neck, went into the pot. When mealtime arrived, the chicken was removed and hung in a nearby tree, and broth was served to the battery. Later the chicken went back in the boiling pot, I assume in preparation of the next meal. We were not interested in knowing what this meal might be like.

We learned our next position—Firebase Tomahawk. We started planning our move back to the one firebase we all knew was not a good position to occupy.

WE MOVE AGAIN

I was assigned to take a crew of about 10 men back out of the valley to Firebase Tomahawk to establish a new firebase. We left camp early one morning following a stormy night with heavy rain. We rode in a 548, an ammunition track carrier for one of the guns. Almost immediately, we found fresh tiger tracks. I had the vehicle stop and got off to look at these tracks.

They were huge, about the size of a dinner plate. On top of that, the area of the track made by claws of the tiger's foot was slightly caving in as I watched, indicating the animal had just passed through only seconds before. We never saw the tiger, but I am sure he saw us. This trip took the better part of a day to complete and we arrived safely at Firebase Tomahawk with a new position to construct before the remaining battery joined us a week later.

Our job was to construct a new fire direction center bunker and have it ready to occupy as soon as the battery arrived. We did this during daylight hours in sweltering heat. At night, we slept on top of an abandoned bunker, because it was too hot inside to sleep. One night I woke up to a series of explosions that sounded very different from anything I had ever heard. I woke up the others and moved everyone inside the abandoned bunker. An enemy somewhere in the jungle had just mortared us. The first rounds landed on the slope below our position, successive rounds walked up the slope, and the last round landed on the hill just a few feet from where we had been sleeping. We were lucky that evening as the enemy simply overshot our position. The platoon from the 101st on the highest part of the hill saw the mortars flash as they were launched and fired a machine gun in the general area with no known effect. We stayed up and alert for the rest of the evening and early morning until daylight, when we continued work on the bunker.

This bunker and others were constructed using eight-foot long, 12-by-12-inch timbers, as both posts and beams. Perforated steel plate, an interlocking system used as airstrip surfacing in combat zones, covered the spans. On top of this plating, we used plastic and tarpaulin, covered with three layers of sandbags to ward off an attack from RPGs. We were about half-finished with the work when the rest of the battery arrived to occupy Tomahawk.

Once the rest of the battery arrived, the gun positions were completed, and we continued our mission of supporting the 101st Airborne Division in their daily operations. Life was normal again as we fired hundreds of rounds daily.

Our mess section set up a nice kitchen and mess hall. Sleeping quarters were fashioned as bunkers for each of the gun sections: maintenance section, communication section, fire direction center, exec post, and headquarters. Everyone had his own small space to call home, at least temporarily, including fighting positions in the event of an attack. We finished the set-up not a moment too soon.

A LIFE-CHANGING EVENT FOR BARDSTOWN

For several weeks, FDC had planned to provide charcoal-grilled hamburgers with all the trimmings for the battery. To this end, we had had conversations with the soldiers in control of some of the food stored in Phu Bai, and we were allowed basically unfettered access to those stores of food that presumably were earmarked for the officers' club. We acquired two cases of hamburger patties, some potatoes and other trimmings, onions, tomatoes, pickles, and the like, and a considerable amount of ice. Next, we went to the PX storage yard called the beer depot. We helped ourselves to several cases of our favorite beers, sodas, and the like, and then we went back to Tomahawk, about 20 miles or so away. When we acquired the hamburger patties, we decided that we also needed one of the metal shelves from the freezer to use as a grill. We gave all this to the mess section, some of the scrap dunnage lumber was converted to charcoal, and we were set.

On the evening of June 18, 1969, we had a large meal of hamburgers and all the trimmings, a real treat. There were beer and soft drinks for those who wanted them, and then we showed a movie in the maintenance section tent, where vehicles were serviced and minor repairs made. I believe the movie was *You Only Live Twice*, and every space was taken. Meanwhile, there was a rainstorm raging outside, as hard as any rain I had ever witnessed. Little did any of us know the rainstorm was just the cover Charlie needed to take positions against us without anyone's knowledge.

When the movie ended, it was late and those of us not on duty that night returned to our bunkers for some sleep. The rain had stopped only a few minutes before.

At about 1:45 the next morning, June 19, there were several explosions, all of them sounding strange. At the same time, Specialist Tom Raisor was waking me for the next shift change, which was to occur at two o'clock. It is far too simple to say that all hell broke out; that is a trite expression for what happened. From this time until a little after five o'clock, there was shooting, firing of RPGs, satchel charges, and hand-to-hand fighting as we struggled to survive for another day. In the end, 14 Americans died, another 44 were wounded, many critically. Four of the six guns were destroyed, and all bunkers were destroyed except the fire direction center. Since FDC was the only bunker still intact, the men brought all of the wounded to us, and our medic and others gave first aid treatment until help arrived and medevac helicopters evacuated the injured.

This story cannot be told properly without including the real heroics of our medic, Specialist Roger Coffey. He was a trained medic from Louisville and a member of Headquarters Battery, assigned to Charlie Battery for the duration of our tour of duty. Like all of the others in Charlie Battery, he became alert instantly on hearing the first round of enemy fire. He immediately dressed, picked up his medical bag, and awaited his call to a horrendous duty. He treated several men soon after the battle started. He came to the FDC bunker when he realized that all hell was breaking out, that the FDC was the best-defended bunker on the hill, and that wounded were already being brought there. A total of 44 wounded men were brought to the FDC; at least one of them later died from his wounds. All were comforted and treated by Coffey. Those of us who were not shooting out doors and vents at the enemy assisted. While there were some wounds that were not life threatening, many were horrific and life drained out of several men with every beat of their hearts.

Somehow, Coffey was able to sort these people out and treat those in the worst condition in a bunker designed to house 10 soldiers, under the most impossible conditions of darkness, foul air from explosions all around us, and unbelievable over-crowding. He went from one to another, seeking the most critical cases, and then pressed others into service, some of them wounded themselves, to hold a flashlight or to keep pressure on a blood vessel to control bleeding. Use of flashlights was limited by having to keep any light from the enemy's view that might invite an attack on us, further complicating his work.

Coffey's adrenaline was apparently flowing at peak levels, and he is credited with saving many lives. I recall one man with a terrible leg wound who was laid on my bunk. His blood completely soaked through my sleeping bag and ran onto the floor beneath my cot. It was difficult to control his bleeding, but our medic finally was able to save this man's life and his efforts led to a full recovery. Several similar stories come to mind, but the bottom line is that without expert services provided by Roger Coffey on that terrible night, the death toll of 14 Americans certainly would have been a great deal higher. He is credited with saving numerous lives, and at the same time, he provided care to those not critically injured. He dressed their wounds and helped many up the hill to the air ambulances once they began to arrive.

Coffey was awarded the Silver Star because of his service that night, but he earned a great deal more than that. He probably should have been awarded something a great deal higher, but the Army higher-ups had become stingy by then when it came to awards. He certainly won the hearts of those in the battery, and many people in Bardstown and environs when their loved ones came home, due to his tremendous service.

Sergeant Jerry Janes, on gun number one, had been firing our self-defense plan and had run out of ammunition when things got hot. He and others in the gun decided that they needed to get out of the gun and fight from a position in the bunker area. As they ran for the cover of the soil berm that surrounded the gun, a rocket-propelled grenade hit the gun, killing two who not yet made it out. They were Private Gerald Daley and Private Larry Kinder, two of the infusees who had entered the battery a month or two earlier. One of these men was scheduled to leave for home the next day, his one-year tour completed. This was also true for another regular army man who had transferred into Charlie Battery.

Janes suffered non life-threatening burns that took him out of Vietnam for good. After a stay in an American military hospital in Yokohama, Japan, he returned to the states for the balance of our tour. His new station was Fort Knox, Kentucky.

Our only source of help during the three-and-a-half-hour attack was the radio we had in the FDC and a call went out immediately. Several gunships arrived to help fight off the enemy. A couple of infantry units on the ground started making their way toward us, but they were quite a distance away and would not be useful. Sometime during the fight, the batteries used to power the radios went dead; the radios were our lifeline to our headquarters and infantry units. The batteries needed to be recharged. It was my job to go outside to start the generator to restore power, since I was chief of section and knew how the generators functioned. I certainly was not going to send someone else out into such an embattled locale, so I donned my flak-jacket and helmet, and carrying my M-16, left the safety of the bunker and made my way to the generator pit several yards away.

Staff Sergeant Charles "Skippy" Stone saw my movement in the darkness. He aimed his rifle at my silhouette, thinking I was an enemy soldier, but did not pull the trigger when he determined his target might be one of his own. Lucky me. Stone fired at a lot of enemy soldiers that morning, but I do not know how many he might have hit. The generator started easily, and I made my way back to the bunker. I didn't know what Stone had done until Jim Wilson was told while researching his book, *The Sons of Bardstown.*

One remark that I will never forget came from Specialist Jodie Haydon, who was beside me most of that night during this fight. Referring to news of the disaster, he said, "This is going to kill a lot of people in Bardstown."

Certainly, people in Bardstown and nearby areas were very concerned for the safety of loved ones serving in Vietnam. The news was, in fact, devastating to our friends and loved ones back home. It did not take long for the information to arrive in Bardstown through the news media, and the damage back home was soon underway.

With radio communication intact, we were able to call for help and communicate with headquarters back in Camp Gia Le. Help was sent as quickly as it could be scrambled into action. While it seemed like hours before helicopters circled us, they actually arrived within 30 minutes or so. There were at least two Cobra gunships firing rockets, mini-guns, and grenades; medevac or air ambulances; and an old Army C-47, known as "Puff the Magic Dragon," carrying four mini-guns and illumination flares. This incredible hell-raising fighting machine was most welcome since the flares not only illuminated our perimeter so we could see to fire on the enemy, the mini-guns fired all around our hill, killing anyone unlucky enough to be on the acre or so of land devastated each minute the firing continued. I feel certain that arrival of these instruments of war prompted the enemy to quit and leave. However, there is still debate over this issue.

As it turned out, the enemy left shortly after a green flare was fired into the night sky. The lone prisoner taken from this battle confirmed that was the signal to withdraw. He explained that the signal should have been red since the enemy had the upper hand, and a lot of our unit was no longer able to fight. Another battalion of the North Vietnamese Regular Army was to come in and finish off every living person. What can you say to that?

As it turned out, the enemy was a very well organized army unit from North Vietnam, with one battalion, about 250 to 300 men in the initial attack and a second unit of similar size in reserve. Had the second unit entered the hill that night, I would not have written this, but instead some Vietnamese soldier would have written of his victory.

Could it be that their intent was to bring devastation to a small town because they knew of our National Guard status? We do not know, but such a calamity would have been a major victory to the Vietnamese if they had been able to wipe out the entire battery. As it was, they did a pretty good job of disabling a firing battery that was a serious threat to them.

In the aftermath, we learned that the NVA had entered from high ground and immediately killed two guards of the 101st Airborne Division at our southern edge, while other elements climbed up the hill on three sides and laid in wait—all of this during the heavy downpour. As soon as the battle erupted, a call on the radio alerted our headquarters and they sent several gunships and alerted those needing to know. While we were fighting for our lives, there was another coordinated attack a few miles up the road at Firebase Roy where an eight-inch howitzer battery was located. This unit was therefore unable to fire in our defense, part of the enemy's well thought-out plan.

Perhaps one of the most remembered sights on the hill following the battle was our American flag still flying at the command post. While it had never fallen, there were numerous bullet holes and burns from flying hot shrapnel, marking forever the effects of a night many of us thought would be our last night in this world. With determination, fortified by God, our battery of men was able to fend off this attack and live to fight another day.

Father Resch, who had previously been our chaplain, was leaving Vietnam, his tour completed. Father Resch was a Catholic chaplain for the 101st Airborne Division, and he visited our firebases weekly to say mass. He stopped by on his way to the Da Nang airport to express his condolences and offer a prayer for those who were lost. He was a favorite among all of us, regardless of which faith we followed, and we have never forgotten him.

HEROES OF CHARLIE BATTERY

Apparently, the alarm was sounded because Specialist David Collins had gone to the mess hall to pick up a snack or cup of coffee. He discovered an enemy soldier standing there eating something he had stolen from our food supplies. Items had been found missing a few days before, but no one imagined enemy soldiers had breached our defenses. Collins apparently yelled to his fellow guardsmen that there were gooks in the mess hall. Collins was shot from behind by an enemy soldier, and fell in the entrance of his own bunker. His discovery and sounding of the alarm probably saved many of the other soldiers on the hill that night. Collins was the first to die that deadly morning.

Specialist Joseph Ronald (Ronnie) McIlvoy was sleeping in his bunker when the attack was unleashed. He woke up, along with other guardsmen, at the first sounds of disaster. Sappers with satchel charges unmercifully attacked the communication bunker. We suspect that the NVA thought this was the location of the fire direction center and that destruction of this element would disable the entire battery. All within had no choice but to run out another exit to escape the enormous explosions and terror.

As McIlvoy ran from the bunker in the dark, he was beside Specialist Larry Johnson. They ran for cover in another area, probably the fire direction center, which was closest to them. Only a few yards outside their bunker, a satchel charge went off, knocking both of them to the ground. Apparently, McIlvoy fell on another satchel charge and his body took the greatest force of the explosion, thus protecting Johnson. Johnson suffered only damage to his ears; McIlvoy died instantly.

Staff Sergeant Jim Moore was asleep in his bunker, since he was on the day shift, and woke up to the explosions. He ran immediately to his howitzer, and "buttoned up." He got inside and closed the hatches, and proceeded to fire a defensive plan that we had prepared earlier. I don't know if he got off any rounds or not, but soon afterward, his gun was hit by a rocket-propelled grenade, and the spewing molten metal ignited powder inside the gun. The resulting flash fire fatally burned him and the other men inside.

Moore was a big, tough, but gentle man, and he was the only one who exited the gun. He walked into the FDC bunker, which was filling with men with all sorts of serious wounds. I spoke to him and did what I could to make him comfortable. He was evacuated later in the morning by a Huey medevac helicopter. He died on a hospital ship in Da Nang harbor five days later; the cause was third-degree burns over most of his body.

Ronnie Simpson was sleeping in his bunker with others in communication. In his efforts to escape certain death inside the bunker, he ran toward the exec post and was the victim of rifle fire. Anyone leaving the communication bunker who survived action in this area was fortunate. The previous firing battery had left this bunker intact. It was the one we occupied when we started building the new firebase, the same bunker that protected the guys and me.

First Sergeant Luther Chappel was shot just outside his bunker. He was apparently trying to move to the exec post to help direct defenses against an overwhelming enemy. It was his job to see to the defense of our position no matter where we were located.

Men were brought into the FDC with an enormous array of wounds and burns. One of the devastating tools of war, the satchel charge, was used extensively on Tomahawk. When a satchel charge landed on the ground in a bunker, the explosion loosened the ground itself, blew it in all directions, and drove it deeply into human flesh, blinding some victims.

Staff Sergeant Buck Harned was chief of the firing battery, and had a terrible amount of this soil, consisting of sand and fine gravel, blown deep into his body, particularly his arms. For the rest of his life, about 35 years, Harned found grains of this debris working out of his body. It would first become a lump under his skin, then the skin would rupture, and a small rock or grain of sand would come out.

When the fighting stopped, daylight soon followed. With first light, choppers began to arrive at the top of the hill where the 101st was located. Several of the survivors manned stretchers. The mess hall screen door, blown off during the attack, was also pressed into service as a stretcher. Several of the wounded were transported to a chopper aboard the screen door, others on the available stretchers. There was a seemingly endless parade of medevac helicopters arriving, picking up the wounded, and leaving for a hospital back in Phu Bai. Forty-four wounded and 12 dead were evacuated to the rear in Phu Bai, and two of the wounded later passed away.

A couple of days later, there was a memorial service for our fallen comrades. Unfortunately, the entire battery knew how to prepare for this ceremony, having done a similar one when our battery commander, Captain Lyle Thompson, lost his life. In this ceremony, there is a display of a poncho—rain gear folded and placed on the ground—on which the victim's boots are displayed. His rifle, with bayonet attached, is stuck in the ground, and his helmet placed on top of the rifle. This ritual allows the surviving comrades an opportunity to mourn the soldier's death and to remember him in any way they see fit. On this occasion, there were 10 such displays set up as a temporary memorial to our fallen comrades. Four more would be located somewhere with the 101st Airborne Division.

Looking back on the deaths of these brave fighting men, I draw one conclusion; none of them could have predicted the circumstances that led to their deaths. This was different from that fateful decision made by Captain Lyle Thompson. His choice to fly in dense fog played at least some part in his death.

However, there are too many circumstances in war that end in wounding or death to analyze and determine what should or should not be considered. In a war situation, there is a general plan based on many years of experience by past military commands that dictates how we are to proceed, and then there are new circumstances that cause a change in this plan, sometimes resulting in adversity.

Soon after the events of June 19, 1969, we learned of the deaths of Specialist Jim Wray and Staff Sergeant Harold Brown. I met Brown on the night of April 20, 1964, when I was sworn into the National Guard by then Captain Harold O. Loy; Brown was the only other man sworn in that night. We became instant friends from that time on; he was from Mount Washington, Kentucky, and I was from Bardstown. Brown was among the first wave of soldiers to be infused out of the battery and he was not happy about it. In another firing battery somewhere else in Vietnam, his unit came under attack one night. I understand he was ordered by some lieutenant to send someone outside his protected position in a bunker to get a flashlight that was lying on the ground and turned on. Brown, a very good NCO, was unable to order anyone to such a dangerous duty and so did it himself. While outside his bunker, he was fatally shot. This was another situation in which one might have predicted impending doom, and it was obviously a bad decision by his commander. Perhaps his commander should have asked someone to shoot the light out rather than place an American life in peril.

Jim Wray had transferred out of the battery when infusion started. He lost his life on July 2, 1969, serving in B Battery, First Battalion of 40th Regiment, 108th Artillery Group. Cause of death was "non hostile, other—accident, ground casualty." We had all heard that he was killed in a friendly fire incident, but no other details were ever made available to us.

Friendly fire is something that is unavoidable in the heat of battle and occurs more than anyone wants to admit. While it is a terrible abuse of good soldiers, the cause, while it may be friendly fire of some sort, is still attributable to enemy action; otherwise, there would be no fire of any kind.

Several other men were burned when powder was ignited inside the howitzers. Some of these men died, while others were burned to varying degrees. Any such form of a burn was an automatic trip back to the States, because the environment in Vietnam was not conducive to healing deep burns. Infections occurred frequently if these patients were allowed to remain in country.

Bullets caused several wounds, but huge explosions of RPG rounds and satchel charges caused many more. One of the infused soldiers had a bullet wound in the upper arm near the elbow that missed any bone, and was a simple wound to treat. A small bit of muscle exited with the bullet and was hanging outside his skin. A few very serious gaping wounds were due to flying debris. Many of these people owe their lives to our medic.

The next day, replacement guns and crews arrived from each of our sister batteries. We hurriedly cleaned up the aftermath of the previous evening's attack; bodies of 28 dead Vietnamese were dragged off and unceremoniously disposed of. Bunkers were minimally repaired, wire communication was reestablished, and the battery was ready for fire missions by around noon. There was some firing, mostly H&Is, but there was a lot more going on in the minds of those who had just survived the most intense night of horror imaginable.

The soldiers who were lost were friends and relatives of the survivors. The wounded that had been evacuated were sorely missed; many of them would not return to do battle with us again. Our overall effectiveness was questionable soon after such a fight. Then there was nightfall to deal with once again, coming much too quickly after the attack. Those of us who remained and those who were temporary replacements felt an enormous amount of trepidation and fear. During this first night, there were many sounds indicating the enemy was not far away. I am certain this was an effort to further reduce our effectiveness as a fighting unit. Several gunshots rang out during the evening, probably more out of fear than anything else. Nobody slept that first night, whether on or off duty.

CONCLUSIONS

All of this speaks to the enormous ability of the Vietnamese, in this case the North Vietnamese Army regulars, to plan and conduct battle in their homeland. Therein lies the problem we faced the entire war, namely that we were involved in a civil war, that this war was on the homeland ground of our enemy, and that the enemy was a very well-trained and formidable force. I am not certain that our leadership ever thought of the enemy as being so well prepared to fight, and that the fight on their homeland was an enormous disadvantage to us. Our efforts to change the government surely could never have met with success because of the immense dedication the Communist government had instilled into their large and well-trained army, on their homeland soil. We were simply at a disadvantage from the start.

Not only were the NVA regulars a well-trained and expertly led army from the North, they were also well supplied with weaponry. Many of them carried Russian AK-47 rifles; others carried the Chinese Communist SKS, both firing a 7.62-mm round. These weapons operated at top efficiency regardless of weather, dust, and dirt, or other issues that were always a concern with our weapons. The craftsmanship of these rifles was dedicated to efficiency of operation, while no consideration was given to looks. The soldiers also carried a crude, but effective, grenade provided by the Chinese. It was made of cast iron and wood, filled with black gunpowder, and had a primitive fuse that might or might not go off. This grenade also had an eyelet cast into the body that would allow the small bomb to be hung above the ground. A string was tied to the fuse and strung across a path, creating a perfect trap that killed and maimed many American and South Vietnamese soldiers.

The rocket-propelled grenade (RPG) was the enemy's most devastating weapon; it was fired using a launcher resting on a shoulder. Some of these launchers were merely a section of bamboo with a triggering device attached. This round was similar to the bazooka used in World War II and contained a shaped charge that, upon making contact with one of our howitzers, would instantly burn a small hole through the armor, spraying hot molten metal inside, burning the men, and igniting gunpowder.

The satchel charge was another devastating weapon; it was a very simple, but deadly, block of TNT with a fuse. Soldiers called sappers carried these charges in bags. Sappers would enter under the cover of fire from all directions and throw one of these satchel charges through a doorway into a bunker. The explosion would pick up anything inside, and slammed items and debris in all directions. Impact from these flying items was frequently fatal, as was the concussion of the blast. With perhaps 20 or so of these sappers running in all directions, throwing satchel charges here and there, the enemy certainly had the upper hand during the confusion. Satchel charges and RPGs caused a great deal of damage to Firebase Tomahawk.

As a defense against RPGs, chain link fencing was installed around some of the gun positions. Following the battle, several RPGs were found hanging in the fencing; their targets were protected from those particular rounds. This was a defensive move on the part of American forces not used as frequently and as well as it might have been.

Looking back on our experiences at Firebase Tomahawk, I recall several things that were just not right. For example, the guard bunkers we had erected around our unit were quite ineffective since they each contained 50-caliber machine guns that could not fire in a depressed condition, pointing downhill. This use of manpower, as well as the guns, was a waste under these circumstances. Several 55-gallon barrels of jellied gasoline had been delivered some time before our attack. However, these were never installed with the needed triggering devices. The battery commander had used some of our available manpower on otherwise idle days to paint white the rocks that lined either side of a path leading to the command post. This seemingly silly action was of no apparent benefit in the end, and only pointed out the location of those in command of the unit. This is where our First Sergeant Chappel died on the 19th. Our battery commander, Captain Charles Harbin, was on emergency home leave at the time, attending the funeral of his sister who had died in an auto accident in Kentucky.

It is difficult to determine if any of these issues really contributed to the events of June 19, 1969, since the enemy had time during the rainstorm to deactivate the defensive weapons. I am not certain how we could have defended our position, given the fact that higher ground was found in most all directions, and defense of such a position is automatically more difficult. I just know that none of this would likely have happened if we had still been located on Firebase Denise. We will never know for sure.

OPINION

We had it good on our firebases, unlike grunts, or foot soldiers who were in the bush for days or weeks at a time. Our day was somewhat predictable and we were relatively safe from attack most of the time, with notable exceptions. We usually had hot meals while the infantry had C rations perhaps once or twice a day, and little else. C rations were not bad for the most part, but a steady diet of them would get old very quickly. We had a defensive position that we could depend on for basic safety and relative comfort. The grunts were constantly in a dangerous position and unpleasant conditions of rain, cold, and terrible heat. Our position was easily resupplied with food, ammunition, and other supplies, and daily mail. The infantry frequently had to wait for a week or more for any of these items. Tension was certainly a greater issue with the infantry, but the guys handling 98-pound projectiles on a busy night were probably more worn out at shift change. There were many differences between the two offensive military units, but we probably had it better in the end.

General Hal Moore, a lieutenant colonel in 1965, and battalion commander of the First Battalion, Seventh Cavalry, learned just how well trained this enemy was. On one of Moore's seven return visits to North Vietnam and South Vietnam, he met with the commander of the forces he fought off in the Ia Drang Valley in the Central Highlands in November 1965. The enemy had his unit outnumbered by eight to one, but the largest number of casualties was on the side of the North Vietnamese regulars. This might not have been the outcome had it not been for the immense dedication Moore had instilled in his men, as well as the new tools of war—the helicopters. On his return visit, he learned firsthand just how dedicated the enemy was, and how well trained and disciplined they were.

General Moore is a former Bardstonian, and a graduate of Saint Joe Prep High School and West Point Military Academy. The two books describing his unit's actions in 1965 are required reading for anyone entering military academies in all US military armed forces. They are a great read for anyone wanting to know important details of the Vietnam War.

US involvement in the war resulted in many awards to various members of Charlie Battery. I received the Army Commendation Medal and a Bronze Star with V Device, as did others in the battery. I am quite proud of my service in this time of war and the service of all of my brothers in combat.

However, the fact is that the war was conducted with anything but military objectives being at the core of decisions. I am not quite sure just what was behind the war, but military decisions were supplanted by some force here in the US, whether the US Congress, or some other force, leaving many people wondering just why we were there in the first place. This leads one to wonder if the 58,000-plus deaths of Americans, seven of whom were guardsmen from Charlie Battery, carried a justifiable worth. It is hard to imagine that these lives were, in fact, of any value to this nation's objectives, leading one to wonder if there was any right in what we were doing there in the first place. I had always tended to think that we were, in fact, there for a good purpose, but little doubt remains that our losses in that war were for the wrong reason or for no reason.

REST AND RECUPERATION

While in the war zone, all members of the armed forces were entitled to one R&R in a country on that side of the planet, and another located in a "safe" area of Vietnam. Trips were available to places such as Sydney, Tokyo, Seoul, Hawaii, Bangkok, and Hong Kong. While expenses at these sites were all on the soldier, our armed forces paid for the trip.

These trips lasted for five days and were always welcome by the weary soldier who had seen much too much death, injury, and destruction. There were many opportunities for us to see sights that we might not otherwise see in our lifetimes and have some most memorable experiences. Similar experiences were available with the in-country R&R, usually at China Beach or another location further south. While I never was able to go to the in-country location, I was fortunate to experience two trips to Tokyo. I suppose this was because there was no room at the in-country site, but I never did know for sure. These trips allowed a soldier to relax and clear his mind before returning to the scene of destruction and resuming his job. No one ever complained about a trip away from war.

PROBLEMS

Drugs were never an issue with our guys until the infusion program picked up speed, and more and more draftees and regular army soldiers arrived, some of them bringing their bad habits with them. Even then, I'm not aware of any major issues with drugs and heavy drinking. There were those few who would drink too many beers on occasion, but I never found anyone who was unable to function and do his job properly and accurately. Probably this is a result of our chiefs of sections, the non-commissioned officers and original National Guardsmen, who were with the battery from call-up until time to go home. Liquor and beer were both available from the PXs located in areas where there were greater concentrations of soldiers, such as Phu Bai, Da Nang, and Camp Eagle, home of the 101st Airborne Division.

Beer was delivered on very large pallets and handled with big forklift trucks, and was available in several brands. The alcohol content was low in this beer; I believe it was 3.2 percent. Several brands came in at the same time and there was a scramble once a shipment arrived. Soldiers able to travel to the beer depot tried to get there as soon as possible so they could pick up their favorite brands. Carling Black Label was always the last of the beer to be sold. When they were out of Carling, they were out of beer.

The PXs were great places to break monotony while shopping among the bargains for photographic equipment, stereo apparatus, and clothing that might be used on upcoming R&Rs. We could get pictures developed and buy snack items. We were out from Phu Bai about 40 miles away, so visits to such places were not frequent, but the few times we were able to go there, the PX was a welcome short relief.

BROTHERS IN BATTLE

National Guard military units are quite different from other units consisting of career soldiers, draftees, and others who volunteered for the military (or who were told, in a few cases, to join the military or go to jail). Guardsmen are all volunteers, are most often older by a few years, and are usually better educated. They are also closer—the men are often related or grew up together, and stayed together throughout their military obligation.

Family connections are regularly found throughout the National Guard, including cousins, uncles, in-laws, and brothers. Charlie Battery had their fair share of these relationships, both family and friendships stemming from childhood. Most of these men were well acquainted with one another through neighborhood connections, and had been educated in the same schools long before joining the Guard. In our case, we also had seven pairs of brothers, in addition to all the other associations. All of these relationships served our mission well, since there were few if any situations where there were disagreements or other issues that interfered with our day-to-day activities. In fact, this closeness to one another contributed in no small way to our extreme effectiveness as a battle unit.

In the end, after the battles and bloodshed, we regarded almost everyone as a brother.

AFTER OUR TOUR

Surviving members of Charlie Battery have held reunions every five years since we returned home in October 1969. Events of this sort have been great for maintaining the friendships that developed because we were placed into a very dangerous and difficult position when we were activated. We all emerged as brothers in every sense of the word. As with almost any organization, not all of the members of our unit take advantage of the opportunity to remain close to one another by attending these reunions. While some only renew these relationships every five years, others have remained very close in friendship.

Whiskey City Cruisers, a club of vintage car owners, has as its core membership several of the guys from Charlie Battery. They meet regularly to discuss restoration of old cars or other pertinent issues, and show off their work at monthly "cruises." It is likely that this organization got its start solely from relationships rooted in service in the National Guard, and a tour in a war-torn region.

In 1994, Jim Wilson released his book, *The Sons of Bardstown,* in conjunction with our 25th anniversary reunion. We had the pleasure of the company of the author and other dignitaries. Wilson was the photo editor for the *Los Angeles Times* newspaper at the time and this was his second book; his first book, about the Korean War, was entitled *Retreat, Hell!.* Wilson was in Korea as a news correspondent and got firsthand training in what war was really about. He was in a great deal of danger for a considerable time and that experience was invaluable to him in writing of our experiences in his second book.

Wilson called me one Sunday afternoon in 1981 to make an appointment to speak to me the next Sunday. He had been lounging on the couch in front of a TV and saw me being interviewed on CNN. His telephone call the next Sunday from California lasted for more than three hours as he asked me various questions and I gave him my account of what had happened. I gave him names of a number of others to contact, and I know he did that. His writing was very accurate, and his attention to detail and truth was of the highest order. He insisted there be no mistakes in his writing. The project took 13 years of part-time effort and the resulting book is accurate to the tiniest detail. Several of us read the manuscript of his book as many as six times, looking for the tiniest detail that might not be correct, including spelling and punctuation. He visited Bardstown four or five times, and I took him to various places to take photographs and conduct interviews. He was stunned with the Bluegrass Parkway and the fact there was virtually no traffic on the road. California was not this way at all.

On his last visit to Bardstown when releasing his book, he heard me speaking of a return trip to Vietnam, and he indicated his desire to return to this country with a group of us. This was not to be; he died in September of that year with a brain aneurism. I spoke with his daughter some time later and she gave me the details of his death. I told her she should be proud of her father because he took every possible measure to be accurate in his reporting of the events surrounding Charlie Battery's ordeal in the Far East. We appreciated this attention to detail and accuracy.

SOME RETURN TO VIETNAM WITHOUT WAR

Rachel Platt, morning news anchor for Louisville's WHAS-TV, had seen some of our interviews on our 25th anniversary reunion. She called to see if she could go to Vietnam with us to do a documentary of our experience. After a few conversations with her and her producer, the game was on and there was a crew of three from the TV station going with us to Vietnam. Rachel's father had done a tour there himself and that was another motivation for her to see the place he had spoken about so much. Each of us paid our own way, and the travel arrangements were made by an agency at the request of the television station. These arrangements included mini-bus rides at all of the major stops, an interpreter/tour guide who lives in California and makes return trips for a living, and provisions for hotel and restaurant stops. These preparations certainly made planning such an adventure a lot simpler. Many thanks to our new friends for making this a 10-day excursion unforgettable.

Our return trip took place in October 1995. We checked with various members of our battery, and seven of us made the decision to go back to Vietnam. We wanted to try to get to all of the major positions we had occupied in 1968 and 1969. The trip was planned in the greatest detail, and was executed on schedule with stops in Saigon, Hanoi, Da Nang, Hue, Hoi An, and back to Saigon. The results were wonderful.

Those returning to Vietnam included seven of our battery who had been there for the entire tour. Kent Bischoff was our supply sergeant. Ronnie (Smiley) Hibbs was a member of one of the gun crews. He was wounded on Tomahawk and sent home early. Jodie Haydon and Tom Raisor were in the fire direction center. Sam Boone was a forward observer who was on Tomahawk during the attack. Joey Keeling was with maintenance section, caring for all of our mechanical equipment, and I was chief of the fire direction center. While all of us except Kent Bischoff were on the hill during the attack, Kent's role as supply sergeant was to be there the next morning with help and new supplies for those items destroyed in the fighting.

The trip was somewhat grueling, since the plane ride was 26 hours long. We boarded a plane in New York on Tuesday evening, and got off the plane in Hanoi on Thursday night after crossing the International Date

Line. We rode in a bus to our hotel and found the accommodations were like a nice hotel in the states. It was a little unnerving to note that the bathroom fixtures used in a hotel in Hanoi, Vietnam, were made by American Standard, a company in Louisville, Kentucky.

Hanoi is a large city with about three million people, occupying an area a little bigger than Bowling Green, Kentucky. However, Hanoi appeared to be very much behind the times in technology, with an electric system barely able to function, and smelly sewers that ran in the gutters of the streets. The water system functioned okay but the water was not pure enough for us to drink, requiring that we drink bottled water everywhere we went. Restaurant food was okay, as long as it was cooked thoroughly. We didn't touch any uncooked food. We didn't want to get sick.

Residents traveled in the city almost exclusively by bicycle; some used mopeds and a three-wheel cyclo, a sort of a taxi driven by the owner and carrying one or two riders. Very few automobiles were seen, only thousands of bicycles and our mini-bus. Supposedly, there were only three traffic lights in the city, and that might be true. Left turns were interesting. A virtual sea of bicycles would simply open up and allow the bus to move slowly among them, horn tooting all the way.

Further south, the traffic became more mopeds, fewer bicycles, and an occasional automobile. In Da Nang and Hoi An, there were also some of the trucks we left behind when American forces left the country for good. Virtually all American military trucks larger than three-quarter-ton pickups were tandem-axle trucks. The Vietnamese had removed the front axle of each of these trucks and converted them to single axle, placed an old 55-gallon steel drum on the roof for fuel, and then were able to move about the country delivering goods and people. Some of these trucks had even been modified to use engines out of tanks and other track vehicles. They are a versatile people who accommodate whatever life has thrown at them.

Perhaps the most memorable site we visited was the prison in Hanoi known as the "Hanoi Hilton." The actual name is Maison Centrale. Thousands of soldiers were held there at one time or another during the war, including prisoners from America and its allies, as well as from South Vietnam. Many of the prisoners died from poor treatment and disgusting living conditions. Treatment there was as bad as it gets. The walls were made of brick, plastered and painted, and topped with a continuous row of broken glass embedded in a concrete cap. There was also a post-and-wire system atop that wall, electrified by a direct connection to the electric power with no obvious switch to disengage the electricity. Bars covered what few openings there were. It was the epitome of hopelessness.

The building was being torn down, at least the rear portions. However, as we were taking pictures, the communist guards quickly stopped us and closed whatever openings there were. They did not like us recording this event. I understand that the plan was to build a luxury hotel. A Hilton might be appropriate.

Air travel in Vietnam is limited to Vietnam Air, and I must admit the service was quite well done. All personnel on the planes were very polite and helpful. The one disconcerting point was that at every airport we went to, there was frequently no other plane in sight. We did see several other jet passenger planes parked off the runway. We assumed they were beyond further use and were a source of parts for those still able to serve their passengers. I really had no complaint for their transportation system; we had smooth flights that were on time.

There is also a train, a narrow-gauge railroad used by locals carrying their goods, chickens, pigs, and whatever else, or the mini-bus, the same ones that we all saw during the war. These were not as comfortable a means of travel as we were accustomed to.

When traveling up the mountain toward Hai Van Pass (or Rabbit Ears Pass, as it was known to us) with its two switchbacks, we encountered a truck that had turned over on the mountain road. It was very close to the edge of the bluff, several hundred feet high, and blocked the right lane. It had happened shortly before we arrived, and people were standing around looking at the vehicle. Apparently, no one was hurt. I asked the bus driver if there was a wrecker to handle such events and he said no. He went on to say that the only way to deal with this accident was to take the truck apart and reassemble it back upright on its wheels. When we returned late that evening, the truck had been disassembled; righted; put back together; reloaded with cargo and passengers, and was gone. They have hidden talents we cannot imagine.

Museums are located in each of the larger cities. They are styled as museums to the American aggression in Vietnam, and are called war crimes museums. Not surprisingly, they depict Americans as the enemy who caused unspeakable terror and chaos in their country. Various captured weapons, and supply items are on display, along with several aircraft and helicopters we left behind.

In Hanoi, the museum included a pile of scrap aircraft elements—rudders, wing parts, and engines—that were allegedly the wreckage of a B-52. Nothing about this pile of scrap resembled a B-52, especially the radial piston engine that probably was built for a single-engine plane in the 1940s. The overall effect of the museum was to make Americans out as demons of the highest order.

The Saigon museum had perhaps the most sobering of display items—the guillotine used to execute prisoners. The guillotine traveled from city to city in Vietnam, and executed as many as hundreds at a time on its stops. This grisly thing was used up into the 1950s.

While this return trip to a now peaceful country was quite emotional for each of us, it was a rewarding experience. Meeting the people, who spoke perfect English in most cases, made us aware that they are no different than we are. They simply go about their daily duties and are happy no one is shooting at them. The work ethic there is as good as it gets, and entrepreneurism is the order of the day, with everyone doing something to earn an honest living.

Emotions ran high when we returned to Firebase Denise, and even higher once we climbed to Tomahawk and toured that infamous position. Some of the men found closure in Vietnam. Seeing one more time where an unspeakable battle had occurred that took the lives of lifelong friends seemed necessary for all of us.

A typhoon hit Vietnam while we were there. The lowlands flooded, resulting in a mass evacuation of the residents. We watched these families leave. In one trip, they would carry all of their possessions to higher ground, although I am not quite sure where. Their possessions were scant in quantity. In a hotel in Hue, there was a television on in the lobby with a news program showing footage of a schoolroom with students seated at their desks, a teacher at the blackboard, and more than a foot of water all around them. The teacher waded in water, the students sat with their feet and legs in water, and education continued uninterrupted.

Visits to our two principal locations, firebases Denise and Tomahawk, were filled with interest and emotion. On both sites, we found evidence of our past presence. There were depressions in the ground where we had established bunkers and gun positions. In the case of Tomahawk, I found rusted hinges from 105-howitzer shell crates in the depression that was our bunker. These had to have come from two of the crates we used to create windows in our bunker. The hinges were attached to the lids of the boxes, and the bottoms were cut out, making a window/fighting position that could be closed. Nearby we found an unfired M-16 cartridge. We also found the end of a ridgepole that was used in a general purpose (GP) tent, likely the one we used as a mess hall, which was destroyed by the enemy attack 26 years earlier. Several other recognizable pieces of equipment were found, including expended rifle shells. Evidence of war and disaster could not hide from us. The road leading up to the firebase was eroded in some places more than four feet deep, and climbing to our former home was difficult.

The Catholic Cathedral in Hue was one of the sites we visited. In the 1950s, Air France paid for and erected this huge church. Most of us had visited there in 1969 when we took two truckloads of children's clothing to a nearby orphanage. The people of Bardstown had collected the clothing and shipped it to us. We took these clothes to an orphanage, operated by a group of Vietnamese Catholic nuns, not far from the church. The staff included men and women who had their own children in the orphanage, but had lost their spouses in the war. This facility has since been converted into a hospital.

Curiously, the pastor of the church during our visit in 1969 was still there in 1995, and he remembered our kindness from so long ago. We learned he was wounded during an attack that resulted when an artillery round pierced one of the huge stained glass windows in the church. He was not badly hurt and he continued with his mission while the window was restored. He allowed us to climb a rickety staircase that led to the bell-tower where we got a bird's-eye view of the city while the typhoon was still raging.

I have never spoken to anyone who spent a tour in Vietnam who did not praise the country for its beauty, both during the war and afterward. In addition, the friendliness of the Vietnamese people is beyond my fondest hopes. I am convinced they do not care what form of government they live under as long as they are not involved in fighting. Almost everyone spoke English, as this is taught in all of the schools as an international language.

While I treasure my experiences in Vietnam, I would never want to do it again, nor do I ever want anyone else to have to experience what we did. This war is still taking lives. A recent experience connected me to a lady whose fiancé was killed, and apparently, while she is happily married and living in a different state, she has not yet gotten over the loss of her high school sweetheart who was one of the four infantry men killed on Firebase Tomahawk. While speaking to her on the phone, I heard her emotions break out and real pain is yet with her. Her sweetheart's mother committed suicide a couple of months after the loss of her son.

Today, the veterans' hospital is monitoring several of the members of Charlie Battery, because of our placement in I Corps in areas where there was concentrated use of Agent Orange as a defoliant. Many cancers have developed in men stationed in this area, and several of our battery's members have contracted this disease. While there is not definitive evidence that this defoliant is the direct cause, there is serious reason for concern. The war continues to kill.

While in the war zone, we made friends with commanders of several infantry units. With the high level of camaraderie, we were quite effective as an artillery support unit. When the infantry was in trouble and needed help from artillery, we were always the first to be called if the action was within our range.

Once a nighttime ambush went bad and the infantry platoon was in real trouble; a large unit of the enemy was firing on them. They frantically called for illumination rounds, and there were not nearly enough available from a nearby mortar platoon. We heard this action over the radio. I had a chart operator plot the site of the battle so we could try to help. As it turned out, we were just able to reach this area and we fired for over an hour, supplying light for our infantry. This additional light helped save lives and the infantry let us know it.

The battalion commander visited the next day and personally thanked me and the others involved. He said that this was unprecedented in other artillery units. A little later, he presented us with an award as a thank-you for our attention and helping his men out of a difficult situation. There were several presentations to our battery for our service. This battalion commander came to Bardstown from his home in Alexandria, Virginia, to celebrate the 25th anniversary of our service in Vietnam.

Press exposure has been with us ever since we left home on our way to Vietnam and continues even today, although it has decreased. Bardstown was unique in that so many of its residents were lost, and that so many were sent there in the first place. It was highly irregular for a National Guard unit to have seven casualties, as our unit did.

The press has made much out of this. There have been more than 100 interviews by television stations from all over the United States, as well as several from Europe. Magazines and newspapers have published countless stories about Charlie Battery, largely because of the high number of casualties, and because it was unique to have a National Guard outfit involved in combat. Members of Charlie Battery have been very cooperative, and this exposure has been quite positive in general.

As time moves on, there is less interest on the part of the public and the interviews have declined a great deal. There may be more coverage at some point, but will the public care? Continuing friendship of all those who served together is the greatest reward today as we all become closer as brothers who were in a terrible war a long time ago.

Battery C, Second Battalion, 138th Artillery, Kentucky National Guard, Bardstown, Kentucky: Members who went on Active Duty in Vietnam

Captain Samuel Thomas McClure

Second Lieutenant Thomas R. Ice

Sergeant First Class Joseph Patrick Simpson

Staff Sergeant Harold M. Brown

Staff Sergeant William K. Harned

Staff Sergeant Joseph K. Ice

Staff Sergeant James T. Moore

Staff Sergeant Charles M. Stone, Jr.

Staff Sergeant Charles G. Taylor

Sergeant Walter Kent Bischoff

Sergeant Glen A. Brown

Sergeant Freddie A. Bunch

Sergeant Earl L. Doyle, Jr.

Sergeant Robert S. Filiatreau

Sergeant Jerry Janes

Sergeant Charles Thomas Riggs

Sergeant Michael H. Simpson

Sergeant Ronald Simpson

Sergeant David G. Stone

Sergeant Bobby E. Stump

Sergeant Wendell C. Thomas

Sergeant Louis B. Thompson

Corporal Evan L. Crowe, Jr.

Corporal William G. Hamilton

Corporal Joseph C. Moore

Corporal John W. Rizer

Corporal James D. Simpson

Corporal Billy R. Snellen

Corporal Charles F. Stansberry

Corporal Jerry L. Thomas

Specialist James F. Barnes

Specialist Thomas D. Ballard

Specialist Alan T. Brewer

Specialist Cecil Robert

Specialist David E. Collins

Specialist Theodore H. Collins, Jr.

Specialist Wayne Collins

Specialist Harry T. Downs

Specialist Thomas R. Downs

Specialist Joseph T. Drury

Specialist William R. Greenwell

Specialist Bernard L. Hall

Specialist Kenneth T. Hardin

Specialist Joseph Haydon

Specialist Ronald R. Hibbs

Specialist Joseph R. McIlvoy

Specialist Francis L. Johnson

Specialist Joseph Keeling

Specialist Bruce L. King

Specialist Julian Lewis

Specialist James D. McGee

Specialist William F. Osborne

Specialist Donald J. Parrish

Specialist Charles T. Raisor

Specialist Joseph L. Shelburne

Specialist Kenneth A. Shelburne

Specialist William D. Stone

Specialist Jim A. Wray

Private First Class Robert A. Atwood

Private First Class Joseph H. Bartley

Private First Class Gary W. Bickett

Private First Class David R. Bishop

Private First Class Louis Blanford

Private First Class Samuel R. Boone

Private First Class James C. Bradbury

Private First Class Joseph W. Brown

Private First Class Danny D. Cheatham (promoted to corporal)

Private First Class George W. Clan

Private First Class Donald R. Coomes

Private First Class Larry B. Cornish

Private First Class Charles Coulter

Private First Class Roger R. Coulter

Private First Class Donald R. Cox

Private First Class Martin P. Duffy

Private First Class Robert G. Durr

Private First Class William B. Hurst

Private First Class James L. Ice

Private First Class Larry C. Keeling

Private First Class Charles R. Linton

Private First Class James Livers

Private First Class Robert Lyvers

Private First Class Joseph T. Marshall

Private First Class Edgar Stewart McClasky

Private First Class Joseph D. Nally

Private First Class Joseph Nation

Private First Class Joseph Neel

Private First Class James P. Newton

Private First Class Joseph Newton

Private First Class Hark W. Parrish, Jr.

Private First Class William L. Peake

Private First Class William D. Puckett

Private First Class Ronald G. Rexroat

Private First Class William K. Roberts

Private First Class Steve Robinson

Private First Class John W. Roby

Private First Class Stanley Stone

Private First Class Thomas L. Smith

Private First Class David A. Unseld

Private First Class William F. Welch, Jr.

Private First Class William R. Yates

Private Donald R. Allender

Private James N. Hutchins

Private Gary Lewis

Private Wayne Lewis

Private William Lewis

Private Paul L. McClintock

Private Joseph R. Newton

Private John R. Simpson

Gulf of
Tonkin

DEMARCATION LINE

● Quang Tri

● Hue
Phu Bai
● Roung   Firebase Tomahawk
Roung ★ ★   Firebase Denise
A Shau
Valley   ● Da Nang
                       ● Hoi An
                    I CORPS

LAOS

CAMBODIA

Ia Drang

● An Khe

**SOUTH
VIETNAM**

II CORPS

● Cam Ranh Bay

III CORPS

● Cu Chi

★ HO CHI MINH CITY
(SAIGON)

● Vung Tau

South China
Sea

ulf of
ailand

○ **IV CORPS**

Mekong Delta

Map by Carolyn Parrish

Bob Hendren, with the team, before leaving for Vietnam in 1965
Front L-R: Monty Frye, Gordon Jennette, Joe Drost, Bill Britton, Bob Hendren, Bill Boggs.
Back L-R: William Robinson, James Jackson, Bob Cherry, Eugene Angstadt, Hubert Van Poll, Joe Phillips

Lieutenant Kenneth Simpson was in Operation Starlite and was awarded the Bronze Star.

Memorial on Tomahawk Hill for those killed during
June and July 1969

Colonel Hal Moore, now Lieutenant General, Retired.

Specialist Raymond Ford was
killed in Operation White Wing
on February 20, 1966.

Corporal William Russell Taylor died in Da Nang, Vietnam, August 28, 1966.

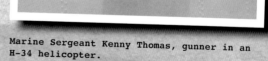

Marine Sergeant Kenny Thomas, gunner in an H-34 helicopter.

Marine Sergeant A.B. (Buddy) Grigsby (right) with other members of platoon
L-R: Lance Corporal Williams, Corporal Zattua, Corporal Thomas, Sergeant Grigsby

Specialist Ronnie Greenwall, Ninth Division, in Mekong Delta

Marine Sergeant Kenny Nevitt, First Division, with grenade launcher

Chief Warrant Officer Denny Howard, helicopter pilot with over 100 assault missions. He was awarded the Distinguished Flying Cross, two Bronze Stars and ten Air Medals.

E4 Donald Holbert, 26th Marine Regiment, Khe Sanh siege

Staff Sergeant Raphael Norris died of wounds November 3, 1968. He was awarded the Silver Star

Lieutenant Colonel Jimmy Bean with F-105 fighter bomber. He was shot down over North Vietnam and spent four years in captivity.

Lieutenant Colonel John Finn Hurst flew in over 200 missions in B-52 and EB-66 bombers. He was awarded two Distinguished Flying Crosses and 20 Air Medals.

Sergeant Bobby Ballard, with A-1E fighter bombe
was at Tan Son Nhut Air Base during Tet Offensive

Specialist David Collins
Killed June 19, 1969

Specialist Ronnie McIlvoy
Killed June 19, 1969

Staff Sergeant Jim Moore
Wounded June 19, 1969
Died from burns June 24, 1969

Specialist Jim Wray
Killed July 2, 1969

Specialist Barry Neal Thompson
Killed June 25, 1969

Sergeant Ronald
Simpson Killed
June 19, 1969

Specialist Charles David St. Clair (left) was
awarded the Bronze Star.
Killed January 16, 1971, at Con Thien

Don Parrish, with flag from Tomahawk Hill.

Staff Sergeant Nick
Johnson, Ninth division
Killed August 13, 1970

Captain James Crawford
Killed in crash in Laos
February 3, 1972

CHAPTER 16

1969: CONTINUED

Unabated small unit attacks continued in 1969. These were pressed primarily by the NVA and the Vietcong. Convoy attacks were one of the most persistent problems for the Americans. They had been an ever-present problem, but in 1969, the enemy increased their number and scope, trying to isolate distant outposts, and even cities such as Pleiku and Kon Tum. Highway 19 from Qui Nhon to Pleiku was the most frequently hit route; bases in the highlands were also targeted.[266] Most supplies had to be transported by trucks. Planes were helpful, but could carry only a small fraction of the food, arms, and ammunition required. Almost a million troops, American and Vietnamese, had to be supplied.[267]

To protect these convoys of supplies, the army had to devise tactics not used by American forces since the Indian wars, when wagon trains had to be protected. The methods used by the Vietcong and the NVA were much more sophisticated than any the Indians ever thought of. In Vietnam, the highways were narrow, and lined by jungle, rocky defiles, and heavy brush, which made good cover for the enemy. They used the same tactics they had used against the French, but which they had perfected over the years.

The enemy set up ambushes with men on either side of the road. With a rocket or mine, they would knock out the lead truck and the rear vehicle. The convoy, unable to move forward or back, could then be dispatched one vehicle at a time. If trucks tried to get around, they received special attention.

By knocking them out, the enemy blocked both sides of the road. Bombs or other explosive devices, buried and hidden in the roadbed, were often used, much as they were later used in Iraq.

At first, MP units provided protection, but they were inadequate in number. Brush and undergrowth along the road were cleared. Later on, trucks were sandbagged on their sides and armor plated, with armor plating even underneath. Gun trucks were given extra ammo, usually at the ratio of 1 to 10 that of the normal amount, and loaded with all sorts of weapons, such as multiple machine guns. Helicopters helped, but it was impossible to over fly every convoy. Trucks were loaded with necessary staples in the front of the convoy, and gas and explosives in the rear. If the rear trucks were hit and exploded, they would not block the rest of the convoy.[268]

Personnel carriers were also used for convoy support, but in well-organized attacks, they were knocked out first. They helped, but were not the whole answer. A new gun, the Vulcan, which could put out 1,000 rounds of 20-mm cannon fire a minute, was used with partial success in riddling the sides of the road and ditches harboring the enemy.[269] These guns were first used in 1969. The last major convoy attack in 1969 was on November 22 when a 300-vehicle convoy of mixed 48th Transportation and Engineer companies was traveling from Long Binh to Song Be.

The bravery of the long-haul drivers was common. MACV gave them a special patch. One driver even received the Congressional Medal of Honor. The ability of the convoys to get through varied considerably. Sometimes they ended up in disaster for friendly forces, but sometimes the enemy's attacks were complete failures.

A number of Nelson Countians served in transportation units.

Michael Robinson was in transportation at Nha Trang. Sergeant William S. Smith was in the supply depot at Qui Nhon. Private First Class Kenneth Mattingly was with the 363rd Transportation Company. Staff Sergeant Marvin Littlejohn was with the 27th Transportation. Phillip Metcalf was with the 47th Transportation. Sergeant John McCubbins and Private First Class Danny Taylor were with transportation in Thailand. Private First Class Henry Hayden was with the 57th Transportation Company.

Hayden joined the army in November 1966. He shipped to Vietnam in February 1968, and for four months, his truck company transported supplies from Da Nang up Highway 1 to various destinations all the way up to Quang Tri. They usually were part of a multiple-truck convoy with other transportation companies, and were on the road every day, mostly to Phu Bai.

Armored personnel carriers escorted the convoys for security. The country was open and they had no real ambushes. However, the enemy frequently mined the road at night, and about twice a week, trucks would hit mines with resulting deaths and wounded drivers. According to co-author Don Parrish, Highway 1 had minesweepers on it daily, but sometimes they missed some mines.

After four months, Hayden was transferred to the 39th Regiment of the Ninth Infantry Division. He was stationed at the army base at Bearcat, about 30 miles south of Saigon. He was in an armored personnel carrier unit, and their job was to make sure that the bridges in his area of the Mekong Delta stayed open. They were on the road for three days, and spent four days in camp. Occasionally they were fired upon, but had no serious trouble. One bright spot in his tour was a week of R&R in Sydney, Australia. He went home in October 1968, and was discharged shortly thereafter.

One of the bigger operations of late 1969 occurred in the Hiep Duc area when the 196th Light Infantry Brigade and an ARVN regiment ran into strong VC entrenchments. A grisly slugging match followed off and on for two weeks. The Second Battalion of the Seventh Marines was thrown into the battle before the enemy was cleared out of the area. It was called Operation Frederick Hill.[5] Shortly after that, a persistent enemy attacked Firebase Siberia in the same area, but was repulsed. Meanwhile, in the highlands, desultory fighting ensued with many small unit confrontations.

Corporal Gerald Ashby worked out of the post office in Pleiku, getting the mail to the soldiers out in the field. He also took care of sending money orders. The soldiers in Vietnam couldn't use regular American money for fear that it would end up in the black market. They had to use scrip. On one occasion, when taking mail out to a small firebase, Ashby noticed a bunch of mortar shells holes. He asked how often the base was mortared, and was told two or three times every night. He was going to spend the night, but decided not to.

Ashby and a friend from another state have remained close over the years, occasionally visiting. The friend, however, got leukemia, which was attributed to the large amount of Agent Orange used around Pleiku.

Sergeant Harold O'Bryan also served in the highlands in the same Fourth Division. He received the Combat Infantry Badge serving with Company B, First Battalion, First Brigade.

The year 1969 was the most costly to Nelson County in deaths and other casualties; the majority occurred on that one terrible night on Tomahawk Hill. Nelson County would lose more, but never would it grieve on such a massive basis again. Nelson County lost more of its sons that one day in Vietnam than it did on any other day in any war, except at Goliad in the Texas War of Independence.

Ho Chi Minh died September 3, 1969. His death didn't have any effect on the war except for a two-day truce for his burial. In 1969, 60,000 troops came home as a result of the first big drawdown of American forces, and the increasing Vietnamization of the fighting. However, combat deaths were still high, though not as bad as in 1968: 9,414 combat deaths in 1969 as compared to 14,592 the previous year.[270] Up to this point, 40,000 lives had been lost and 260,000 people wounded.

Other Nelson Countians who served in Vietnam in 1969 include:

Private First Class Kenneth Brown: wounded and taken to hospital ship *Sanctuary*

Sergeant John Calbert: 22nd Artillery, Company C, Fourth Battalion

Private First Class George Dennis: received Air Medal for meritorious service in aerial combat

Private First Class Charles Durbin: received multiple shrapnel wounds on his body and extremities from a booby trap

Specialist Larry Goode: re-enlisted for a second tour of duty

Specialist John E. Greenwell: stationed at Phu Bai

Sergeant John T. Greenwell: squad leader, Company C, First Battalion, Fourth Infantry Division. Earned a Combat Infantry Badge near Pleiku.

Sergeant Joseph Raymond Hagan: received Army Commendation Medal with V for valor for meritorious service

Lance Corporal Robert Janes: served a 13-month tour

Father James Litchfield: Qui Nhon 67th Evacuation Hospital

Sergeant Joseph E. Lyvers: aircraft mechanic at Da Nang

Airman First Class Joseph E. Masterson: Combat Support Group, Nha Trang

Lance Corporal Joseph F. Price: First Amtrac Battalion, A Company

Specialist James K. Simpson: 247th Signal Company, Long Binh

Dennis H. Smith: received a Bronze Star serving against hostile fire

Private First Class Mark Spalding: First Aviation Battalion

Private First Class James Winninger: Company C, Fifth Battalion, 12th Infantry

Private First Class Arthur Wiseman: mechanic, 12th Maintenance Company

CHAPTER 17

THE NAVY

In Vietnam, the navy played a relatively unsung, but necessary and effective role. First, the navy helped bring many of the men and most of the supplies across the Pacific. In the early war, it brought over the Army First Division, and the First and Third Marine Divisions. Although many of the supplies were later brought by private freighters, naval control was vital. Naval LSTs (landing ship tanks) often moved supplies up and down the coast.

Lowell T. Linney was on the LST, the USS *Madera County*, which operated the whole length of the coast from the delta all the way up the DMZ (*Kentucky Standard*, May 2, 1968).

The navy was also the first to bomb North Vietnam. After the 1964 *Maddox* and *Turner Joy* incidents in the Tonkin Gulf, navy planes bombed the oil storage area at Vinh, as well as the patrol boat base from which the attacking North Vietnamese boats came. A navy pilot, Lieutenant Everett Alvarez, was the first pilot shot down, and ended up in the infamous Hanoi Hilton prison.

All during the war, the navy operated off the coast at Yankee Station. Aircraft carriers, two or three at a time, were on constant duty, and flights went out daily, weather permitting. At first, they were part of Rolling Thunder, but continued after that. They supplied ground support when needed, hit the Ho Chi Minh Trail, and, at the end of the war, helped knock out SAM sites when the massive B-52 bombing finally brought the North Vietnamese to the peace table. The carriers were always in danger of fire, because of the constant loading of fuel and bombs on the planes.

Tommy Bullock and John Stiles were on the USS *Franklin Roosevelt*, when a fire broke out and caused multiple explosions. Eight sailors were killed and 14 wounded (*Kentucky Standard*, November 3, 1966).

Just after that, a fire broke out on the USS *Oriskany* during which 44 were killed. John McCain, later a presidential candidate, was of the *Oriskany* and suffered burns.

James S. Donahue was an aviation electronic technician on the USS *Kitty Hawk*, and worked on A-6As and F-4U Phantoms (*Kentucky Standard*, May 17, 1966).

Various aircraft carriers rotated off and on at Yankee Station. The *Ticonderoga* launched the first attack. The *Ranger* made several tours. Radar man John C. Edelen was on the *Ranger* and Francis D. Hall was on the assault carrier, the USS *Princeton* (*Kentucky Standard*, December 29, 1966).

The USS *Okinawa* was also an assault carrier. Marine Sergeant Kenny Thomas served on the Okinawa and flew off it as a helicopter crewman. The navy operated closely with the marines and supported them. They were vital in flying into isolated LZs and firebases, bringing in supplies and reinforcements, and evacuating troops when necessary. Ships such as the *Okinawa* were mother ships with helicopter mechanics and crewmen who gave a mobile base for marine helicopters.

The navy also had the gunships of the fleet, guarding the coast and giving support where possible. Engineer's Mate Third Class Carl Pash was on the cruiser *Canberra*, whose eight-inch guns could fire 12 miles inland. The *Canberra* was the flagship of the fleet and brought the Third Marines in as the first American land force. The *Canberra* later provided eight-inch fire in the retaking of Hue, during the Tet Offensive.

The guided missile destroyer *Robinson* provided sea-to-land bombardment on numerous occasions. When Joseph Rogers was on the *Robinson*, they gave fire support at Dong Ha during one of the DMZ battles. Yeoman Joseph Rapier was on the *Robinson* when it gave naval support for Operation Sea Dragon, which involved the Third Marine Division, the First Cavalry Division, and the ARVN Tiger Division.

Fireman Paul Miller and Ensign Joseph Leo Smith also served on ships that gave shore bombardment (*Kentucky Standard*, December 29, 1966). Miller was on the cruiser USS *St. Paul*, and Smith on the destroyer the USS *Turner Joy* of the Tonkin Gulf incident. The *Turner Joy* bombarded targets in both North and South Vietnam.

Daniel Brown served on the destroyer USS *Henry Tucker*, which gave fire support to the Americal division (*Kentucky Standard*, November 10, 1968, and September 5, 1968).

Even the massive battleship, the USS *New Jersey*, gave shore bombardment with one-ton, 16-inch shells, knocking out targets impervious to smaller artillery. The *New Jersey* could hit targets 20 miles away with relative accuracy.

Navy personnel watched the coast and gathered intelligence.

Various navy personnel, often non-coms, learned Vietnamese. They were posted along the coast to learn about any local enemy activity, and to pick up messages that could be transferred by Morse code to navy ships offshore. (The remarkable story of Bill Huston appears in the chapter on Intelligence.)

The navy also engaged in river warfare. Vietnam had a number of rivers emptying into the sea, but of course, the largest and most difficult to secure was the Mekong. It was the biggest river in Southeast Asia. As it left Cambodia, it spread into numerous branches that fed the Mekong Delta, the most fertile and populous part of South Vietnam. Saigon was on the northern edge. There were few roads in the delta. Most transportation and movement was done by boats of various sizes, from the good-sized junks to the small, oar-powered sampans. The delta was a good, inaccessible site in which the Vietcong hid, and from which they operated.

The navy developed a Riverine Force to help establish some control over the area. They worked in concert with the Army's Ninth Division. The fleet had numerous boats of various sizes. The workhorse was the fast, well-armed "swift boats" on which John Kerry (later a presidential candidate) served during his Vietnam tour. Their small, rapid-firing cannon and 50-caliber machine guns could put out a lot of firepower. Some were even armed with flamethrowers.

The navy also had landing craft known as LCMs (landing craft mechanized).

Joseph D. Rapier, then a petty officer who had served in operation Sea Dragon in the North, later served on LCMs in the "Game Warden" operation at Dong Tam in the delta (*Kentucky Standard*, March 20, 1968).

Chief Boatswain Mate Thomas Underwood served with the Riverine Force, as did Gunner's Mate Stuart Wade Maddox, who served on the Advisory Group River Patrol 31, training the South Vietnamese how to operate the Riverine Force (*Kentucky Standard,* July 27, 1969). The navy also had large barges in the delta that served as barracks.

The navy had aircraft flying over the delta and other waterways, such as the helicopter flown by Lieutenant J.G. Lud McKay.

The navy's role was multi-faceted, and vital for American functions in Vietnam. Their casualty rate was not as bad as that of the army or the marines. They had approximately 2,500 deaths, about 5 percent of the overall total for Vietnam.

According to the *Kentucky Standard,* others from Nelson County who served with the navy in Vietnam include:

Air Apprentice Theodore Burgin: Navy Air Operations on aircraft carrier *Constellation*

Petty Officer 2 Ronald Keith Coomes[1]: carrier USS *Hornet*

Joseph Farnsworth: carrier USS *Kitty Hawk*

Petty Officer Tony Graham: destroyer escort *Sample*

William Hall: destroyer USS *Prickett*

Petty Officer Second Class James Hodge: aircraft carrier *Ticonderoga* (*Kentucky Standard,* February 25, 1968)

Milburn Howard: Company A of the Navy Construction Battalion

Lieutenant J.G. Thomas M. McGinnis: Naval supply in Da Nang

Lieutenant Commander Michael E. O'Bryan: in charge of Sealift Command at Cam Ranh Bay; had 15 men under him controlling docking and operations at a massive port (*Kentucky Standard,* December 21, 1970)

Joseph Sympson: carrier USS *Kearsage*

Signalman Sheridan Talbott: Amphibious Transport
(*Kentucky Standard*, April 17, 1969)

CHAPTER 18

1970: CAMBODIA AND DRAWDOWN

As 1970 started, there was still a sizable force of Americans present in Vietnam—330,000 army soldiers and 55,000 marines[273], in addition to the air force and navy personnel. Some of these were preparing to leave. The last of the Third Marine Division was leaving. All but one brigade of the Ninth Division was gone.

Despite the drawdown, Americans were still dying. Approximately 100 died in the first week of the year. In the first month of the year, there were more than 100 rocket, mortar, and ground attacks against allied bases from the Mekong Delta to the DMZ.[274]

The enemy pressure was not letting up. The enemy was also losing men. On February 15, 145 communist soldiers were killed in a battalion preparing an ambush near Da Nang by combination US and ARVN units.[275] It was a war of give and take with many small unit actions. American units were increasingly used to train and equip South Vietnamese troops to assume the greater part of the fighting.

American army and marine action was tentative. After Hamburger Hill, commanders were reluctant to face the criticism of wasting their men in senseless battles when the only object was to kill enemy soldiers, or take territory they would later abandon. The army and marines in most of the country were in a holding pattern. They had enclaves around the big population areas, and scattered LZs, firebases, and supply bases, many of which were outposts to help interdict enemy movements or to serve as listening posts.

A great deal of effort was also spent trying to stop the flow of enemy supplies down the Ho Chi Minh Trail. Air attacks were bombing it almost daily; some of the attacks were by B-52s with massive payloads of bombs.[276] B-52s also sometimes bombed North Vietnamese and Pathet Lao troops close to the Plain of Jars in Laos to help the Royal Laotian forces.

In March, the North Vietnamese-leaning Cambodian leader, Prince Norodom Sihanouk, was ousted, and the West-leaning General Lon Nol assumed command of the country.[277] The treaty that allowed Communist use of the country, and even some of its ports for passage, was rescinded. Vietnamese embassies were ordered closed, and the embassy personnel were to leave within a week.

Despite these changes, the enemy continued to use the Ho Chi Minh Trail, and stock its bases along the South Vietnamese-Cambodian border, particularly in places that stuck out into the country close to Saigon—places called Fishhook and Parrot's Beak, because of their geographical configuration.

On April 14, 2,000 ARVN soldiers attacked across the Cambodian border in a surprise action and reportedly killed 179 North Vietnamese soldiers.[277] Following reports that the communists from the north had doubled their forces in Cambodia, General Lon Nol asked for American aid. South Vietnamese army forces made two more raids across the border, as action heated up in mid April.

President Richard Nixon gave permission for a cross-border attack of US forces into Cambodia to bring the enemy to battle, and to destroy the enemy bases that threatened the Saigon area.[278] On May 1, Operation Toan Thang 43, the First Cavalry Division's armor burst across the border with Task Force Shumaker leading the way. Hundreds of helicopters bore First Cavalry troopers and ARVN troops, and leapfrogged out ahead of them, hoping to ensnare enemy battalions. Fighter-bombers led the way, blasting potential enemy troop positions.

Private First Class Daniel White of Company B, Fifth Battalion of the Seventh Cavalry Regiment, was with the First Cavalry (*Kentucky Standard*, September 13, 1970). During this action in Vietnam, he earned an Air Medal for 23 helicopter missions. For the Cambodian action, he received an Army Commendation Medal with a V for valor, and a Bronze Star for neutralizing an enemy threat, saving comrades and rescuing wounded.

Staff Sergeant Larry Holbert was also with the Fifth Battalion of the Seventh Cavalry Regiment (*Kentucky Standard*, April 23, 1970).

Specialist William Durbin was wounded near the border in the Cambodian action (*Kentucky Standard*, May 19, 1970). He ended up in a hospital in Japan. Durbin received the Purple Heart and Bronze Star for outstanding meritorious service.

Enemy opposition was light, although vicious on occasion. Most of the NVA left to fight another day. The Air Force and the 11th Armored Cavalry Regiment pursued them, but most made good their escape.[279] The supply depots the enemy left behind were enormous. Americans found large stores "beyond belief"[280] of all sorts of foodstuffs, and all sorts of supplies, including many trucks. It was obvious that the enemy left in a hurry.

On May 6, the First Cavalry leaped across the border to air assault two battalions for the second time. Another large supply dump was found, and engineers had to build a road so the captured materials could be brought out over land. It took nine days to empty that base. Whatever rice could not be brought out was contaminated and made unusable. As the First Cavalry was moving forward, the Fifth Battalion of the 199th Light Infantry Brigade fought off several determined enemy attacks to recapture the caches.

Specialist John B. Cecil, with Company C, 22nd Aviation Battalion, served with the First Cavalry (*Kentucky Standard*, October 7, 1970).

Specialist Joseph Winninger earned the Army Commendation Medal serving with the 199th Light Infantry Brigade (*Kentucky Standard*, May 5, 1970).

Second Lieutenant Jimmy Brown was another Nelson Countian who was in the Cambodian invasion. He joined the army in January 1969, but didn't go active until later in the year after he had finished college at Eastern Kentucky University. He joined as a private first class, and was sent to Fort Dix. From there, he went to Officer's Candidate School at Fort Benning, Georgia. In January 1970, he went to Fort Hood in a signal battalion, where he was cleared in crypto clearance (code reception and transmission). He next went to Fort Lee when the Army was putting everything on computers, and served in the quartermaster.

His MOS (military occupational specialty) was changed, however, to an infantry officer when he was sent to Vietnam. He was assigned to the First

Cavalry Division. He was a second lieutenant in the infantry, a position with one of the highest mortality rates in any war.

When Brown got off the helicopter at his assigned company, the man he was replacing got on. The next day, a group of Vietcong with AK-47s spotted Brown and his commanding officer as the CO was showing Brown the vicinity. Brown and his CO had only pistols, so they dove to the ground for cover. Friendly forces came to their rescue, and for a while, they were in no-man's land with bullets whizzing over their heads from both sides. He was as scared as he was at any time during his tour. It was a good introduction to Vietnam.

Brown's captain was a Hungarian. He had been in the field for several years, and wore a yellow towel around his neck as a scarf, which seemed to give him some immunity from fire.

At first, Brown was a platoon leader of 30-plus men, and they spent a lot of time in the field, sometimes away from the rest of the company. One night, they got a call that they were going to be extracted, and were taken out by helicopter. He said they were lucky. They had camped over a large tunnel complex—headquarters for more than 300 North Vietnamese. They could have been slaughtered.

When the First Cavalry went into Cambodia, Brown's unit ran into numerous caches of weapons, most of them covered with Cosmoline™ for preservation. He guessed there were 50 caches spread around. They didn't meet any opposition, because the North Vietnamese had pulled out. He said the Cambodians were friendly and disliked the Vietnamese. He also said that when they were there, he read in an army newspaper that President Nixon said American troops were never going into Cambodia.

During his stay, he lost few men out of his outfit, and that included when he was first lieutenant and executive officer of his company. Out of his battalion, however, he estimated there were close to 50 percent of the casualties in other companies. He credited two things for saving lives. One was that he didn't take any chances. If there was any movement in the bush, and if it was a free-fire zone, he would fire into it and told his men to do so. If he were sending a message, he'd hunker down in the grass, and bend his radio antenna down so it couldn't be seen.

Brown came into the country with two other lieutenants who went into other units. A B-40 rocket killed the two men after they had been in Vietnam only a few days when they exposed their location with maps and a 12-foot radio antenna sticking up in the air. Brown took every possible precaution to protect his men. He also attributed his safety to the perpetual novena said by his mother and her friends.

He was promoted to executive officer of his company, and continued to be involved in firefights and helicopter assault missions. He was involved in 38 combat helicopter assault missions, and received an Air Medal. He also earned two Bronze Stars for meritorious action. On one of his assault missions, his helicopter came under heavy fire, despite helicopter gunships pounding the proposed landing area. The pilot pulled up, and told them that two men had to jump out to lighten the load because of damage to the aircraft. He and another man jumped out over a river. Because of a flotation device in his rucksack, he popped right up to the surface, and was able to rejoin his unit.

Periodically, Brown's unit would go back to a firebase, where the men could relax, and have a few beers. He would often play poker with the other officers, including the battalion commander and the brigade colonel. Then

Brown's unit would have to return to the more exposed area.

For the last few weeks of Brown's service in the field, he had a new company commander, with whom he had friction. They had trip flares and Claymore mines around their perimeter to detect enemy movement. One night, the Claymore mines were set off, and the company captain ordered Brown to call in parachute flares for illumination, and to send the company to check the body count. Brown disagreed, saying that their whole perimeter would be lit up and they would become perfect targets. The order was rescinded only after the matter was taken up with the battalion colonel. The next morning when they checked for a body count, they found only a few dead chickens. The company commander never forgave Brown for correcting him, and even tried to get him court-martialed, but failed.

Brown recalled the frequent rains, sometimes four to five times a day, and the termites that ate even his air mattress. He was glad when an opportunity occurred for him to transfer out of the field.

There was a scandal about slot machines and other fraudulent actions in the officers' clubs. An officer was needed to clean up the mess, and since Brown had a degree in business administration, he applied to a Colonel Carter with whom he had played poker, and got the job. He was transferred to the First Aviation Brigade at Long Binh. He was told that if he didn't do the job well, he would be sent back to the field. That didn't happen. He ran the clubs well. He was in charge of food service, and even went to Vung Tau on the coast for fresh fish. He also installed a drive-in window in the officers' club as he had seen at the Snappy Snack in Bardstown, where enlisted men could pick up hamburgers and French fries. It was a first in Vietnam, and the men paid for them with army chits.

While at the First Aviation Brigade, which was responsible for all helicopters in Vietnam except for the First Cavalry, Brown ran into Lieutenant Joe Howard from New Haven, Kentucky. Howard had gone to helicopter school, and he and Brown became fast friends. Howard was later the best man at Brown's wedding. Howard made the army his career and retired as a colonel.

Brown had a chance to return to the states and be assigned to Fort Polk, Louisiana, but he decided to sign up for another six months in Vietnam with the First Aviation Brigade. Finally, his time was up and he flew to Fort Lewis, Washington. There he was discharged in April 1972, as the American army was gradually pulling out of Vietnam. He had served his time well, and received two Bronze Stars, a Commendation Medal, and an Air Medal, fighting in the Cambodian invasion and numerous other places.

Operation Toan Thang 44 began on May 9 with the 25th Division jumping across the border in their area. Following a tactical air attack, two battalions were air assaulted into the heart of one base area. Huge Commando Vault bombs blasted LZs in the dense jungle.[281] Another battalion was air assaulted across the Rach Beng Go River at the border and a bridge was built over the river for the Second Battalion of the 22nd Regiment of the 25th to storm into Cambodia. Helicopter gunships tracked down enemy soldiers retreating westward. There were many brief but violent firefights as the enemy attempted some rear guard defense.

Specialist James Olds served with the 25th Division's 22nd Regiment. He received a Purple Heart while serving as a forward artillery observer (*Kentucky Standard*, September 22, 1970). Private First Class Donald Cheek was also with the 25th Division (*Kentucky Standard*, April 23, 1970), as was Private Stephen A. Vittitoe (*Kentucky Standard*, January 29, 1970).

Sergeant Robert Hutchins earned a Bronze Star while serving with Company B, Third Battalion, 22nd Regiment (*Kentucky Standard,* May 7, 1970). Hutchins was a radioman in his company. As such, he was always with his lieutenant; the enemy frequently targeted lieutenants. He was in a number of helicopter assaults and firefights. One benefit of being a radioman was that in an assault, he was not at the door of the 'copter, but in the middle, and often the last one out. Hutchins will never forget his first action, when they were flying into their landing zone. The machine gunner started spraying the perimeter of the landing area. The noise was loud and unexpected, and scared him. He soon got used to it. He continued as radioman for seven months of his tour. The other five months he served as company clerk, a less dangerous job.

Although the cross-border Cambodian attacks reaped massive amounts of material from NVA bases that had been and probably would be springboards for future enemy offensives aimed at the critical Saigon area, they were disappointing in the number of enemy brought to bay. Most escaped. The excursions ended for the American units on May 29. They were only allowed to go about 20 miles into Cambodia. Some South Vietnamese units remained for offensive actions.

President Nixon got worldwide criticism for his decision to attack into Cambodia. There were many protests in America, including those on many college campuses. A confrontation between students and National Guard troops occurred at Kent State University in Ohio during such a protest, and several students were killed.[282] Between 75,000 and 100,000 protesters marched in Washington. About 100,000 construction and dockworkers paraded in New York City, backing President Nixon's policies. Nixon claimed the Cambodian victory was necessary to expedite the withdrawal of American troops.

In the central front, the Fourth Division took part in the insertion of American troops into Cambodia to destroy enemy military and supply bases just across the border. On May 6, they started Operation Binh Tay (Tame the West).[283] Unlike in the area further south, the enemy stayed to fight, or at least to confront the landings. The Fourth Division helicopters were met with fierce fire at many LZs. Some had to go to alternative LZs. The Third Battalion of the Eighth Infantry Regiment ran into trouble after it put 60 men on the ground, and a fierce firefight developed, but the enemy eventually withdrew. All of this NVA resistance occurred despite intensive pre-attack bombing by B-52s. Despite all of its difficulties, the Fourth Division found numerous caches of enemy supplies. None was as large as those found in the Fishhook or Parrot's Beak areas further to the south. After about 10 days, the Americans pulled back, and left the ARVN troops to search for more caches.

In these and subsequent operations, Specialist Joseph H. Bryan earned the Air Medal for participating in aerial flights in support of ground operations with the 14th Infantry (*Kentucky Standard,* January 29, 1970). They flew into many hot LZs.

Specialist James Tingle earned an Army Commendation Medal with the 47th Engineers (*Kentucky Standard,* November 5, 1970), and Sergeant Charles Rogers received a Bronze Star for meritorious action against the enemy (*Kentucky Standard,* August 30, 1970).

Private First Class Joseph E. Roby earned a Combat Infantry Badge with the Eighth Infantry, Fourth Division, for sustained ground combat with the enemy (*Kentucky Standard,* October 20, 1970).

On April 15, 25 Americans died and 54 were wounded in the Americal Division sector, the highest one-day casualty number for the year.

Fourteen of the men were killed by a 105-mm artillery shell, which the enemy had rigged as a booby trap. The explosion caused two 81-mm mortar shells to explode, which in turn, caused Claymore mines in some of the soldiers' packs to detonate. Booby traps killed an increasing number of men.

Fighting raged from May 3 to May 5 in the town of Jiep Duc in the Americal Division's area, where the North Vietnamese held three hamlets. Two-hundred nineteen NVA soldiers were killed, compared to seven Americans and 12 South Vietnamese soldiers.[284]

Specialist David Ingraham was with the Americal Division (*Kentucky Standard*, February 2, 1970). Private James Bose was also with the Americal Division and received the Army Commendation Medal (*Kentucky Standard*, June 28, 1970).

Private First Class Joseph L. Ball was with the First Battalion, Sixth Regiment, 196th Light Infantry Brigade, and Private First Class Phillip Lyvers was with Battery D, 77th Artillery in support of the Americal (*Kentucky Standard*, August 20, 1970).

Private First Class Larry Reinle of the 57th Intelligence Patrol also served in the Americal Division (*Kentucky Standard*, March 12, 1970). He worked with scout dogs, including many German shepherds. The dogs were trained to sniff out the enemy, hidden mines, trip flares, and booby traps. They were usually in the lead of patrols on the point. When the enemy or other devices were found, the dogs would be moved back out of danger. They were a valuable asset.

Lance Corporal Robert Searcy also worked with dogs with the First Marine Battalion at Da Nang. He reported that on 45 missions, the dogs were responsible for 67 enemy dead, 230 wounded, and 261 captured.

A story appeared in *Time* magazine[285] about the South Vietnamese popular Self Defense Force in the Mekong Delta. Tom Hayden, who graduated from St. Joseph Prep in Bardstown, Kentucky, was training irregulars into a disciplined fighting force.[286] He helped build a force of 3,000 irregulars to defend themselves against the Vietcong. These men were unpaid and had to furnish their own uniforms. One of the said, "I protect my city. If during the Vietcong Tet Offensive, we had a self defense, the Vietcong could not have come in. Now they can't burn our houses again."[287]

Tom Hayden was serving as a civilian with the Agency for International Development (AID) at the time. He had previously served with the marines, and had earned two Purple Hearts. He also earned the Bronze Star with V for valor for saving four wounded South Vietnamese troops. He retired as a lieutenant colonel in the Marine Corps, after putting in 35 years of government service, much of it in intelligence and special operations. He has written two books about special operations and low-intensity conflicts. Even though the Popular Self Defense Force was effective locally, it did little to change the war. It was too little, too late. By 1970, the war had lost its credibility for a large number of Americans.

In the north, the Fifth Infantry Division was hit in defensive positions west of Con Thien. Air support repulsed the attack. The next day the NVA hit again at Cam Lo.[288] An intense firefight lasted three hours, during which a Sheridan tank and two armored personnel carriers were destroyed before the NVA was driven off.

Specialist Joseph F. Pardieu, with the Fifth Division, earned the Army Commendation Medal with V for valor for meritorious action against a hostile force (*Kentucky Standard,* August 6, 1970).

On March 9, the marines turned over control of I Corps to the US Army. The commanding general of the five northernmost provinces was to be Lieutenant General Melvin Zais of the 101st Airborne Division. From April 1, the 101st would be engaged in various operations, including Operation Texas Star and Operation Glen. One brigade of the 101st kept the responsibility for pacification and development support in Thua Thien Hue province, while the other two brigades conducted offensive operations in the western portion of Thua Thien Hue and Quang Tri provinces.

Offensive operations of the 101st included sweeps through the rugged jungle and mountainous parts of northwest South Vietnam, close to the Laotian border. They even ventured back into the ever-dangerous A Shau Valley. Operation Jefferson Glen, which lasted six months, and consisted of patrolling and sweeping the rocket belts around critical installations, followed these operations. These belts were areas from which the enemy could launch rocket and mortar barrages into cities and military bases.

Private First Class Jerry Howard, with Company K of the Airborne Rangers, was with the 101st in these actions (*Kentucky Standard,* April 16, 1970). He stepped on a punji stake, got a severe infection in his foot, and ended up in the hospital. He received the Purple Heart.

Mike Jameson also served with the 101st. Jameson enlisted in November 1969. He volunteered with four others, Mike Fogle, Jerry Blanford, Gene Cammack, and Jimmy Bose. He was sent to Fort Knox for basic training. From there went to Fort Polk in Louisiana for infantry training in the Armed Individual Center for jungle warfare. He then shipped out to Vietnam, landing at Long Binh, a replacement center. He had bunker training for two weeks, and was assigned to the 101st Airborne Division. (Some called it the 101st Air Mobility Division.) He was in country for four days before he was sent to Bien Hoa, which had been hit by the North Vietnamese and suffered a number of casualties.

Jameson was assigned to a roving brigade of 35 men, about platoon size. He stayed with them for most of his tour. Around Phu Bai, his group worked off Tomahawk Firebase. This was the same base where the enemy attacked the Bardstown National Guard company and caused so many losses. The firebase had been moved back to the top of the hill, to be less vulnerable. His group primarily worked around artillery firebases in sweeps trying to draw fire so that the enemy would expose itself and could be pounded by artillery fire. They moved from place to place where they were needed. Most of their action was in the Third and I Corps areas. However, they even went south to around Tay Ninh and into Cambodia, where they stayed four days before pulling back. Another time, they went up around Quang Tri in the north. At one time, Jameson's platoon was down to 12 men due to casualties.

The largest firebase Jameson was at was Birmingham, but the worst was Firebase Brick at the head of the A Shau Valley, where they went for several sweeps. The valley was one of the main ways for the North Vietnamese to enter South Vietnam. It was heavy jungle with a triple canopy.

Jameson's unit tried to avoid the few trails because of booby traps, and cut their way through heavy jungle with machetes. Movement was very slow, sometimes only a few hundred yards in a day. It was hard to keep their bearings, and sometimes they had to ask artillery to fire an airburst to get their coordinates. He was the squad leader, and as such was often the point man, leading the squad and cutting jungle undergrowth. His was also the most dangerous position. Jameson was wounded twice, both times in the right leg, and had to be medevaced out once. He walked point for the better part of eight months, and was in many firefights.

Many Vietnam veterans thought the A Shau Valley was the worst place to fight; it was never completely conquered. The North Vietnamese fought tenaciously to hold it.

Jameson's platoon was airmobile and had to be ready to fly by helicopters in a few minutes' notice. They flew into hot areas laced by enemy fire several times. Everybody in his group got Air Medals. He and his platoon had to stay together, and got close. When one of several of the short-timers was allowed to go home, they always picked married men with children, and took care of each other. Short-term soldiers were put in safe places by their buddies.

Occasionally on their patrols, they ran into tunnel entrances. Jameson, as the smallest, became a "tunnel rat" for the patrol, and climbed down to investigate. He never ran into the enemy in the tunnels, but one time he discovered a large complex in the A Shau Valley, with a hospital room, and a cache of weapons, ammunition, dressings, medicine, and food. When the patrol found such tunnels, they pulled out and specialists destroyed the tunnels.

Jameson had great respect for the North Vietnamese. They would hole up in bunkers with extended tunnels, and no amount of shelling, rockets, or air bombs could get them out. He remembers B-52s dropping such a great amount of ordnance that it looked as if they had blown off the top of a mountain. However, when the American infantry charged the hill, they were still caught in crossfire from the mountain. He also respected the sappers. One time when he was on Tomahawk Hill, enemy sappers snuck in with wire cutters, and satchel charges strapped to themselves, and blew up the whole side of the hill.

Jameson felt that a lot of damage was done to the Vietcong and North Vietnamese during his tour of duty in Vietnam. They took many casualties, but they were always ready to regroup and replaced their losses shortly. They had the uncanny sense of knowing how long to stay in a firefight, how long they could inflict damage.

Jameson came home in June '71. From the time he got word, went to Phu Bai and Cam Ranh Bay, and flew out, he was home in four days. He had spent most of his time in high country and had seen more than his share of battle.

Sergeant Paul Johnson was another member of the 101st Airborne Division (*Kentucky Standard*, August 13, 1970). He joined the army on November 2, 1968, and had been in Vietnam since January 1970. He had just returned from a 30-day leave when he died. He was a member of a reconnaissance helicopter company, Troop 2/17 Cavalry, attached to the 101st Division. They were the eyes of the division, scouting in front of it, and often engaging in firefights against isolated enemy troops. He was killed June 28, 1970, probably in one of these firefights. He was from New Haven, Kentucky, and his remains were brought back there. He was one of four men from New Haven who lost their lives in Vietnam.

Another was Staff Sergeant Nicholas Johnson (*Kentucky Standard*, August 20, 1970). Nick Johnson was born in October 1944. He was one of 10 children and had children of his own, which should have kept him out of Vietnam. He also had a brother serving in the navy off Vietnam, and there was a rule that siblings should not serve in a hostile area at the same time, but despite both, he ended up in Vietnam. When he went there in 1969, he was assigned to the Ninth Division, serving in the Mekong Delta. He had attended NCO candidate school stateside, and was a squad sergeant. He later became a staff sergeant and a platoon leader.

General Westmoreland assigned Johnson's Ninth Division to help control the Vietcong in the delta, the most populous and productive part of South Vietnam. When Johnson joined the Ninth, the Vietcong had been decisively beaten on several occasions, usually with moderate to severe losses on both sides. Most often, the Vietcong got the worst of it, but they snuck back in, and it finally became obvious that it wasn't a war of body counts, but one of perseverance.

If the war was to be won, it became obvious that the enemy's ability to wage war had to be eliminated. The enemy's communications and their supply lines had to be disrupted, and the Vietcong superstructure had to be dislodged. In the summer of 1970, this had become the task of Gen. Creighton Abrams, Westmoreland's successor.

When President Nixon approved the invasion of the Cambodian supply bases, the last brigade of the Ninth Division still in Vietnam was to attack south of the 25th Division. It's impossible to say what Johnson's role was in that action, but the action was a success. His unit probably endured the physical demands of patrolling through jungles and swampy land, working cooperatively with the Riverine naval forces to help clear the canals of enemy interdiction, getting muddy up to their chests, picking leeches off at the end of the day, fighting where necessary, and doing all of the things that a platoon had to do.

In early August, Johnson went to Australia on R&R. After returning, and while on patrol on August 13, 1970, one of his men set off a bouncing Betty booby trap—a fiendish device that bounced up when activated, and exploded about two feet off the ground. It blew off the man's legs, and a piece of shrapnel hit Johnson in the head, causing almost immediate death, probably hitting the vital centers in the brain stem. Once again, booby traps claimed more victims. An increasing number of American casualties was due to them.

Johnson had only a few weeks left on his tour. He became the fourth Vietnam death of his hometown, New Haven. It was particularly sad because of his family with small children.

Johnson was a platoon sergeant, respected by all of his men. Two members of his platoon later visited his family. They were complimentary of Johnson, and his leadership in showing them the ropes. One was the soldier who had had his legs blown off.

The air force was still flying missions out of Thailand in support of ARVN and American units, hitting the Ho Chi Minh Trail, and bombing North Vietnam. They were still flying over Cambodia and Laos, although their flights were never publicized or even acknowledged. When they did go down in Cambodia and Laos, they were said to have gone down in Southeast Asia. When they went down, efforts were made to extract personnel if it was deemed that the pilot and crew were still alive. Even though Cambodia and Laos were supposedly neutral, they had communist insurgents, the Khmer Rouge and the Pathet Lao, ranging the countryside. Being captured by them was frequently worse than being captured by the North Vietnamese. When American planes went down, long-range helicopters were sent in to North Vietnam, Laos, or Cambodia to try to extract any Americans, if possible.

Such was the situation Major Hubert Berthold found himself in (*Kentucky Standard*, April 30, 1970, and July 9, 1970). He had been a teacher and assistant coach at Old Kentucky Home High School in Bardstown, and had married a Bardstown girl. After joining the service, he served in both Germany and Vietnam. He had three tours in Vietnam.

On this particular tour, he was the pilot of a large rescue helicopter called the "Jolly Green," when a call came that two men were down in "Southeast Asia." Other helicopters had tried to rescue them, but enemy fire drove them off. Major Berthold made desperate and heroic attempts to save the two men on several tries, each time taking heavy enemy fire. Finally, his helicopter was so shot up he had to give up or risk the lives of his crew. His helicopter was riddled with holes. Even his gas tank had been punctured. He received a commendation for the mission that said that it was only with heroism and skill that he got his helicopter and his men safely home to their base. He received the Silver Star and the Distinguished Flying Cross.

Airman First Class John C. Forsee also served with a rescue unit in Thailand.

In the latter part of 1970, Vietnamization was going full swing, and American troops were coming home. The First Division, the Big Red One, one of the first to go to Vietnam in the spring of 1965, was packing up and leaving.[289] Their area of combat and protection north of Saigon was turned over to the 22nd ARVN Division, which they had helped train. The First Marine Division was packing up and leaving, with only a few units left behind. The Fourth Division that had fought so bravely and doggedly to subdue the enemy in the highlands around Pleiku and up to the Cambodian border, also left after four years of meritorious duty.[290] The last brigade of the Ninth Division, which included the 60th Regiment that Nick Johnson belonged to, was to leave by the first of 1971.

Some of the navy's Riverine Force stayed in the delta, and would work with ARVN units. The 25th Division, which had fought all over, from the Cambodian border to the highlands and as part of the initial Task Force Oregon on the coast, was leaving to return its old base in Hawaii.[291] The 199th Light Infantry Brigade was leaving to return to Fort Benning to have its colors retired. South Vietnamese Divisions replaced all of them.[292]

The First Cavalry Division, "The First Team," remained to give stability to the central part of Vietnam. The 101st Airborne Division, which didn't come as a whole until late 1966, was still there to guard the northern five provinces, the most threatened part of South Vietnam. The Fifth Infantry Mechanized Brigade was still stationed along the DMZ, securing the area for which the Third Marine Division had fought for five years. The Americal Division remained to guard the coast around Chu Lai. Numerous other smaller outfits also remained: the aviation assets so necessary for the support of the ground troops, artillery units, and back-up units such as the engineers, transportation, MPs, and the Signal Corps. They would assist the South Vietnamese as much as they could, and guard American facilities. Special Services advisers remained to give their vital service.

Over the next two years, American ground forces would become only a skeleton of the mighty army of a half million men. Enough remained, however, of the muscle to guarantee security for South Vietnam, and hold the enemy at bay in 1970 until the South Vietnamese army could take over.

Nelson County continued to be well represented in Vietnam in 1970. In addition to those already mentioned or who were closely associated, were:

Sergeant Vella Boblitt: 6994 Security Squad; earned Air Medal f or reconnaissance flight

Sergeant Joseph E. Clayton: 173rd Airborne Brigade

Sergeant William T. Davis

Private First Class Carl Borland: 67th Evacuation Hospital

Sergeant Mike Fowler: Commendation Medal

Private Tommy Girdley: First Battalion, Fifth Marines

Sergeant Ed Boblitt Hart: First Division Operations and Intelligence

Sergeant William D. Holt: Bronze Star earned against hostile forces, 563rd Transportation Company

Terry Jones: Company A, 84th Signal Battalion

Private First Class Kenneth Mattingly: Nha Trang, 864th Engineer Battalion

Staff Sergeant Joseph L. Mudd: 6225 Air Squadron

Specialist David L. Newton

William Shields: 93rd Engineers

Private First Class Keith Spalding: 564th Transportation Company

CHAPTER 19

INTELLIGENCE

_____

It's important in any war to know where the enemy is, how many of them there are, and what their plans are. This has been true ever since wars have been fought, back to the Egyptian Hittite wars and beyond. Initially, this required spies, and personal observation, both of which are still important methods. The practice of surveillance has gotten ever more sophisticated with time, from the use of balloons, and tapping telegraph wires in the Civil War, the use and breaking of codes in World Wars I and II, and spy planes during the Cold War.

In the Vietnam War, intelligence gathering rose to a new level of sophistication. The enemy's main weapons were secrecy, surprise, and small group attacks; gathering information about them was all the more difficult. In Vietnam, the enemy looked, talked, and acted just like friendly forces. It was complicated to tell friend from foe and who was or wasn't a mole.

In an effort to develop the best intelligence about the enemy and assist friendly forces, new levels of sophistication were developed, and old methods were refined. Highly tuned listening devices, movement devices, and all sorts of instrumentation were used. Perhaps one of the biggest boondoggles of the war was Defense Secretary Robert McNamara's planned line of movement protection devices all across the DMZ. It was never completed because of its expense and impracticality.

By far, the most-used and most effective method of finding the enemy was simple patrolling with bodies on the ground, foot soldiers who became the eyes and ears of larger units, whether they were the size of companies or regiments. It was also the most dangerous.

The second most-used method was probably aerial reconnaissance, using observation planes from small Piper Cub-type planes to helicopters, to T28 observation jets, on up to larger planes with the most advanced cameras and lenses. However, the thick jungle canopies that covered much of Vietnam limited aerial reconnaissance. Newer techniques were developed to detect movement, heat radiation, and infrared radiation below the trees and vines. These methods were imperfect at best, but better than nothing.

Other methods were used. The experiences of several servicemen from Nelson County demonstrate the diversity in intelligence gathering methods. Intelligence gathering is a day-in and day-out examination of monitored data, a large part of which is seemingly unusable. However, when the information is assembled on a master plot or map, a better picture is obtained.

One of the most unusual stories to come out of Vietnam was that of Bill Huston, a retired Coast Guard captain and the current president of St. Catherine's College, just 16 miles from Bardstown. He was born in Canada, and his first introduction to Nelson County was when he attended St. Joseph Prep School in Bardstown. He went to school there for four years, graduated in 1965, and became a loyal alumnus.

After graduating, he went to Murray State College and Lindsey Wilson College. Not too successful or happy in college, he joined the navy in 1968.

After basic training at Great Lakes, he was sent to visual communication school in San Diego, where he learned Morse code and semaphore. He did well and he credited discipline learned at St. Joseph Prep for preparing him for anything that came at him. He was to spend 36 years in the service—six in the navy and 30 in the Coast Guard.

His first assignment after communication school was Vietnam. He almost became a corpsman in the marines, but his actual assignment was just as grueling and dangerous.

He was placed in a 12-foot boat with two other men, in an inlet off the South China Sea at about the level of the DMZ that divided North and South Vietnam. Their work was clandestine, picking up all transmissions, whether Vietnamese or American, and transmitting them to an intelligence ship, the *Bonner*, 12 to 13 miles out to sea. Silence was the most necessary part of their work. They could not talk, even among themselves. Their communication with each other was semaphore, using their hands.

Huston's job was to listen on earphones all day for messages. These were transmitted to a boat mate by semaphore, who wrote them down for later transmission.

They had a nine-and-a-half horsepower motor on the boat, but they never used it because of the noise. At dusk, they would paddle from their upstream hiding place down to the sea. This usually took two hours, and Huston slept while his two mates paddled. After reaching the sea, Huston signaled the day's messages to the intelligence ship by means of a flashing light with an infrared screen. About four o'clock in the morning, when all of the transmission was done, he slept again while the other two paddled back upstream to their hiding place.

They did this day in and day out for 22 months without letup. They didn't shave or cut their hair during that time, and grew long ponytails. They looked like Robinson Crusoes. Their baths consisted of slipping over the side of their boat and rinsing off. They couldn't use soap, for fear that the enemy would detect the suds downstream. Their boat wasn't made for comfort. They had only a 21- by 23-foot tarpaulin to protect themselves from the rain, and the hard boards on the bottom of the boat to sleep on. About every two to three weeks, a plane would come over and drop supplies on the beach from which they did their nightly transmissions. It contained only their food, chlorinating pills for drinking water, malaria pills, and the most meager of supplies.

They transmitted all messages they picked up, regardless of how unimportant they may have seemed. These, in turn, were sent to higher intelligence for decoding. Troop movements, raiding parties, artillery placements, offensive movements and plans, and messages from downed American pilots were just some of the information they passed on. Frequently, the messages didn't mean anything, but they were passed on anyway. Huston learned the parties on the other end of the transmission by the way that they answered, and occasionally would get non-military news back, such as ball scores.

They were in constant danger of capture, but the Lord was with them. One night, North Vietnamese troops camped right above them on a 20-foot bank. Huston could hear them popping open something that sounded like beer cans, and then using something that sounded like poker chips. In the morning, they were gone.

The only weapon Huston and his shipmates had was a 45-caliber pistol with six shells, more for self use than for any other purpose, if capture was imminent and if they so desired.

They were supposed to be there for a six-month tour, but ended up spending 22 months on one of the most intriguing assignments of the war. Despite the appalling conditions they had to live in, and the lack of normal human communication, they survived without psychological problems. It was an almost two-year chapter of Huston's life marked by void and isolation. When they finally got word they were to be taken back to civilization, they were pulled out in 24 hours. Huston came home after debriefing at Pearl Harbor and San Diego.

He was supposed to have a four-week home leave, but in two weeks, he got orders to report to Bath, Maine, to serve on a newly commissioned guided missile armed frigate, the USS *Reeves*. On this ship, he was to serve as an E5 signalman. After a shakedown cruise at Guantanamo Bay, the frigate sailed to Pearl Harbor. Once back in the western Pacific, they sailed off Vietnam for a 13-month cruise, primarily using their missiles to protect aircraft carriers, and larger ships from air attack. With their Terrier anti-aircraft guided missiles, they shot down about 20 enemy planes.

Their primary port was Subic Bay in the Philippines, but they went to other harbors such as Hong Kong, Taiwan, and Japan. Huston hoped to get to Australia, but never made it. After their first tour, they were sent on another 13-month tour.

In all, Huston spent 48 months in and around Vietnam. He had one scary occasion on board the USS *Reeves*. One of the Terrier missiles didn't disengage from its launcher after it started firing. It had almost enough destructive power to cripple the ship and the order was given to abandon ship, but the missile fizzled out without mishap. Huston was persuaded to serve two more years in the navy after his initial enlistment, because of his crucial MOS.

After his stint in the navy, he went back to college and got his degree. He went from there to form the first Coast Guard station in Paducah, Kentucky, becoming an officer. He went steadily up in the Coast Guard to become a captain, the equivalent of an army colonel, and became commanding officer at St. Louis and Huntington, West Virginia, covering the Ohio River from Pittsburgh to Louisville.

After 9/11, he was reactivated, and served at Scott Air Force Base, coordinating movement of equipment all over the world. He served five months the first recall time and three months the second.

Virgil O'Bryan was drafted and entered the service on April 29, 1970, after two years of college (*Kentucky Standard,* March 21, 1968). After completing signal corps and intelligence schools, he was sent to Vietnam on September 7, 1970. He landed at Long Binh, and was stationed at Camp Debeau on the edge on Tan Son Nhut Air Base. Tan Son Nhut was the nerve and intelligence center for most of Vietnam. His mission there was primarily as a decoder for all of the messages sent in from army, marine, and coast guard outposts, and air force and naval reconnaissance flights. This information was relayed on to infantry, artillery, and air bombing units.

O'Bryan also acted as a courier from Tan Son Nhut to various other American bases, such as those at Da Nang, Nha Trahn, Long Binh, Can Tho, Vung Tau, and Cu Chi. Usually, he traveled by jeep, but sometimes by helicopter, particularly to Da Nang and Nha Trang. He was shot at by snipers, and frequently found holes in the jeeps and helicopters. Five people from his section were killed, and three committed suicide. He also flew missions delivering crypto gear (KA-7) to various stations. This was highly secret equipment, and had a self-destructive device that could be set off by touching two wires together. None of the devices was ever captured by the Vietcong or the North Vietnamese.

O'Bryan recalls several happenings. The tower of Camp Debeau collapsed due to the Vietcong inadvertently tunneling under its piers. In the tunnel, they found a large cache of captured American arms, M-16s, and grenade and rocket launchers. Camp Debeau was struck by several Vietcong rockets, and was bombed once by a South Vietnamese pilot. Tan Son Nhut and Saigon were rocketed almost daily. There were no safe places in Vietnam.

He remembers once while driving back from Da Nang on a courier mission, the sky lit up and the ground shook as the ammunition dump at Cam Ranh Bay, 50 miles south, blew up.

O'Bryan signed up for a second tour, and for the last six months worked out of the US Embassy. The embassy was a cover for his intelligence work. He drove around in a black embassy jeep, sometimes in street clothes. Off duty, he ventured into the pleasure part of Saigon. He was twice robbed and once knocked out. One time, he inadvertently walked into a hotel room where a black market deal with the Vietcong was going on. The *mama san* of the hotel quickly ushered him out.

After coming home, following his discharge, he was unable to get a good job, and rejoined the army for a three-year stretch. This time, however, he did his intelligence work in Hawaii. He was there when the released POWs arrived at Hickam Air Force Base. He was part of the guard. He saw Lieutenant Colonel Jimmy Bean, but was unable to talk to him. He said they were all smiling, gaunt, and gawking around at all of the changes that had happened during the long period of their imprisonment.

He was offered an opportunity to go to Virginia Military Institute for officer training, but decided to get out of the service in 1975. He was tempted to stay in because he liked intelligence work, but his hometown beckoned.

Corporal Tyre G. Forsee (Terry) was born April 15, 1945. After his schooling, which included three years of college, he joined the marines on June 26, 1963. After completing boot camp at Parris Island, he went to radio school in Pensacola, Florida. There he specialized in radio direction finding for eight months. He was sent to Hawaii as a member of the First Radio Battalion. For the next two years, he operated out of that battalion, going to Vietnam for two tours, the first for four months, and the second for 13 months.

On Forsee's first tour of Vietnam, he landed at Da Nang and was sent to Phu Bai on temporary additional duty with the army. There he worked with a scope picking up enemy transmissions. On the scope, he was able to determine the direction (zero to 360 degrees) from which the transmission came. This finding was triangulated with the findings of other scopes up and down the coast to fix the position of the transmitter. In the course of an eight-hour shift, 200 to 300 transmissions were detected. In an adjacent room, the army would pick up the messages for encoding, writing them down in blocks of five.

Forsee worked at Phu Bai for four months, and then returned to Hawaii. He recalled that the code listening people at Phu Bai got so good they could determine the sender by the way the messages were sent, and could follow him around in his unit's movements.

After a few months in Hawaii, Forsee was sent back to Vietnam. There he worked in marine bases, and was shifted around from Da Nang to Chu Lai, and Quang Ngai. Everywhere he went he had to have his helmet on and carry his M-14, even to the beach. The men did the radio direction finding work in trailers, often on hills and as much as five miles from the perimeter where Forsee lived. The marines lived in tents, but the army had concrete barracks at Phu Bai. When he was at Da Nang, their perimeter on Hill 327 was alerted one night about a possible attack. It was the policy of the marines that when under attack, the men would take their weapons and go to the perimeter. That was the only time he felt threatened.

In Chu Lai, Forsee's trailer was situated in front of a hill where a battery of 155 howitzers was located. The reverberation from the 155 shells passing overhead exploded one of the radio scopes, and put them temporarily out of action. Sappers with satchel charges attacked the same artillery base at night. The attack was unsuccessful, but his unit's generator was damaged. The attack happened at night when they were not in the trailer, but five miles away in camp. The damage was repaired and the direction went on without missing a day.

Forsee was a corporal during most of his stay, but was promoted to sergeant before his discharge. After Vietnam, he went back to Kaneohe Marine Air Corps Base in Hawaii, where he finished out his term in the marines. He had served four years.

Despite all of the efforts to gain intelligence of enemy plans and dispositions, often the intelligence was faulty or absent altogether. Perhaps the worst example was the Tet Offensive.

The United States had no idea of its timing, size, and scope of all of the urban areas to be affected. Forty-three urban areas were attacked; none of the attacks was expected. Thousands of Vietcong infiltrated Saigon, Hue, and all of the provincial capitals. Stocks of arms and ammunition had been placed in many of the cities in advance. The Vietcong were in the center of many of the cities, and had a chokehold on them before the US troops knew what was happening. Over 80,000 Vietcong were involved. It boggles the mind, and defies common sense that so many men could be moved into position, and not anticipated.

The South Vietnamese army, supposedly guardians of the cities, was at half-strength because of the Tet holiday. Good intelligence is always active even in the calmest of times, but it was an abject failure in predicting the Tet Offensive.

General Westmoreland had shortly before said that America was winning the war, and could see the light at the end of the tunnel. It was obviously a case of overconfidence, and not seeing the forest for the trees.

The Tet Offensive turned out to be a tactical defeat for the Vietcong. The populace had not risen up to join them, as it had not joined in mind and soul with the South Vietnamese government and forces before Tet. Locally, Vietcong forces were gutted with enormous losses. It was estimated that over half were killed or captured. However, strategically and internationally, particularly within the United States, it was a master stroke, as it shook American confidence and diminished backing for the war. The failure of intelligence had a near crippling effect on the American war effort.

Intelligence also failed in predicting where the enemy was, and how well dug in he might be in bunkers and tunnels. Time after time, the facts were found out the hard way, by stumbling into a well-emplaced enemy, and suffering a withering sheet of multiple weapons fire. Even though both sides set up ambushes, the enemy seemed more expert in laying them. American troops could and often did have a general idea where certain enemy units were, but unfortunately, approximation wasn't good enough. Foot soldiers on patrol had to do their own intelligence, and often paid for it with casualties.

Intelligence was successful in telling where major enemy formations were, such as the build up around Khe Sanh and north of the DMZ. It could tell where the major supply dumps were in Cambodia and Laos. It could also tell the approximate location of Vietcong battalions and regiments. However, approximations were the best that intelligence could do most of the time. Direct questioning of prisoners also helped, but it was sketchy. In a war where the enemy could be anywhere, intelligence was doubly difficult. Special Forces camps along the Cambodian and Laotian borders helped to gather information on enemy movements. Overall, considering the type of war that it was, intelligence was a mixed bag, with both successes and failures. They did the best they could.

Marine Corporal Samuel Lawrence, from Nelson County, served with intelligence, and Sergeant Ed Bobblitt Hart was with the First Division Operations and Intelligence (*Kentucky Standard*, April 4, 1968).

CHAPTER 20

MEDICAL CARE

Medical care in Vietnam for acute care wounds showed considerable improvement over previous wars. The changes often saved lives or limbs. There were four areas of medical care, which were interdependent on each other.

The first was the medic or corpsman assigned to platoons. Their fellow servicemen often called them "Doc." They were well-respected because the line soldiers knew their lives were dependent on their doc's actions. The medics were well trained in first aid, and in most areas of primary care for battlefield wounds. They were taught the proper use of tourniquets to stanch bleeding, and the use of rapid intravenous fluids to prevent shock. They were taught to treat chest wounds with bandaging to prevent sucking wounds and tension pneumothorax, which caused lung collapse and pressure on the other lung, a rapidly fatal injury. They were taught positioning to allow for proper ventilation of the non-injured lung. In neck wounds, they had to maintain an airway, usually by positioning, but sometimes by tracheotomy—cutting directly into the windpipe if there was an obstruction from blood clots or destroyed tissue. In neck injuries, direct pressure was necessary to stop bleeding, and proper positioning was necessary to prevent further spinal cord injuries.

In limb injuries, proper positioning and splinting were necessary to try to save the limb, prevent complications, and take pressure off arteries that gave vital blood to the distal limb. In all injuries where the skin was penetrated, the gross removal of dirt and the use of antibiotic powder and dressing helped prevent infection.

Medics and corpsmen were taught all of this. Doing these procedures on the battlefield was easier said than done. It was most hazardous to do these procedures while bullets were flying, and mortars and grenades were exploding all around. The mortality and morbidity rate of docs was much higher than that of the average line soldier.

The Vietcong and the NVA learned early that Americans were trained to take care of their downed fellow soldiers. They would wound a soldier, and then pick off those coming to his aid one by one. Sometimes the wounded would live and the doc would die. To the everlasting glory of the medics and corpsmen, they kept trying to save their charges in the platoon. They were in a position to do more than any other medical personnel in the chain of care to save a soldier from going into shock. The GIs knew it. The docs were most revered. They were often the difference between getting home or not. The docs also helped get the injured to the rear, where they could be evacuated, which was another extremely dangerous chore. Some men from Nelson County and men closely associated with the county served as docs, such as James M. Morton with the marines and Specialist David Blair with the 173rd Airborne Brigade (*Kentucky Standard*, April 10, 1969).

Once the wounded were taken to the rear, they needed to be transported to an evacuation hospital. When the battle was going on all around, getting a helicopter in to pick them up was often most hazardous, and many helicopters were shot down in the process. Some medical evacuation companies would not fly into hot LZs, but it was amazing the number of pilots who would, day or night. Their exploits were legendary.

Chief Warrant Officer Denny Howard and Lieutenant Lud McKay did it time after time. Others flew in as crewmen, including William Tichenor, who was commended by a lieutenant general for saving his son's life.

Hueys, the workhorse of the army, and H-34s for the marines, were converted for medical evacuation purposes. They were equipped with all sorts of life-saving equipment. Most importantly, there was often another doc on board to give the necessary continuity of care. It was a little higher level of care than could be given on the battlefield, and the rapid provision of fluids could keep men out of shock long enough to get them to the hospital for more definitive care. In desperate situations, men were loaded on the helicopters any way they could get them on, up to eight at a time. Once the wounded were loaded, the medic aboard had to triage, and take care of the most seriously wounded and savable first.

Sometimes because of heavy ground fire, the helicopters would touch down or hover only for a few seconds, and the wounded were loaded without the gentlest of care. Sometimes, they would be hit again, and the medics, as well. Sometimes the medic would have to unstack bodies to give care. With critically wounded soldiers and marines, every minute was important in the saving of lives. The pressure on the docs was tremendous, but most often, they did amazingly well in their blood-saturated situation.

Once the helicopter was in the air, the evacuation hospital would be forewarned what was coming in. Teams of nurses, both male and female, and emergency triage doctors would be waiting to give the best care available to the wounded. Those with shock, chest or belly wounds, or major severed arteries would be treated first, but all would be taken care of with the best medical care available. Nurses were dedicated, and some would even go out on helicopter evacs when necessary. Nine army nurses were killed in Vietnam.

Once the wounded landed at the area evac hospital, they were quickly triaged by doctors and nurses. Those in the worst condition—soldiers with complicated chest or belly wounds, those in shock, those with acute respiratory distress, and those threatened by immediate limb loss due to arterial damage—were rushed to emergency surgery after they were stabilized. In most cases, the care was life saving, but sometimes even with the best of care, patients died, such as Staff Sergeant James Raphael Norris of New Haven, Kentucky, whose multiple injuries were too much.

Those patients with less serious injuries were cleaned up and patched up until more definitive surgery could be carried out. These included those with fractures or deep muscle wounds, and stable chest and belly wounds. These patients were supported by IV fluids, analgesics, splinting, and other ancillary measures.

Closed head wounds were observed unless signs were seen of increasing intracranial pressure. Occasionally, emergency trephining, or drilling a hole in the skull, was necessary to relieve pressure on the brain. Open head wounds had to be cleaned and closed.

All wounds were considered dirty wounds, and were vigorously cleaned, debrided of dead flesh, and treated liberally with antibiotics. Drains were inserted in body cavities associated with wounds to prevent formation of abscesses.

Often nurses cleaned and sutured superficial wounds, and removed shrapnel if it was not too deep or life threatening.

The evac hospitals also saw non-surgical cases, such as malaria, pneumonia, skin rashes and infections, and a whole gamut of medical infections.

Those who needed long-term care—fractures, amputations, colostomies (where a section of the gut is externalized), severe head injuries, etc.—were sent to regional long-term care hospitals in Okinawa, the Philippines, Japan, or the states.

Dr. James Brashear, stationed at Cu Chi Evacuation Hospital 12, was one of the Nelson Countians who was involved with medical care in Vietnam (*Kentucky Standard*, March 21, 1968).[294] His story was written by another doctor and sent to the *Kentucky Standard*, and was printed in the US Congressional Record. This information is drawn from those accounts.

In the 10 months Dr. Brashear was at Evacuation Hospital 12 at Cu Chi, more than 6,000 inpatients and countless outpatients were treated. Patients included American military, Vietnamese military and civilians, and Vietcong. Treatment was mainly limited to acute cases, the majority of which were injuries sustained as a direct result of the war.

Brashear recalled that the surgical capabilities of the doctors serving with him were excellent, and that the services rendered by the helicopter pilots and crews in evacuating the wounded were beyond belief.

The lives of three young men with heart injuries were saved when he was at Evac 12. All three were in surgery within 15 minutes of when they were wounded. These and many others would have died if their treatments had been delayed even a few minutes.

According to Brashear, supplies were always a problem, and X-ray and laboratory were very poor when the hospital started, but improved steadily. He was in the first group that reactivated the 12th Evac Hospital at Cu Chi. The unit had not treated any casualties since World War II. When he left the unit in September 1967, the hospital facilities were still below what could be expected, but the situation was undoubtedly better than it had been in any previous war.

Even though the hospital was a model pacification center, it suffered mortar and sniper attacks intermittently. Even though the hospital was considered secure, one mortar attack killed 20 people and snipers killed many, many more.

Brashear felt that, after two years of effort, the US and Saigon governments had not been able to say to the peasants, "You are safe to go about your daily affairs." The same was true of the military, and was a constant source of frustration as snipers and land mines killed people in and around their encampments. This was especially true since it was impossible to tell the friendly villagers from the deadly Vietcong, and searches were almost always fruitless.

According to the letter in the *Kentucky Standard*, Dr. Brashear said, "Observing casualties taken in day after day disturbs the peasants. As a result, the populations are extremely reluctant to rally to either the Saigon or US cause. Yet our presence in Vietnam has made a Vietcong victory impossible. They live and fight under unbelievable conditions. It is impossible to understand their motivation to continue the conflict."

He said that the Vietcong could severely beat a South Vietnamese army unit on Friday afternoon, but come Saturday, the South Vietnamese would take off for the weekend, and do no more fighting until Monday.

Brashear noted that the village chief—as the only representative of the Saigon government—collected taxes, and paid his own expenses by taking a cut, which could average $100 a month, a veritable fortune there. With the money, the chief could buy loyalty for himself, the Saigon government, and the US government. The more ruthless and corrupt the village chief, the more powerful he was. The chief was a virtual dictator, able to keep power so long as a rival or the Vietcong did not kill him. The VC rounded up very corrupt chiefs and killed them in the village square to the clapping of hands of every prefect in the district.

If the chief was effective, he kept the Vietcong populace down by offering a bounty to informers. The going rate was $100 to $150 per Vietcong. The problem was identifying the Vietcong. Thugs took advantage of the situation; who was to say whether the people they killed were Vietcong or not.

When Brashear came home in 1967, he had the satisfaction of knowing that he had participated in saving many lives. However, he was pessimistic about the lack of support by the Vietnamese people for the efforts of US and South Vietnamese armed forces.

Private First Class Carl Borland, of Nelson County, worked in an evacuation hospital. He worked on a ward of the 67th Evac Hospital (*Kentucky Standard*, February 5, 1970).

With each war, medical care has improved, and in Vietnam, it was as good as could be under the circumstances.

CHAPTER 21

1971: SOUTH VIETNAMESE OFFENSIVE

By 1971, Vietnamization was in full swing. American forces were down to 270,000, and more were leaving all the time. American deaths were down to 4,204 in 1970[295], the lowest since 1965, and a sign of the decreasing number of Americans in combat. South Vietnamese troops were still in Cambodia, just across the border. Communist insurgents and North Vietnamese were attacking elsewhere in Cambodia. Loyal Cambodian troops and ARVN battled three battalions of NVA and the Khmer Rouge, attempting to keep Route 4 open between the capital, Phnom Penh, and its sole port facility. American planes, including B-52s, flew in support, and the fighting slacked off.

In the north along the DMZ, the North Vietnamese frequently probed the allied line, part of which was held by the Fifth Division's Mechanized Brigade. In January, one of these probes resulted in the death of Specialist David St. Clair. He would be the last soldier from Nelson County, Kentucky, killed in ground action.

Charles David St. Clair was born in Cox's Creek, Kentucky, on January 9, 1950 (*Kentucky Standard*, February 18, 1971). He graduated from Old Kentucky Home High School in 1968. The following summer, while playing softball for Heaven Hill Distillery, he was chosen for the league all-star team. He volunteered for the army on September 23, 1969. After training, he ended up with the Fifth Division, assigned to Company B, First Battalion, 61st Regiment. He started his tour of duty in Vietnam on September 19, 1970. He was a specialist 4 and became a squad leader. His division was assigned to the northernmost part of South Vietnam. This area had previously been assigned to the marines, and they had had many bloody battles there, repulsing the enemy.

While serving in Quang Tri province, close to the DMZ, only a few miles above the old marine base of Con Thien and Fire Support Base 4, St. Clair led his squad on a search-and-clear mission. The North Vietnamese frequently crossed the DMZ, attempting to control the area, and had recently probed the jungles around Con Thien.

On this particular mission, a platoon-size force of North Vietnamese regulars, using automatic weapons, small arms, and rocket-propelled grenades, ambushed Company B. When the initial burst of fire raked Company B, St. Clair immediately braved the incoming rounds to direct his men in returning fire, and providing flank and rear security. Under his direction, his squad was able to provide such overpowering fire superiority that they virtually silenced the enemy's positions.

He was then ordered to lead his squad in a sweep of the area from which the enemy fire had emanated. With the sweep only partially completed, friendly forces were subjected to a concentrated 82-mm mortar attack. Ignoring the obvious danger to himself from enemy mortar fire, St. Clair remained in the open to ensure that his men had taken proper cover from the incoming rounds, and to check for wounded personnel. He was mortally wounded by mortar shrapnel. He was taken to the 18th Army Surgical Hospital, where he was pronounced dead. He died on January 16,

1971, just short of four months into his tour.

According to the *Kentucky Standard*, his courage and leadership under enemy fire was "in keeping with the highest traditions of the military service, and reflected credit upon himself, his unit, and the US Army." He was 21 years old when he died. He earned a Bronze Star with a V for heroism, a Purple Heart, and other medals. His body was returned to be buried in Nelson County. He embodied the best of American youth.

Mike Guthrie was another Bardstown native who volunteered. He enlisted on January 26, 1970. After six weeks of basic and three months of radio operator training, he was sent to Vietnam on December 4. In Cam Ranh Bay, he was assigned to the Americal Division at Chu Lai. His assignment officer was undecided whether to send him or another man newly arrived in country to an outpost artillery base. Guthrie had just received supplies, including a deck of cards, and suggested that they cut cards. He won. He was a free spirit, and chose the lax atmosphere of Hawk Hill, where he could wear cut-off fatigues. He was assigned to C Company.

Jungle surrounded Hawk Hill, and rockets and mortars bombarded it every night. The men lived mostly in underground bunkers with steel matting and three layers of sandbags overhead. The bunkers were fairly impervious to the shelling, and the men got used to it. A time or two during monsoons, the bunker was flooded out. Hawk Hill was never attacked outright while Guthrie was there, but a nearby artillery LZ, Mary Ann, was overrun completely with over 60 percent casualties. Phantom jets flew frequent sorties in the adjacent country, and their bombing, particularly napalm, could be seen from Hawk Hill.

For the first six weeks, Guthrie went out on patrols as a radioman.

Then he became a teletype operator, and incoming messages came through him. Some of it was top secret, and went through crypto clearance. These were need-to-know messages that could be given to only about a dozen people on the hill.

On Hawk Hill, they were sprayed a number of times with Agent Orange. They were told it was an insecticide, but obviously it was a defoliant as all of the vegetation for a couple of hundred yards outside the compound was gone. The hill was denuded. Guthrie understood the use of a defoliant. It helped save American lives in Vietnam.

After four months, his company moved to Da Nang as the marines moved out and the Americal Division took over. Hawk Hill was turned over to the ARVN. It was overrun several months later.

At Da Nang, Guthrie worked in communication, doing teletype work at first, but soon became an air courier. He took reports twice daily in a two-man helicopter from Da Nang Air Force Base to Monkey Mountain, across the Da Nang Bay. Occasionally he was shot at. No place was safe. For the last five to six weeks of his Vietnam stay, he was the company clerk.

He commented on the use of heroin, which some of the men smoked. Although it was fairly common, he never used it. He estimated that one out of every five used heroin due to frustration, boredom, the ease of getting it, lack of discipline, and America pulling out of the war.

After the war, he painted signs for a while, and eventually went to California to do artwork for Disney.

In the northern section of Vietnam, MACV and the South Vietnamese command decided it was time to strike the NVA supply lines across the Laotian border, and onto the Ho Chi Minh Trail. Their target was to be Tchepone, about 12 miles into Laos. American forces would open the way to the border, and then the built-up ARVN would push into Laos to destroy enemy supply bases, much as the 25th, First Cavalry, Ninth Division, and ARVN troops had done in eastern Cambodia with such good results. It was time to test the true fighting ability of the South Vietnamese army. Their attack would be without American advisors.[296] The most elite of the South Vietnamese divisions were to be used.

First, the way to the border had to be opened. American troops would do this without world protests about an invasion of Laos, as had occurred after the Cambodian incursion; US troops would stop at the border. The American action to get to the border was called Operation Dewey Canyon II. It involved the Fifth Infantry Division Mechanized Brigade that thrust down Highway 9, past Khe Sanh, and on to the border. Engineers cleared the main road and built a secondary flanking road called Red Devil Highway. Enemy opposition was light and was thrust aside easily. The 101st Division made a feint toward the A Shau Valley.

Specialist James Sims was with the 101st Division and was promoted to sergeant (*Kentucky Standard*, April 21, 1970).

Some 9,000 American troops opened the way for 20,000 ARVN soldiers. Since the US Senate prohibited American troops from entering Laos, American support consisted of cross-border artillery firing 175-mm long-range cannons, fighter-bombers, B-52 bombings, and helicopters ferrying the ARVN soldiers in. The 17th Air Cavalry Squadron, to which Sergeant Paul A. Johnson had previously belonged, was out front reconnoitering and shooting the enemy where they were found.[297] The men saw a lot of NVA armor on the trails, but ran out of ammunition before they could knock them all out.

The invasion of Laos started well for the South Vietnamese. They crossed the border with very little opposition. LZs and firebases were established. However, opposition stiffened and vicious firefights resulted. The North Vietnamese anti-aircraft fire, which had become expert using Russian-made weapons, made successive landings and the establishment of LZs difficult and costly. The outer flanks of the advance came under counterattack.

A battalion of the First ARVN Division was air assaulted close to Tchepone; 11 helicopters were lost and 44 more were damaged. Three days later, another unit was airmobiled into Tchepone.[298]

The unit found some caches, but after a few days, they were pulled out because of increasing NVA pressure. Unfortunately, the ARVN troops were not well trained in orderly withdrawal. The most elite of their divisions, with ARVN marines, paratrooper, and Ranger units gradually came apart under fierce North Vietnamese pressure. Rear guard outfits had varied results. Those that stayed were badly chewed up. Others just bugged out and ran. In the end, it turned into a rout. American air assets and artillery saved it from complete disaster. Many trucks, tanks, personnel carriers, and artillery pieces were left behind, and had to be destroyed by American bombs and rockets to keep them from falling into enemy hands.

The first major South Vietnamese offensive action had been a miserable failure. It was like the rout of American forces at the Kasserine Pass in World War II. The major difference was that American troops learned and got better, and overcame their enemies in the end. The South Vietnamese didn't. It appeared that Vietnamization had a long way to go. The operation was called Lam Son 19. There would be a Lam Son 20 later, which wasn't nearly as large or disastrous, but that would have little effect on the war.

Throughout 1971, there were few major encounters between the American troops and the NVA. It seemed that the NVA was avoiding the American army and biding its time until the American withdrawal. The 101st Airborne made a few forays into the rugged mountains of the northwest, but the enemy was evasive. This was all part of Operation Jefferson Glen, which started in 1970.[299] The operation would end in late spring 1971, and would be the last official American operation of the war. The 101st continued sweeping the rocket zones around Da Nang and other enclaves. Later the 196th Light Infantry Brigade would take over the duty of rocket zone sweeps.

First Lieutenant Stephen Knopp was serving with the 101st as a forward observer of the 319th Artillery (*Kentucky Standard*, September 2, 1971).

All throughout Vietnam, the American army was gradually disengaging and going home. In late February, the 11th Armored Cavalry "Black Horse" Brigade started the slow process of disengaging and shipping out.[300] It was still in the process in May when Warrant Officer Preston Miller earned a Distinguished Flying Cross as a helicopter pilot (*Kentucky Standard*, September 30, 1971). Miller flew 10 missions in a battle, delivering weapons, ammunition, and medical supplies, and evacuating the wounded. He also flew low-level missions marking enemy positions with smoke grenades. He even flew the squadron commander over the combat area, so he could direct artillery fire.

The 25th Division remnants pulled out in April, and rejoined the rest of the division in Hawaii.[301] That last brigade performed well until its departure. The bulk of the First Cavalry Division also departed in April. It left behind one large brigade to serve as a fire brigade. In May, the last of the First Marine Division pulled out.

Petty Officer Sheridan Talbott was on the transport, the USS *Duluth*, which brought home 1,600 marines and 750 tons of equipment (*Kentucky Standard*, June 3, 1971).

Private Tommy Girdley came home with the First Marine Division (*Kentucky Standard*, August 13, 1971). He had served with the Fifth Regiment. The regiment gained fame as the fire brigade that helped save the Pusan perimeter in Korea, and as heroes of Belleau Wood in World War I. In that campaign, when the French told them to retreat, they said, "Retreat hell! We just got here."

Raymond D. Jones was with the First Marines, and had seen service close to the Laos Vietnam border (*Kentucky Standard*, August 13, 1971).

Some of the Seventh Marines had participated in Operation Dewey Canyon II. Joseph Henry Greenwell also served with the marines and left in 1971 (*Kentucky Standard*, August 13, 1971).

In May, the NVA made numerous attacks against the allied DMZ bases that lasted three weeks. As the United States continued its withdrawal, the enemy increased their activity. The First Brigade of the Fifth Infantry Mechanized Division had been holding the part of the DMZ closest to the coast, including the embattled Con Thien. (It was there that David St. Clair was killed.) That brigade was notified on June 17 that it was going home. By the end of August, the brigade had completed its slow disengagement procedure, and had moved all of its men and equipment 100 miles south to Da Nang.[302] As the Fifth Division left, the NVA slowly moved south to occupy Dong Ha and the old marine outposts along Highway 9.

In August, the 173rd Airborne Brigade, "The Herd," left the country. They had been the first army unit dispatched to Vietnam in early 1965, and had fought some of the most vicious battles, particularly that of Dak To.

Sergeant Joseph E. Clayton served with the 173rd in Company A (*Kentucky Standard*, April 20, 1970).

With the departure of the marines, the security of the Da Nang area and the Chu Lai area was under the control of the American Division, in conjunction with the Second ARVN Division. The divisions did dynamic defense operations with sweeps of the rocket belts, and general defense of those two enclaves.

Sergeant Joseph L. Ball of New Haven, Kentucky, received an Army Commendation Award for service with the American Division near Chu Lai (*Kentucky Standard*, May 20, 1971). He was with Company B, First Battalion, Sixth Infantry of the 196th Light Infantry Brigade as a radio operator, one of the special targets of the enemy.

Specialist Russell Thurman of C Troop 1, First Cavalry, Second Platoon, operating with the American Division, received shrapnel wounds to his head and leg (*Kentucky Standard*, July 29, 1971). Because of the head wound, he ended up with a slight paralysis of the left leg.

Army Captain Edward Corrothers received a Bronze Star with the American Division for meritorious service in military operations. He was part of Battery A, Second Battalion.

Most of the Americal Division pulled out in November. The 196th Light Infantry Brigade remained, as did some of the 101st Division and the Third Brigade of the First Cavalry Division.

At the end of the year, American forces were down to 159,000 men; most were in support units.[303] In addition to the above-named ground troops, army and marine advisors to the ARVN units remained, as well as air force personnel, some artillery units, signal, engineer and transportation companies. American losses for the year were down to 1,386 men killed in action.

CHAPTER 22

1972

The US ground forces still in Vietnam were mostly in a training and defensive attitude. In January, with the heaviest shelling of American forces in months, 18 US soldiers were wounded in a mortar attack at Firebase Fiddler's Green, 20 miles northeast of Saigon. Overall though, the enemy avoided American forces as they were being withdrawn, realizing they still had a sting. Ten thousand ARVN troops began a sweep around Saigon to prevent another Tet Offensive. The 101st Airborne was involved in a five-hour battle against a communist bunker line.

Sergeant Joseph Boone of Howardstown, Kentucky, received a Combat Infantry Badge for active combat against a hostile force; he was with Company A, First Battalion, 501st Infantry, 101st Airborne Division (*Kentucky Standard*, January 13, 1971). Boone had earned a Bachelor of Science degree from the University of Kentucky before he was drafted.

The United States continued to bomb and fly reconnaissance over the Ho Chi Minh Trail, along the Laotian border, to prevent enemy attacks into the highlands and to interdict supplies. Captain James Crawford was likely killed on such a mission.

James J. Crawford was born in Missouri on December 6, 1941, the day before the Japanese bombed Pearl Harbor (*Kentucky Standard*, February 16, 1971). He was raised in Missouri, and graduated from college there. He had always wanted to fly, and after talking to a recruiter and being tested, he was sent to Lackland Field in San Antonio, Texas. After basic training, he went to Enid Air Force Base in Enid, Oklahoma, for pilot training. After graduating, he went to Valdosta, Georgia, where he trained pilots in cross-country navigation. On one such flight, he landed in Dayton, Ohio, at Wright-Patterson Air Force Base. While there, he met his future wife, who was teaching home economics and science in Dayton. After a whirlwind romance, they married.

Rebecca (Becky) was from Bardstown, Kentucky. The couple initially lived in Valdosta, where he was stationed. After he went overseas, his wife came back to Bardstown and it became their home address.

When Crawford went overseas, he was sent to Udon Air Force Base in Thailand. When he learned that he was to train pilots there in T-42s, he was disappointed. Officially, that was all he did; actually, he did a lot more. In all probability, he was flying reconnaissance flights over the Ho Chi Minh Trail in Laos. Officially, though, he was only doing training, as Laos and Cambodia were considered neutral, and off-limits to the US Air Force.

Halfway through his tour, he came home on R&R. It was the last time Becky would see him. She was supposed to fly to visit him in Asia later, but because she was expecting, and had previously had a miscarriage, she decided not to go. It would have been about the time of his last flight. He was reported missing on February 3, 1972, and later declared killed in action. He had only a few months left in his year's tour in the Vietnam theater. He was another man who would have a child born while he was serving in the war—one he would never see. Becky recalled that he loved flying; he wanted to fight in the war and make peace in the world. Becky continues to live in Bardstown.

Another air force officer in his plane was also killed; one of his stabilizers was torn loose in Laos.

In late March, the North Vietnamese began a three-pronged, six-division attack, invading South Vietnam. It was called the Nguyen Hue Offensive. It blasted down into the Quang Tri province from the DMZ, supported by tanks and heavy artillery. Within four weeks, they pushed the ARVN through Quang Tri City, the provincial capital, and beyond.[304] American units were prohibited from joining the fight, although US advisors stayed with their charges. After Quang Tri City fell, most advisors evacuated. Eighteen advisors chose to stay. American support was mainly from the air. United States marine and army helicopters were involved extensively, trying to support the faltering ARVN divisions, mainly the shattered South Vietnamese Third Division. Air force and navy fighter-bombers also flew in support missions to hold back the enemy.

Chief Warrant Officer Bernard S. Reed of the Second Squadron, 17th Cavalry of the 101st Division, received two distinguished Flying Crosses, a Bronze star with a V for valor, a Purple Heart, and a Vietnam medal, for flying a Cobra gunship in support of the ARVN (*Kentucky Standard*, February 24, 1971).

First Lieutenant Joseph C. Howard of the H&H Company of the First Aviation Brigade, was also involved in the American aviation support (*Kentucky Standard*, February 10, 1971).

The enemy attacks throughout the south in the middle of April were the highest they had been since the 1968 Tet Offensive. There were 107 attacks in 24 hours. The northern offensive turned toward Hue, but the South Vietnamese defense stiffened, aided by US air power. The US 196th

Light Infantry Brigade was moved north to shore up defenses around Phu Bai, north of Da Nang. Despite some dissension, they probed the hills north of Phu Bai, and discouraged enemy action in that area.

About the middle of April, the enemy attacked cross-border into the Central Highlands against Kon Tum and An Khe. B-52s and fighter-bombers succeeded in slowing attacks toward Kon Tum, but An Khe was encircled and put under siege. More B-52s and fighter-bombers assisted in its support. Two more squadrons of B-52s were orderd to Indochina.

Lieutenant Colonel John F. Hurst of Nelson County, who had been a pilot and squadron commander of B-52s, had been moved to Korat Royal Air Force Base in Thailand. He was placed in the Tactical Command, supporting allied ground troops (*Kentucky Standard*, June 29, 1971).

The tank-supported 320th NVA Division, near Dak To and Kon Tum, resumed their attack and put Kon Tum under siege. Both Kon Tum and An Khe continued to hold out with air support and supply.

Offshore, the navy had built up its force on Yankee Station to six aircraft carriers for the first time in the Vietnam War. At least two Nelson County men were on board some of these carriers. Petty Officer James B. Hodge was on the USS *Ticonderoga*, which had participated in the Gulf of Tonkin incident in 1964. Air Apprentice Theodore Burgin was on the USS *Constellation* (*Kentucky Standard*, February 10, 1971).

Navy planes gave continuous support in South Vietnam, in addition to hitting targets in North Vietnam. Two squadrons of Marine Skyhawks were moved to the Bien Hoa Air Base, close to Saigon, to give tactical support in the north and in the Mekong Delta, where the enemy was active.

In the north, with US air support, ARVN marine and army troops counterattacked successfully, and drove back the NVA almost to the DMZ after much give-and-take action. They recaptured Quang Tri City, and most of the province, but Dong Ha and the old marine outpost line south of the DMZ remained in North Vietnamese hands. In the Central Highlands, the sieges of Kon Tum and An Khe persisted.[305] In An Khe, NVA troops entered the city, but were driven out. Eventually both sieges were broken.

American air support played a critical and decisive role in stopping the North Vietnamese offensive. Under President Richard Nixon, the number of fighter-bombers had tripled, the number of aircraft carriers had tripled, and B-52s had quadrupled in number. Because of the USAF commitment to battlefield support, navy planes were flying two-thirds of the sorties against North Vietnam.

The US Army continued to pull out its forces throughout the first half of 1972. The 101st Division officially departed in March, but many of its soldiers were rolled into the Third Brigade of the First Cavalry Division. That brigade continued its mobile defense, securing Long Binh, Bien Hoa, and the Saigon area. The Third Brigade left Vietnam on June 26, 1972. It left a small garrison battalion, which left in August.

The last to leave was the famed First Battalion of the Seventh Cavalry. Colonel Harold Moore helped make the battalion famous at Landing Zone X-ray in the Ia Drang victory, where his men were outnumbered four to one.

The 196th Light Infantry Brigade in the northern part of the country was pulled out a little earlier. Only MPs, advisors, support troops, and helicopter crews remained of the powerful 500,000-man army in Vietnam at the peak of the war. On November 11, the US Army turned over the

Long Binh Headquarters to the South Vietnamese, which symbolized the end of direct US participation in the war. Long Binh had been the biggest US military installation outside of the United States.[306]

CHAPTER 23

AIR WARFARE OVER NORTH VIETNAM AND PEACE NEGOTIATIONS

After the end of Rolling Thunder, there had been little bombing of the north. Negotiations with the North Vietnamese for a peace settlement had been going off and on with very little give or take on either side. The North Vietnamese demanded incorporation of the Vietcong into the South Vietnamese elections. The Saigon government did not consider this an option. In February 1972, talks resumed, but after only 17 minutes, the Communist government walked out.

When the Nguyen Hue offensive started, American bombing resumed on North Vietnam; around the DMZ to start with, but later expanded further up. On April 6, Operation Linebacker I was begun, with air and naval bombardment.[307] It was started on a sustained basis as ordered by President Nixon. The next day, 220 missions flew. On April 14, the use of B-52s 200 miles up the panhandle was authorized, and on April 16, 18 B-52s and 200 navy planes hit Hai Phong harbor, the port of Hanoi. Sixty planes hit oil storage facilities close to Hanoi itself. It was apparent that any place in North Vietnam may be bombed, except close to the Chinese border.

Anti-war protests started almost immediately because of the bombing.

The first was at the University of Maryland, and required the use of National Guard troops to quell it.[308] Other protests spread across the country. Tens of thousands protested in New York, San Francisco, and Los Angeles.

On April 20, the North Vietnamese government formally proposed the resumption of peace talks whether or not the US stopped the bombings. On May 4, however, both sides agreed to an indefinite halt to the talks, since there was no progress. Secretary of State Henry Kissinger and Le Duc Tho, the main Communist negotiator, continued to talk privately off and on with no give. On May 6, President Nixon ordered the mining and blockade of North Vietnamese harbors, announcing that these measures would persist until all American prisoners of war were released and an internationally supervised cease-fire began.

Bombing of the north continued and rose to the levels of Operation Rolling Thunder. Some opposition by MiG-21s was met with varying results. In one air battle, one Phantom jet shot down three MiGs. As the MiG pilots got more experienced, the odds evened. American airplane losses continued; most were due to conventional anti-aircraft fire, but some were due to surface-to-air missiles, and only a few to enemy aircraft. Rescue missions were attempted for downed pilots. Most were unsuccessful, however.

On June 10, US Phantom jets destroyed the Langchi power plant with 2,000-pound bombs. The power plant supplied much of the electricity in the Hanoi/Hai Phong corridor. On June 14, 340 planes, the most ever flown over the north, knocked out the rail line from Hai Phong to Hanoi. On July 24, fighter-bombers were back over Hanoi, and knocked out supply depots with laser-guided bombs, their first use in the war. In August, the number of attacking planes rose to 370. On August 27, the heaviest attack of the four years, since the cessation of Rolling Thunder, destroyed army encampments close to Hanoi and Hai Phong. Practically all flights originated from navy aircraft carriers and out of bases in Thailand.[309] The northernmost Thailand base was Udon Royal Air Force Base, which was at about the same parallel as Vinh, North Vietnam. Bien Hoa Air Base was the only South Vietnamese airport used for military purposes.

Negotiations continued off and on with announcements of false faith on both sides. The South Vietnamese president's demand that all North Vietnamese troops be removed from the south slowed the talks. Intransigence was met with increased bombing. In November, 800 air tactical attacks were made over the panhandle of North Vietnam. Peace talk agreements became very close by the middle of December, but the Communists would not agree to South Vietnamese President Nguyen Van Thieu's demand for the sovereignty of South Vietnam, and left the peace talks. On December 18, the Nixon administration announced that the bombing and mining of North Vietnam would continue until both parties reached an agreement. Thus began the infamous Christmas bombings, despite worldwide protests.

The most concentrated air attack of the North, known as Linebacker II, began.[310] It would drop over 40,000 tons of bombs on the Hanoi and Hai Phong area. It was hoped that the bombing would pull the enemy back to the peace table with acceptable terms. B-52s, with their massive bomb loads, were used over Hanoi and Hai Phong. Three B-52s and two fighter-bombers were lost in the initial raid of Linebacker II. More than 100 B-52s and many other planes were involved. North Vietnam announced that 215 civilians were killed and another 235 injured. Attacks continued almost daily. By December 24, when the US called a Christmas truce, 11 B-52s had been shot down, but 97 percent had penetrated the elaborate SAM defense area of Hanoi and Hai Phong.

On December 26, with no response from the North Vietnamese negotiators, the attacks resumed and were the most violent of the war. Jimmy Bean said that despite the danger, the POWs welcomed the attacks. Planes rained bombs on Hanoi for 40 minutes.[311] The B-52s came in from two different directions; fighter-bombers preceded them, suppressing the SAM sites and other anti-aircraft concentrations. By the end of the bombing, the entire 1,200 SAM supply was gone and much of Hanoi obliterated. It left the enemy virtually defenseless against future bombing. The North Vietnamese negotiators finally agreed to come to peace talks in early January 1973. Nixon's strategy, although questionable, was successful. On January 9, the parties agreed on a peace treaty, and by January 23, they had worked out all details.[312]

On January 27, the United States, North Vietnam, South Vietnam, and the Vietcong signed the treaty.[313] The prisoners of war would be released. All US troops, about 23,000 including advisors, would be withdrawn within 60 days. The US military bases would be dismantled in 60 days. NVA troops in South Vietnam would continue in place. All foreign troops, North Vietnamese, and Americans would be withdrawn from Laos and Cambodia. The 17th Parallel DMZ would remain in place until the peaceful reunification of all Vietnam. President Thieu would remain in office until the next election. An international control commission of neutrals would oversee the agreement.

For America, the war was effectively over.

EPILOGUE

The treaty put off the takeover of South Vietnam by the North for two years. Many people felt that the fall of the Thieu government was inevitable, along with the loss of South Vietnamese sovereignty. Their attacks in 1972 had riddled the North Vietnamese army. By 1975, NVA units were rebuilt and at full strength. They were ready to go, and there was no US Air Force or Navy to contend with. When the initial ARVN defenses were breached, North Vietnamese battlefield success built upon success and eventually it became a rout.

The TV and other media reports showed the hopelessness and panic of the populace, as people hung onto helicopters trying to get away, and thousands of refugees streamed south.

A sideline to this story is that of Sister Susan Carroll MacDonald of Loretto, Kentucky, just across the Nelson/Marion county line. She had gone to Vietnam to be a nurse in an orphanage. When it was obvious that the South Vietnamese government was going to fall, she and her compatriots tried to get the orphans out, fearing for their care under the new regime. Commercial airlines had stopped flying in and out of the country.

An appeal went to President Gerald Ford. Their rescue was authorized as Operation Babylift. Air force transports were sent to carry out the orphans and some of the nurses. Unfortunately, the first load on a C-5 Galaxy ended up in disaster. The plane crashed and 120 of the orphans and their attendants died. Sister Susan Carroll went to the crash site to help bring some of the survivors back in, and provide nursing care. Later flights were successful, and the rest of the orphans were evacuated. Sister Susan Carroll still communicates with some of the crash survivors. She goes back to Vietnam every year to see some of them, as well as those adopted by Americans.

After the fall of the Saigon government, the questions and charges about the conduct of the war became even louder and more vociferous. Many Americans asked, "Why?" and "What have we to show for all of the lives, energy, money, and goodwill lost?" The veterans asked, "Were we right? Was it all in vain?" Most Americans didn't know the answers.

Some felt that America shouldn't have been there at all. Others felt that the United States ought to have tried to stop communism, but failed. Looking at it in the short term, the feelings were negative. The blood spilled wasn't worth any benefit accomplished. It did seem that American troops died in vain. Americans were proud of the service of those who died, but not of the politicians who sent them to Vietnam, nor of the management of the war.

The fact was that America seemed to have lost. The nation that had never lost a war had trouble coming to grips with the results. There were no parades. Some returning servicemen were degraded, spat upon, or called names. The country felt shame.

It can safely be said, however, that in Nelson County, servicemen were never abused. They were respected, and the whole community mourned those who didn't make it back. Nelson County was probably representative of most of the small towns and counties across America. In small communities, people knew the servicemen and their families, and there was an attachment to them as members of the community.

For the Vietnamese, it was a 40-year war. American involvement for ground troops was only eight years of that, from early 1965 to early 1973. Even so, it was the longest war in American history. It was the third most costly in lives lost, surpassed only by the Civil War and World War II (if the influenza deaths of World War I are not counted). It was by far the most unpopular war in US history, and the only one where it appeared that America had lost.

However, if the war is considered in the context of the 40-year Cold War between communism and the free world, it was only a battle in that war.

The United States went into the war to stop the spread of communism in Southeast Asia. By going in militarily and taking a stand, America allowed the other nations of that area to stabilize, and become democratic. When the United States went in, Malaysia, Indonesia, and Thailand were under the threat of communist insurgencies. American involvement gave them breathing time to develop stable, free nations. So, it can be said that *those who died in Vietnam did not die in vain.*

Nelson County, Kentucky, lost more servicemen in Vietnam per capita than any county in the nation. To all of those men and all of the others who served, we owe a deep and lasting debt of gratitude. War is a terrible event, and was a terrible experience for many who served in Vietnam. The Vietnam Wall in Washington, DC, and all of the other Vietnam monuments around the country are testaments of the sentiment held most deeply in the subconscious mind of America. It lingers with a sadness perhaps more than any other war we fought, but those sentiments don't have the pride that has accompanied other wars. That perhaps explains its sadness, and the nation's guilt as a whole for not embracing these men on their return. We must not forget.

THE FACES

How can we forget the faces,
The eyes shining with hope
And belief in their immortality;
The arched thin brows of youth
Strong and smooth and brave,
The full cheeks pink and warm
With blood. And the supple mouths,
Quick to laughter and shouts,
Saluting friends, quick to love,
The faces of comrades that every day
Looked into ours with vigor and life,
And the shared commonweal of care?
How can we forget them in their night
Of flame, and its grim ending;
Their tearless eyes hollow with pain,
Staring through rigid charred masks
Beyond the pleasant sights of yesterday,
And the bold visions of tomorrow.
The days will come bright and promising,
And the clouds will bring gentle rain.
The nights will come restful and cool.
But their faces will shine in the sun,
And their cheeks glisten in the rain,
And their eyes will stare through our dreams.
In all things growing green and strong,
In all things young and full of hope,
In all things wild and full of love
We see their faces looking up from the bush,
And know that we will not forget.

—Dr. Harry Spalding

CONTRIBUTORS

Many people contributed to this book, including Vietnam veterans, their families, and others. We are grateful to all of them. Contributions to the book took the form of personal interviews, letters, and other means. Those interviewed include:

Corporal Gerald Ashby
Sergeant Robert Ballard
Colonel James Bean, retired
Sergeant Joseph Blanford
John Blevins
Mike Cornish
Lance Corporal Ronnie Coulter
Rebecca Crawford, widow of Captain James Crawford
Corporal Tyre (Terry) Forsee (later promoted to sergeant)
Lieutenant Colonel Malcolm Geoghegan, retired
Thomas Goben
Sergeant Ed Greathouse
Sergeant A.B. (Buddy) Grigsby
Dr. Robert Hendren
Lieutenant Colonel Denny Howard, retired
Lieutenant Colonel John Finn Hurst, retired
John Hutchins
Captain William Huston, Coast Guard, retired
Sergeant Robert Hutchins
Mike Jameson
Sergeant Gaylord Mattingly

Rick Molohan

Sergeant Kenneth Nevitt

Virgil O'Bryan

Sergeant Kenneth Thomas

Other Contributors

First Lieutenant James Brown

E4 Gerald Bullock

Charles Dickerson

Mike Guthrie

Private First Class Henry Hayden

Lieutenant Colonel Tom Hayden

E4 Donald Holbert

Jack Johnson, brother of Staff Sergeant Nicholas Johnson

Paul Johnson[314], brother of Patrick Johnson

Corporal Roscoe Norris

Family of Private William D. Price

Family of Specialist Charles David St. Clair

Sergeant First Class Pat Simpson, retired

Lieutenant Kenneth Sympson

Steve Tolliver

SELECTED BIBLIOGRAPHY

Bowman, John S. *The Vietnam War: Day by Day.* Greenwich, CT: Brompton Books, 1989.

Carroll, Andrew. *War Letters: Extraordinary Correspondence from American Wars.* New York: Scribner, 2001.

Christopher, Ralph. *Duty, Honor, Sacrifice: Brown River Sailors and Army River Raiders.* Bloomington, IN: AuthorHouse, 2007.

Doyle, Edward, Samuel Lipsman, and the editors of Boston Publishing Company. *The Vietnam Experience: America Takes Over, 1965-1967.* Boston, MA: Boston Publishing, 1982.

Ellsberg, Daniel. *Secrets: A Memoir of Vietnam and the Pentagon Papers.* New York: Penguin, 2002.

Karnow, Stanley. *Vietnam: A History.* New York: Viking Press, 1983.

Maitland, Terrance, Peter McInerney, and the editors of Boston Publishing Company. *The Vietnam Experience: Contagion of War.* Boston, MA: Boston Publishing, 1983.

Moore, Harold G., and Joseph L. Galloway. *We Were Soldiers Once . . . And Young: Ia Drang: The Battle that Changed the War in Vietnam.* New York: Random House, 1992.

————. *We Are Soldiers Still: A Journey Back to the Battlefields of Vietnam.* New York: HarperCollins, 2008.

Morrocco, John. *The Vietnam Experience: Thunder from Above, Air War, 1941-1968.* Boston, MA: Boston Publishing, 1984.

Sheehan, Neil. *A Bright Shining Lie: John Paul Vann and America in Vietnam.* New York: Vintage Books, 1988.

Stanton, Shelby L. *The Rise and Fall of an American Army: U.S. Ground Forces in Vietnam, 1965-1973.* Novato, CA: Presidio Press, 1995.

Sympson, Kenneth P. *Images from the Otherland: Memoir of a United States Marine Corps Artillery Officer in Vietnam.* Jefferson, North Carolina: McFarland & Company, 1995.

Wilson, Jim. *The Sons of Bardstown: 25 Years of Vietnam in an American Town.* New York: Crown, 1994.

In addition to using printed sources for this book, the authors interviewed many of the Nelson County men who served in Vietnam. Those who were interviewed are listed in "Contributors."

Names of Nelson County men mentioned in the text, but not referenced in the endnotes were obtained from articles in the *Kentucky Standard* newspaper, published in Bardstown, Kentucky.

END NOTES

---

1 Information drawn from various sources, including: Jim Wilson, *The Sons of Bardstown: 25 Years of Vietnam in an American Town* (New York: Crown, 1994), 129; Ancestry. com, "Vietnam War: US Military Casualties, 1956-1998; Bardstown Vietnam memorial plaque; and http://thewall-usa.com

2 Stanley Karnow, *Vietnam: A History* (New York: Viking Press, 1983), 374-414.

3 Ibid., 79.

4 Ibid., 104.

5 Ibid.

6 John S. Bowman, *The Vietnam War: Day by Day* (Greenwich, CT: Brompton Books, 1989), 8.

7 Karnow, *Vietnam: A History*, 88.

8 Bowman, *The Vietnam War: Day by Day*, 9.

9 Ibid.

10 Ibid.

11 Ibid.

12 Ibid.

13 Karnow, *Vietnam: A History*, 138.

14 Ibid., 149.

15 Ibid., 151.

16 Ibid.

17 Bowman, *The Vietnam War: Day by Day*, 9.

18 Ibid., 10.

19 Karnow, *Vietnam: A History*, 154.

20 Ibid., 156.

21 Ibid., 158.

22 Bowman, *The Vietnam War: Day by Day*, 10.

23 Karnow, *Vietnam: A History*, 154.

24 Bowman, *The Vietnam War: Day by Day*, 12.

25 Karnow, *Vietnam: A History*, 189.

26 Ibid., 190.

27 Harold G. Moore and Joseph L. Galloway, *We Are Soldiers Still: A Journey Back to the Battlefields of Vietnam* (New York: Harper Perennial, 2009), 44-47.

28 Ibid., 140.

29 Ibid., 198.

30 Ibid., 204.

31 Ibid., 217.

32 Ibid., 213.

33 Bowman, *The Vietnam War: Day by Day*, 15.

34 Ibid.

35 Ibid.

36 Ibid., 16.

37 Ibid.

38 Ibid., 17.

39 Karnow, *Vietnam: A History*, 224.

40 Bowman, *The Vietnam War: Day by Day*, 18.

41 Ibid., 19.

42 Karnow, *Vietnam: A History*, 238.

43 Ibid., 231.

44 Ibid., 235.

45 Ibid., 238.

46 Ibid., 232.

47 Ibid., 238.

48 Bowman, *The Vietnam War: Day by Day*, 21.

49 Ibid., 22.

50 Andrew Carroll, *War Letters: Extraordinary Correspondence from*

American Wars (New York: Scribner, 2002), 392.

51 Karnow, *Vietnam: A History*, 255.

52 Ibid., 256.

53 Ibid., 259.

54 Ibid., 265.

55 Bowman, *The Vietnam War: Day by Day*, 23.

56 Ibid.

57 Neil Sheehan, *A Bright Shining Lie: John Paul Vann and America in Vietnam* (New York: Modern Library, 2009), 34.

58 Sheehan, *A Bright Shining Lie*, 203-265.

59 Bowman, *The Vietnam War: Day by Day*, 27.

60 Karnow, *Vietnam: A History*, 281.

61 Ibid., 282.

62 Ibid., 284.

63 Ibid., 286.

64 Ibid., 286.

65 Ibid., 290.

66 Ibid., 307.

67 Ibid., 310.

68 Ibid., 295.

69 Bowman, *The Vietnam War: Day by Day*, 29.

70 Ibid., 33.

71 Karnow, *Vietnam: A History*, 227.

72 Ibid., 325.

73 Ibid., 329.

74 Ibid., 384.

75 Ibid., 345.

76 Ibid., 340.

77 Ibid., 334.

78 Ibid., 342.

79 Ibid., 347.

80 Shelby L. Stanton, *The Rise and Fall of an American Army: U.S. Ground Forces in Vietnam, 1965-1973* (Novato, CA: Presidio Press, 1995), 11.

81 Stanton, *The Rise and Fall of an American Army*, 126-127.

82 Hendren had been a member of the Bloomfield basketball team that had gone to the state tournament.

83 Daniel Ellsberg, *Secrets: A Memoir of Vietnam and the Pentagon Papers* (New York: Penguin, 2002), 16.

84 Karnow, *Vietnam: A History*, 361-377.

85 Ellsberg, *Secrets*, 16-17.

86 Karnow, *Vietnam: A History*, 411-412.

87 Ellsberg, *Secrets*, 67-85.

88 Stanton, *The Rise and Fall of an American Army*, 31.

89 Ibid., 32.

90 Ibid., 38.

91 Kenneth Sympson, *Images from the Otherland: Memoir of a United States Marine Corps Artillery Officer in Vietnam* (Bloomington, IN: IUniverse, 2003), 17.

92 Stanton, *The Rise and Fall of an American Army*, 18.

93 Ibid., 22.

94 Ibid., 14.

95 Ibid., 17.

96 Author Harry Spalding grew up across the street from Moore.

97 War Memorial of Mid America, Bardstown, Kentucky

98 Ibid.

99 Harold G. Moore and Joseph L. Galloway, *We Were Soldiers Once . . . and Young: Ia Drang: The Battle that Changed the War in Vietnam* (New York: Random House, 1992), 61-62.

100 Ibid., 65.

101 Ibid., 74-75.

102 Ibid., 78.

103 Ibid., 104-107.

104 Ibid., 78.
105 Ibid., 135.
106 Ibid., 136.
107 Ibid.
108 Ibid.
109 Ibid., 141.
110 Ibid.
111 Ibid., 145.
112 Ibid.
113 Ibid., 157.
114 Ibid.
115 Ibid., 174.
116 Ibid., 175.
117 Ibid., 179.
118 Ibid., 182.
119 Ibid., 193.
120 Ibid., 201.
121 Ibid., 202.
122 Ibid., 205.
123 Ibid.
124 Ibid., 212.
125 Ibid.
126 Ibid., 220.
127 Ibid.
128 Ibid., 235.
129 Ibid., 248.
130 Ibid.
131 Ibid., 254.
132 Ibid., 259.
133 Ibid., 260.
134 Ibid.
135 Ibid., 268.
136 Ibid.
137 Ibid., 281.
138 Ibid.
139 Ibid., 286-289.
140 Ibid.
141 Ibid., 309.
142 Ibid.
143 Ibid., 313.
144 Stanton, *The Rise and Fall of an American Army*, 42.
145 Ibid., 43.

146 Ibid., 69.
147 Ibid., 85.
148 Ibid.
149 Ibid., 86.
150 Ibid., 87.
151 Ibid., 87.
152 Ibid., 65.
153 Terrance Maitland, Peter McInerney, and the editors of Boston Publishing Company, *The Vietnam Experience: Contagion of War* (Boston, Boston Publishing Company, 1983), 35.
154 Ibid., 34.
155 Ibid., 42.
156 *The Kentucky Standard*, August 4, 1966.
157 Moore's brother showed the same determination as Hal by working his way through Notre Dame despite his paralysis.
158 Stanton, *The Rise and Fall of an American Army*, 117.
159 Sympson, *Images from the Otherland*.
160 Ibid., 103.
161 Stanton, *The Rise and Fall of an American Army*, 118.
162 The Fifth Marines had a storied past from World War I at Belleau Wood, World War II across the South Pacific, and at the Pusan perimeter and the Chosin Reservoir in Korea.
163 Stanton, *The Rise and Fall of an American Army*, 100-101.
164 Ibid., 103.
165 Ibid.
166 Ibid., 105.
167 Ibid., 108.
168 Ibid., 126-127.
169 Ibid., 127.
170 Date of death from The Wall-USA website, http://thewall-usa.com, using data from The Combat Area Casualties Current File (Southeast

Asia).

171 Stanton, *The Rise and Fall of an American Army*, 128-129.

172 Edward Doyle, Samuel Lipsman, and the editors of Boston Publishing Company, *The Vietnam Experience: America Takes Over, 1965-1967* (Boston: Boston Publishing Company, 1982), 161.

173 Stanton, *The Rise and Fall of an American Army*, 88-92.

174 Ibid., 94.

175 Ibid., 92.

176 Ibid., 93.

177 Ibid., 95.

178 Ibid., 91.

179 *The Kentucky Standard*, December 29, 1966.

180 *The Kentucky Standard*, October 3, 1968.

181 Stanton, *The Rise and Fall of an American Army*, 134.

182 Ibid., 146.

183 Doyle et al., *The Vietnam Experience: America Takes Over, 1965-1967*, 99-108.

183 Stanton, *The Rise and Fall of an American Army*, 147-153.

184 Doyle et al., *The Vietnam Experience: America Takes Over, 1965-1967*, 111.

185 Ralph Christopher, *Duty, Honor, Sacrifice: Brown River Sailors and Army River Raiders* (Bloomington, IN: AuthorHouse, 2007), 149.

186 Ibid., 189-197.

187 Stanton, *The Rise and Fall of an American Army*, 179-180.

188 Maitland et al., *The Vietnam Experience: Contagion of War*, 163-167.

189 Rank from gravestone, St. Joseph Cemetary, Bardstown, Kentucky

190 Stanton, *The Rise and Fall of an American Army*, 189.

191 Ibid., 156.

192 Ibid., 158.

193 Ibid., 161.

194 Ibid., 164.

195 Ibid., 161.

196 Ibid., 164.

197 Ibid.

198 Ibid., 165-166.

199 Ibid., 168.

200 Ibid., 169.

201 Ibid., 172.

202 Ibid., 174-178.

203 Ibid., 191-192.

204 Ibid., 193-194.

205 Ibid., 195-197.

206 Ibid., 197-200.

207 Ibid., 205.

208 Sheehan, *A Bright Shining Lie*, 719.

209 Stanton, *The Rise and Fall of an American Army*, 205.

210 Ibid., 211-212.

211 Ibid., 220-222.

212 Sheehan, *A Bright Shining Lie*, 714.

213 Ibid., 713.

214 Ibid., 712.

215 Stanton, *The Rise and Fall of an American Army*, 229-231.

216 Ibid., 225-227.

217 Ibid., 227.

218 Ibid., 229.

219 Rank and middle name confirmed on the website of the Vietnam Veterans Memorial, http://thewall-usa.com.

220 Stanton, *The Rise and Fall of an American Army*, 229-231.

221 Ibid., 231.

222 Ibid., 232-233.

223 Sheehan, *A Bright Shining Lie*, 714.

224 Stanton, *The Rise and Fall of an American Army*, 236-238.

225 Ibid., 238-239.

226 When author Harry Spalding visited the city 39 years later, most of the old Imperial City was still in ruins and the Imperial Palace still had bullet holes in the red pillars. The city is slowly being restored with UN help.

227 Sheehan, *A Bright Shining Lie*, 714.

228 Ibid., 717.

229 Ibid., 724.

230 Stanton, *The Rise and Fall of an American Army*, 247.

231 Holbert estimated there were about 200 dead.

232 Stanton, *The Rise and Fall of an American Army*, 254-255.

233 Ibid., 256-259.

234 Ibid., 259.

235 Ibid., 260-265.

236 Ibid., 268-269.

237 Ibid., 273-276.

238 Ibid.

239 John Morrocco, *The Vietnam Experience: Thunder From Above, Air War, 1941-1968* (Boston: Boston Publishing, 1984), 26.

240 Ibid., 28.

241 Ibid., 32.

242 Ibid., 33-36.

243 Ibid., 50.

244 Ibid., 55-57.

245 Ibid., 61.

246 Ibid., 62.

247 Ibid., 66-69.

248 Ellsberg, *Secrets*, 301.

249 Morrocco, *The Vietnam Experience: Thunder From Above, Air War, 1941-1968*, 116-117.

250 Stanton, *The Rise and Fall of an American Army*, 105.

251 Morrocco, *The Vietnam Experience: Thunder From Above, Air War, 1941-*

1968, 65-69.

252 Ibid., 78-79.

253 Ibid., 86-87.

254 He is the son of John F. and Gillie Hurst, and the brother of Julia Hurst Werner.

255 Stanton, *The Rise and Fall of an American Army*, 284.

256 Ibid., 285.

257 Ibid., 285-286.

258 Bowman, *The Vietnam War: Day by Day*, 136.

259 Ibid., 137.

260 Stanton, *The Rise and Fall of an American Army*, 297.

261 Hayden was the son of Cecil Hayden, who was twice wounded with the Ninth Division in World War II.

262 Stanton, *The Rise and Fall of an American Army*, 299-301.

263 Jim Wilson, *The Sons of Bardstown: 25 Years of Vietnam in an American Town* (New York: Crown, 1994), 155.

264 A similar model is displayed at the war memorial on Broadway at First Street in Bardstown, Kentucky.

265 Stanton, *The Rise and Fall of an American Army*, 289.

266 Ibid., 289.

267 Ibid., 289-291.

268 Ibid., 291.

269 Ibid., 305.

270 Bowman, *The Vietnam War: Day by Day*, 156.

271 Rank and middle name from gravestone, St. Gregory's Cemetery, Nelson County, Kentucky

272 Stanton, *The Rise and Fall of an American Army*, 355.

273 Bowman, *The Vietnam War: Day by Day*, 156.

274 Ibid., 159.

275 Ibid.

276 Ibid., 160.

277 Ibid., 162.

278 Stanton, *The Rise and Fall of an American Army*, 337-338.

279 Ibid., 339.

280 Ibid., 338.

281 Ibid., 339-340.

282 Bowman, *The Vietnam War: Day by Day*, 164.

283 Stanton, *The Rise and Fall of an American Army*, 340-341.

284 Bowman, *The Vietnam War: Day by Day*, 163.

285 "The War: Pau Vinh Irregulars," *Time*, November 8, 1968.

286 This was not the Tom Hayden who married actress Jane Fonda.

287 "The War: Pau Vinh Irregulars," *Time*, November 8, 1968.

288 Stanton, *The Rise and Fall of an American Army*, 342.

289 Ibid., 346.

290 Ibid., 347.

291 Ibid.

292 Ibid.

293 Author Dr. Harry Spalding taught Brashear in high school. Spalding recalls that Brashear was a bright, down-to-earth student. Dr. Brashear now practices in Central City, Kentucky.

294 Bowman, *The Vietnam War: Day by Day*, 174-175.

295 Stanton, *The Rise and Fall of an American Army*, 350-351.

296 Ibid., 352.

297 Ibid., 353-354.

298 Ibid., 356.

300 Ibid., 356-357.

301 Ibid., 358.

302 Ibid., 359.

303 Bowman, *The Vietnam War: Day by Day*, 137.

304 Stanton, *The Rise and Fall of an American Army*, 361.

305 Ibid., 361-362.

306 Ibid., 362-363.

307 Bowman, *The Vietnam War: Day by Day*, 182.

308 Ibid., 193.

309 Ibid., 202.

310 Ibid., 208.

311 Ibid., 209.

312 Ibid., 210.

313 Ibid.

314 Not to be confused with Sergeant Paul Allen Johnson.